HELPING FAMILIES WITH
TROUBLED CHILDREN

Second Edition

HELPING FAMILIES WITH TROUBLED CHILDREN

A Preventive Approach

Second Edition

Carole Sutton, PhD

Faculty of Health and Life Sciences,
De Montfort University, Leicester

John Wiley & Sons, Ltd

Other Wiley Editorial Offices

John Wiley & Sons Inc., 111 River Street, Hoboken, NJ 07030, USA

Jossey-Bass, 989 Market Street, San Francisco, CA 94103-1741, USA

Wiley-VCH Verlag GmbH, Boschstr. 12, D-69469 Weinheim, Germany

John Wiley & Sons Australia Ltd, 42 McDougall Street, Milton, Queensland 4064, Australia

John Wiley & Sons (Asia) Pte Ltd, 2 Clementi Loop #02-01, Jin Xing Distripark, Singapore 129809

John Wiley & Sons Canada Ltd, 22 Worcester Road, Etobicoke, Ontario, Canada M9W 1L1

Wiley also publishes its books in a variety of electronic formats. Some content that appears
in print may not be available in electronic books.

Library of Congress Cataloging-in-Publication Data

Sutton, Carole.
    Helping families with troubled children : a preventive approach/Carole Sutton. – 2nd ed.
        p.   cm.
    Includes bibliographical references and index.
    ISBN-13: 978-0-470-01549-0 (cloth : alk. paper)
    ISBN-10: 0-470-01549-7 (cloth : alk. paper)
    ISBN-13: 978-0-470-01550-6 (pbk. : alk. paper)
    ISBN-10: 0-470-01550-0 (pbk. : alk. paper)
    1. Social work with children.   2. Problem children.   3. Family social work.   I. Title.
HV713.S9 2006
362.74 – dc22
                                                                2006001327

British Library Cataloging in Publication Data

A catalogue record for this book is available from the British Library

ISBN-13 978-0-470-01549-0 (hbk)   978-0-470-01550-6 (pbk)
ISBN-10 0-470-01549-7 (hbk)   0-470-01550-0 (pbk)

Typeset in 10/12pt Palatino by TechBooks, New Delhi, India
Printed and bound in Great Britain by TJ International Ltd, Padstow, Cornwall
This book is printed on acid-free paper responsibly manufactured from sustainable forestry
in which at least two trees are planted for each one used for paper production.

'The amount of children's experience with encouraging feedback was strongly associated with the magnitude of their accomplishments at age 3 and at age 9–10'.

(Hart & Risley Meaningful Differences)

To Martin Herbert,
Emeritus Professor, University of Exeter
who played a key role in introducing social learning theory to the
United Kingdom, and so helped to relieve the unhappiness of many
troubled children.

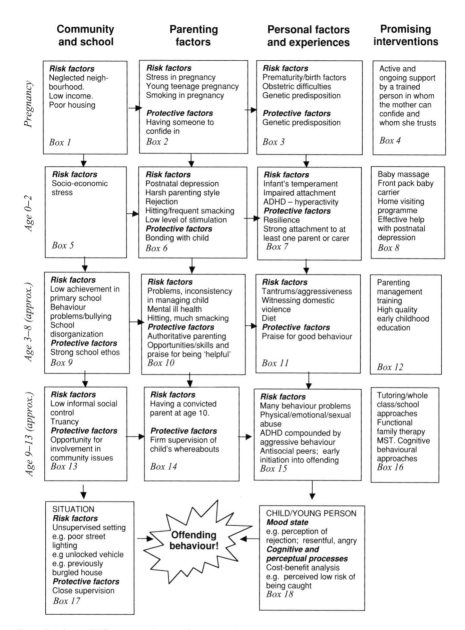

Frontispiece Risk, protection and prevention

Source: Reproduced from Sutton, Utting and Farrington (Eds) (2004). *Support from the Start: Working with Young Children and their Families to Reduce the Risk of Crime and Antisocial Behaviour.* Reproduced by permission of the Crown Copyright Unit, HMSO, Norwich.

CONTENTS

TABLES AND FIGURES

CHAPTER 2   SOCIAL
LEARNING/COGNITIVE-BEHAVIOURAL THEORY

CHAPTER 3   ENGAGING AND SUPPORTING PARENTS
AND FAMILIES

CHAPTER 4   ASPIRE – ASSESSMENT

CHAPTER 5   ASPIRE – PLANNING, IMPLEMENTATION,
REVIEW AND EVALUATION

CHAPTER 6   HELPING FAMILIES WITH CHILDREN WHO ARE ANXIOUS OR DEPRESSED

CHAPTER 7   HELPING FAMILIES WITH CHILDREN'S SLEEPING PROBLEMS

CHAPTER 8   HELPING FAMILIES WITH CHILDREN WITH EATING PROBLEMS

ABOUT THE AUTHOR

Carole Sutton is Associate Director of the Unit for Parenting Studies at De Montfort University. She originally worked as a social worker in the fields of health, mental health and children and families, where her experiences as a practitioner and as a parent led to an interest in preventive work to support young families. She studied for a degree in psychology and then for a doctorate in parent education, working with Professor Martin Herbert. She is a chartered psychologist. This book has grown out of her subsequent experiences of teaching and training professional workers, health visitors, social workers in field and residential settings, psychologists, family therapists, teachers and doctors and supporting parents in helping their troubled children.

ACKNOWLEDGEMENTS

I would like to thank the many students with whom I have worked for the enthusiasm and commitment that they have brought to their studies. I have received some wonderful assignments over the years! Some of the research which the students tracked down is reflected in the following pages.

In addition, I extend my thanks to many colleagues who have encouraged me, provided information and made helpful suggestions about the text. They include Di Hampton, Director of the Unit for Parenting Studies at De Montfort University, Jo Drury, Julie Such and Hellmutt Weich, as well as others in the wider community: the Social Services team at Loughborough, Leicestershire, and Dorsey Precht of On Track, Northampton.

Certain diagrams and charts used in the text are derived from material developed in my teaching and writing within De Montfort University or modified from versions in my earlier publications.

I am indebted to Dr Judy Hutchings of the University of Bangor, for drawing the publication *Meaningful Differences* to my attention.

Finally, I would like to thank Dr Jean Macqueen for indexing this second edition. It is very pleasing when work and friendship come together.

INTRODUCTION

One in 10 children in Great Britain aged 5–16 had a clinically recognisable mental disorder in 2004. This was the same as the proportion recorded in the 1999 survey of the Mental Health of Children and Adolescents in the United Kingdom (Department of Health 2000a).

...SO THE GROUNDS FOR CONCERN ARE STILL SERIOUS

The introduction to the first edition of this book, published in 1999, noted the deep public concern about 'the numbers of children who, themselves clearly unhappy, are causing heartache to their families and exasperation to their teachers'. It reported data from the Department of Health in 1995 indicating that, depending on the location studied, between 6 % and 10 % of 10-year-old children displayed aggressive, disruptive and destructive conduct, whereas between 4 % and 9.9 % showed emotional disorders: anxiety, phobias and depression. Now, well into the twenty-first century, the percentages are almost unchanged. Data from National Statistics Online (2004) are shown in Table I.1.

How has this desperate situation come about and and how is it that, despite considerable efforts in recent years, it is unchanged?

THE BEGINNINGS OF A FOCUS UPON PREVENTION

There have, of course, been huge efforts since the mid-1990s to put in place preventive services, particularly for those living in the most disadvantaged neighbourhoods. The Sure Start initiatives, now developing into Children's Trusts, are attempts to offer services at the point of need: in pregnancy, infancy and in the earliest years of life. How far they will be able to do so will be revealed by rigorous evaluation.

Similarly, establishing Child and Adolescent Mental Health Teams in every part of the country has provided desperately needed resources for supporting the families of troubled children in the community. These teams

Table I.1   Prevalence of psychiatric disorders by sex and age, 2004 (%)

	5–10 year old boys	5–10 year old girls	11–16 year old boys	11–16 year old girls	All 5–16 year olds
Emotional disorders	2.2	2.5	4.0	6.1	3.7
Conduct disorders	6.9	2.8	8.1	5.1	5.8
Hyperkinetic disorders	2.7	0.4	2.4	0.4	1.5
Less common disorders	2.2	0.4	1.6	1.1	1.3
Any disorder	10.2	5.1	12.6	10.3	9.6

Source: Reproduced from National Statistics Online (2004), www.statistics.gov.uk/ccI/nugget. asp?Id=229. Accessed 15 October 2005.

were established following two major publications, *Child and Adolescent Mental Health Services: Together We Stand* (Department of Health, 1995) and *Modernising Health and Social Services. National Priorities Guidance* (Department of Health, 1999).

Considerable progress has been made in putting the above services in place. Despite these, large numbers of young children still appear to be slipping through the nets of available help.

When troubled children first come to the attention of helping agencies they are often at an age when patterns of behaviour are already deeply established and hard to change. Many not only come from disadvantaged backgrounds in respect of low parental income and poor housing but they may also experience much adversity as a result of disrupted relationships with parents or other important people in their lives. *To offer services when behaviours are entrenched is too late.* It is in the earliest years of life when children are at their most vulnerable. We should contnue to focus upon these years in supporting families and providing preventive services. As Bowlby (1979) insisted: 'The

Table I.2   Tiers of provision within child and adolescent mental health services (CAMHS)

Tier	Representative groups of practitioners
1	Social workers, voluntary workers, general practitioners, health visitors, teachers
2	Primary mental health workers, community psychiatric nurses, psychiatrists, clinical psychologists, educational psychologists, etc.
3	Specialist assessment teams, family therapy teams, psychotherapy supervision teams, substance misuse teams, etc.
4	Inpatient child and adolescent mental health teams, specialised neuro-psychiatric services, secure forensic mental health services, etc.

Source: Reproduced from NHS Advisory Service (1995). Child and Adolescent Mental Health Services. London: HMSO.

key point of my thesis is that there is a strong causal relationship between an individual's experiences with his [sic] parents and his later capacity to make affectional bonds'. If children's capacities to make these bonds are damaged by their experiences, then when they become parents their capacities to build bonds with *their* children are already impaired and the vicious cycle may continue generation after generation.

So we must focus our enquiries even more urgently upon what happens in these first seven or eight years – the age when the foundations of children's future health and mental health are being laid down. There are still few answers about how young children develop so quickly from delightful babies and toddlers into deeply unhappy, troubled youngsters, often rejected by other children, disliked by their teachers and even by their parents, but some evidence is now becoming available.

The Costs of Children's Conduct Disorders

A study of the costs of antisocial behaviour was carried out by Dr Stephen Scott from the Institute of Psychiatry and his team. In a longitudinal study in London, 142 children aged 10 were grouped in terms of 'no problem', 'conduct problems' and 'conduct disorder' and were followed until adulthood. Data were gathered in six domains: foster and residential care; special educational provision; state benefits in adulthood; breakdown of relationship; health; crime. By age 28, the data showed that the mean costs of children with 'no problem' were £7,423; the costs of children with 'conduct problems' were £24,324, and the costs of children with 'conduct disorder' were £70,019 (Scott, Knapp, Henderson & Maughan 2001a). These data are entirely in line with those reported from studies from other countries, notably the United States, so I suggest that the case for support from the start is made. *It is just common sense to do all that we can to prevent these difficulties from occurring in the first place.*

SOME COMMON THEMES EMERGING FROM THE RESEARCH

Three themes continue to emerge from the research literature:

1. A multifactorial model of causation.
2. The contribution of structural variables to children's difficulties.
3. The importance of social learning/cognitive-behavioural approaches to helping children.

A Multifactorial Model of Causation

As the quality of research has improved, it has become apparent that a veritable tapestry of variables contributes to the development of distress on the part of a given child. It is no longer a matter of debate as to whether 'nature' or 'nurture' contributes more to the aetiologies of children's difficulties: the interactions have been shown to be of extraordinary complexity.

In 2002, with funding from the British Psychological Society, three seminars were held at the Royal Society at which invited participants discussed the topic 'very young children as potential offenders: preventive approaches'. Discussion focused upon the latest research, starting with the evidence of the impact of influences affecting babies while they are still in the womb, and exploring the effects of risk and protective factors during the preschool and school years until children are aged 13. We developed a report from our discussions: *Support from the Start* (Sutton, Utting & Farrington, 2004) published by the Department for Education and Skills.

We devised a table (see frontispiece) to show how influences from a range of sources, neighbourhood characteristics, parenting styles and practices as well as individual experiences all increase or reduce the probability of a child's becoming an offender. Some influences posed risks; others offered protection. This table is inevitably incomplete, but it provides a 'snapshot' of the key variables suggested by current, rigorous research as contributing to a given child's pathway from conception to becoming an offender at the beginning of the twenty-first century. We shall examine evidence from this table in Chapter 1.

Another important understanding directly relevant to this report has emerged during the last few years. Hagell (2002), writing in *The Mental Health of Young Offenders*, commissioned by the Mental Health Foundation, reports of young offenders:

> The original risk factors that led to their offending also predict, in the general population, to mental health problems. These factors include inconsistent or erratic parenting, over-harsh discipline, hyperactivity as a child and various other types of stressors on families and neighbourhoods, including deprivation.

So the risk factors incurred by children and young people, which predispose them towards offending, are the same as those that predispose them towards mental health disorders. As we shall see in Chapter 1, p. 14, these same risk factors also lead to children failing to reach their cognitive potential.

The Contribution of Structural Variables to Children's Difficulties

Since the mid-1990s, the evidence has continued to accumulate that structural variables, those associated with a child's socioeconomic status, housing and the low income of his or her parents, all contribute substantially to the probability of a child's becoming troubled. The early studies by Rutter, Cox, Tupling, Berger & Yule (1975a) and Rutter et al. (1975b) showed that children in a typical Inner London borough exhibited a level of disturbance twice that of children in the Isle of Wight, and that this increased level was associated essentially with socio-economic factors such as large family size and unemployment. These findings have been confirmed by studies in other countries.

Data supplied by National Statistics Online (2004) offered additional information:

> The prevalence of mental disorders also varied by some characteristics. It was greater among children in lone parent families (16 per cent) than among those in two parent families (8 per cent) and in families with neither parent working (20 per cent) compared with those in which both parents worked (8 per cent).

This book, however, is written for practitioners who are relatively powerless to influence some of the variables included here; we cannot change, except marginally, people's income levels, their employment circumstances or their housing; we cannot change events that have happened in the past – although we can help people talk about these events and their continuing impact upon them, which, as research shows, may relieve some of that stress. For despite their difficulties many parents still seek help; they still want to love their children and to have their children love them. They do not, typically, blame stress as the reason for their difficulties in coping with their children; they are much more likely to blame the children themselves. As I found in my own work with families (among whom many lone parents were particularly successful), enabling them to manage their children effectively both enhanced their confidence and measurably reduced depression.

There are hundreds of children in situations at home that are becoming increasingly difficult for all concerned. One parent said to me, 'They get you to a pitch where you could really harm them . . .' Another said, 'if I don't get away from him, I'm going to kill him . . .' and 'there were times when I could have killed him . . . There were times when I was suicidal – when I was on the point of ringing Social Services and saying, "Take him . . . " ' Now, these were not sadistic, rejecting parents, anxious to get rid of their children. Far from it: they were ordinary mothers and fathers, driven frantic by the aggressiveness and disruptiveness of their children, both to themselves and to people outside the family. Moreover, they were asking, sometimes begging, for help but it was not readily forthcoming. This was not because no-one had tried to help: they had doctors, social workers and health visitors, but in many instances they had used common sense as the basis of their advice and common sense had let them down. What is needed to help these families is *refined common sense*, that is, help based on principles that are not contrary to common sense but which are informed by extensive research in many parts of the world. So this book attempts not only to explore how some children's difficulties develop but also to suggest practical strategies, grounded in research, which parents can use to improve their young children's behaviour. Throughout, the emphasis is upon *prevention and evidence-based practice.*

The Usefulness of Cognitive-behavioural Approaches in Helping Troubled Children

This body of theoretical concepts, which were initially grouped under the generic title of 'social learning theory', has been shown in repeated studies to be of great help in supporting families with troubled children. Table I.3 shows just some of the areas of research where there is firm evidence of their usefulness. Many of these areas will be addressed in this book.

So my forecast in 1999 that cognitive-behavioural approaches are here to stay was accurate. Painstaking research in many countries over the intervening years has confirmed that we now have a body of theory that not only throws light on may children's difficulties but offers ways forward for helping them and their families. A detailed assessment of each child's circumstances is of course essential: organic explanations for a child's difficulties must be explored; 'life events' in the child's past and present must be addressed; but cognitive behavioural theory has been shown both to illuminate the past and to indicate ways forward. Not only can we offer effective help in many existing difficulties but we can begin to undertake preventive work with parents, carers and families in ways that respect culture and tradition and which empower families so that they can work collaboratively with practitioners to help their children.

Table I.3   Areas of research in children's difficulties where cognitive-behavioural theory has been found effective

Area of problem/disorder	Examples of research
Emotional difficulties	Harrington (2002); Klein & Pine (2002)
Eating difficulties	Hampton (1996); Stein & Barnes (2002)
Sleeping difficulties	Ferber (1986); Stein & Barnes (2002)
Interventions in emotional abuse and neglect	Iwaniec (1995, 2004)
Conduct disorders in children	Herbert (1987); Earls (1995); Earls & Mezzacappa (2002)
Attention deficit hyperactivity disorder (ADHD)	Barkley (1995); Schachar & Tannock (2002)
Wetting and soiling	Buchanan (1992); Shaffer (1994); Clayden et al. (2002)

DISSEMINATION OF THE NECESSARY SKILLS

However, recognition of the evidence of what can be achieved by direct work with parents *is* becoming disseminated – witness the Report of the Committee of the House of Commons upon Child and Adolescent Mental Health Services (House of Commons Health Committee, 1997, p. xxiv), which includes the following passage:

> We were impressed with what we heard of Parent Management Training, and recommend that the DoH should support this and similar techniques, while at the same time ensuring that they receive systematic evaluation and monitoring as to their effectiveness and cost-effectiveness.

To critics who point out the stresses under which poor and disadvantaged parents coping with children are living, I acknowledge their case but would point out two things. First, most parents seek to do their best for their children and want to continue to care for their children themselves; they do not want them to be removed by social workers because they are being neglected or maltreated. The body of ideas that I am proposing gives families skills for managing their children in ways which make them easier to handle and easier to love. One mother, whom I have never met, but whom I was able to teach how to manage her very active two-year-old twins by telephone, said 'I used to hate those two, but now I love them'. Second, teaching parents these skills of child management is not in conflict with the provision of better services: social workers and health visitors, as part of children's trusts, can work towards setting up more crêches, more day nurseries, more family support services, *as well as* teaching caregivers how to manage their children's sleeping and behaviour difficulties effectively.

The two approaches should together be among a range of tools in the practitioner's repertoire: it is a matter not of 'either/or' but of 'both/and'.

So I am glad to be able to report that a number of professional bodies have been persuaded by the evidence that other researchers and I have been able to offer and I, with colleagues, am fully engaged in disseminating the skills arising from this body of knowledge among health visitors and social workers in several parts of the country. Now they, in turn, are running sleep clinics and behaviour management groups for parents and caregivers and are reporting the same sorts of success that I have had. My hope is that the second edition of this book will persuade others, both individuals and agencies, to listen to the evidence emerging from the research and seek training to help families to help their troubled children.

I

SOME GENERAL PRINCIPLES
FOR HELPING FAMILIES

1

RESEARCH CONCERNING TROUBLED CHILDREN

The recognition that many of the difficulties experienced by young people and adults have their origins in childhood has led to huge research undertakings within psychology, psychiatry and related disciplines. This research may be divided into four main fields:

- the needs of children
- the nature of children's difficulties
- origins of children's difficulties: risk and protective factors
- the effectiveness of interventions to help children

Each will be considered below.

THE NEEDS OF CHILDREN

There have been extensive investigations of children's needs, because by definition troubled children are those whose needs have not been met. One of the clearest is still that of Cooper (1985) whose conclusions are summarised in Box 1.1.

THE NATURE OF CHILDREN'S DIFFICULTIES

What is Meant by 'Troubled Children'

The expression 'troubled children' means those who have psychological difficulties that interfere with their day-to-day lives but which may or may not show themselves in overt patterns of behaviour. It refers to children whose difficulties are persisting, not to those who show transient upsets and unhappiness. It is known that certain difficulties are more common at certain

Box 1.1: The needs of children

(Reproduced with permission from Cooper, 1985.)

- *Basic physical care*, which includes warmth, shelter, adequate food and rest, grooming (hygiene) and protection from danger.
- *Affection*, which includes physical contact, holding, stroking, cuddling and kissing, comforting, admiration, delight, tenderness, patience, time, making allowances for annoying behaviour, general companionship and approval.
- *Security*, which involves continuity of care, the expectation of continuing in the stable family unit, a predictable environment, consistent patterns of care and daily routine, simple rules and consistent controls and a harmonious family group.
- *Stimulation of innate potential* by praise, by encouraging curiosity and exploratory behaviour, by developing skills through responsiveness to questions and to play, and by promoting educational opportunities.
- *Guidance and control* to teach adequate social behaviour, which includes discipline within the child's understanding and capacity and which requires patience and a model for the child to copy, for example in honesty and concern and kindness for others.
- *Responsibility* for small things at first, such as self-care, tidying playthings or taking dishes to the kitchen, and gradually elaborating the decision-making the child has to learn in order to function adequately; gaining experience through mistakes as well as successes, and receiving praise and encouragement to strive to do better.
- *Independence* to make their own decisions, first about small things but increasingly about the various aspects of life within the confines of the family and society's codes. Parents use fine judgement in encouraging independence and in letting the child see and feel the outcome of his or her own poor judgement and mistakes, but within the compass of the child's capacity. Protection is needed, but over-protection is as bad as too early responsibility and independence.

developmental stages than at others and this must, of course, be taken into account.

In the introduction we considered the numbers of children experiencing difficulties and noted that the prevalence of these conditions had scarcely changed since the mid-1990s (p. 1). We now consider some of the difficulties associated with these conditions. Table 1.1, devised by Rutter (1987) from data drawn from studies of the World Health Organization, spans research endeavours across the world investigating the main broad categories

Table 1.1 Variables differentiating diagnostic categories

Diagnostic group	Age of onset (years)	Gender	Reading difficulties	Family discord	Response to treatment
Emotional disorder (anxieties, phobias, obsessions, depression)	Any	=	−	−	+ + ++
Conduct disorder (aggressiveness, disruptiveness, tantrums)	Any	M	++	++	+
Hyperactivity (ADHD)	<5	M	+ + +	+	+
Autism	<2.5	M	+ + +	+	+
Developmental delay	Infancy	M	+ + +	−	++

Key

−	No association
+	Slight positive association
++	Fairly positive assocation
+++	Considerable positive association
++++	Very positive association

Source: Reproduced with permission from Rutter (1987) *Helping Troubled Children*, 2nd edn. Penguin.

of children's emotional and behavioural difficulties. Indicators concerning associated conditions and the probable response to treatment or intervention are also given. As we saw in the Introduction, boys outnumber girls in many areas of difficulty. Taking as an example the category of emotional difficulties, it can be seen that onset may occur at any time, there is no particular association with reading difficulties or with family distress and there is a very positive prognosis: skilled help given to children with emotional difficulties is likely to be effective and the children are very likely to become less troubled.

ORIGINS OF CHILDREN'S DIFFICULTIES: RISK AND PROTECTIVE FACTORS

I wish now to consider the frontispiece to this book in more detail. It is also the frontispiece to *Support from the Start* (Sutton, Utting & Farrington, 2004). The frontispiece which offers a 'snapshot' of current evidence concerning risk and protective factors, is divided into rows and columns: the first row represents pregnancy; the second the age from birth to 2 years and so on. The columns illustrate different settings upon which the research studies have been focused. The first column shows evidence associated with neighbourhoods or schools; the second concerns parents, their own experiences or their styles of parenting; and the third concerns the babies and young children themselves, their genetic inheritance or their experiences as the children of their particular parents. The figure spans the period from conception to 13 years, the upper limit of the age span addressed by the Children's Fund in the United Kingdom. As mentioned above (p. 4), it is important to stress that the same factors are known to predispose not only towards offending but also towards children failing to meet their educational potential and experiencing mental health difficulties in later life. The various studies and their interactions are discussed in detail in the report but some of the most arresting bodies of evidence will be discussed briefly here.

Pregnancy

There can be no doubt that neighbourhood disadvantage and degradation have damaging effects upon the developing child even during pregnancy. These influences are typically manifest through babies having low birth weight – under 2,500 g or 5.5 lbs, or even very low birth weight, 1,500 g or 3.3 lbs. Sometimes this can be associated with the reluctance of mothers, particularly young mothers, to take up antenatal care services.

Teenage pregnancy may not in itself be a risk but if these young mothers are isolated and particularly if they experience stress that they attempt to relieve by smoking or drinking alcohol, they place their babies at hazard. O'Connor, Heron, Golding Beveridge and Glover (2002) found that if that stress is particularly great in the last 3 months of pregnancy, then the babies born to these stressed mothers were far more likely than the children of unstressed mothers to display symptoms of hyperactivity or attention deficit hyperactivity disorder (ADHD). As we shall see, this is a potential risk for other subsequent difficulties. Studies comparing teenage mothers with mothers who postponed their childbearing beyond the age of 20 have found that teenage motherhood is associated with low educational achievement, low income, low educational status and large family size (Hobcraft & Kiernan, 1999). Later studies have confirmed these data and have shown that the children of very young mothers had lower educational attainment, were rated as having more emotional and behavioural problems, were at increased risk of maltreatment and had higher rates of illness, accidents and injuries. In addition, as the government's Social Inclusion Unit has noted (Botting, Rosato & Wood, 1998), children born to young teenage mothers are more likely to become offenders and to become teenage parents themselves.

There is also strong evidence that smoking during pregnancy is a risk factor for later child behavioural problems. Many mothers may smoke because it helps to relieve the stresses they are feeling but they may be unaware that this poses a serious risk to their babies' health and development. For example, Wakschlag et al. (1997) found that mothers smoking more than six cigarettes daily during pregnancy were more likely to have a child who later developed diagnosable behaviour problems than mothers who did not smoke during pregnancy. Similarly, Brennan, Grekin & Mednick (1999), in a longitudinal study involving 4,000 boys, found a close relationship between differing levels of maternal antenatal smoking (as reported by the mothers) and arrests in adulthood of their children for both violent and nonviolent crime. It appears that nicotine is the damaging agent. While it would be too sweeping to claim that every mother to be who smokes in pregnancy is placing her child at direct risk, the government is right to make very great efforts to advertise the harm that smoking can do to the unborn child.

As for the babies themselves, those who were premature or who experienced obstetric difficulties at birth were found to be at risk of later difficulties, particularly if the obstetric problems were combined with inexperienced parenting. More surprisingly, arising from neurobiological investigations, it has been shown by Caspi et al. (2002), that children who showed resilience under harsh treatment carried a genotype with a high level of a specific enzyme (MAO A); this gave protection against stress for babies fortunate enough to inherit it (Radke-Yarrow & Sherman, 1990). Conversely, those without the specific enzyme were more likely to be affected by stressful events in their lives.

Turning now to research upon helpful influences and strategies, evidence of the most helpful interventions comes from the Elmira studies, summarised in Olds et al. (1998), in the United States. Here some 400 mothers participated and were given 1 of 3 approaches to support:

- fortnightly home visits of about an hour during pregnancy
- fortnightly home visits in pregnancy and continuing during the first 2 years of life
- a comparison group that had no home visits but had standard antenatal care.

At followup it was found in the visited group that, compared with the unvisited mothers,

- teenage mothers had heavier babies
- mothers who had smoked decreased their smoking
- they had fewer premature deliveries
- they had fewer instances of verified child maltreatment in the child's first two years.

A replication of the study in Tennessee found that children of the mothers who received enhanced support demonstrated higher intellectual functioning and had fewer behavioural problems than the children of mothers in the comparison group (Olds et al., 2004).

Birth to Two Years

We turn now to the second row of the frontispiece, concerning babies and tod-dlers from birth to 2 years (Caspi, Taylor, Moffitt & Plomin, 2000). A British study of 3,530 same-sex twins, both identical and fraternal, compared the impact of environment across six different types of neighbourhood, from very disadvantaged to affluent. This showed that children in deprived neigh-bourhoods were at substantially increased risk of emotional and behavioural problems over and above any genetic liability, and that this increased risk was discernible in children as young as 2 years (Caspi et al., 2000). If, in addition to the risks incurred through the locality where the child is born, the mother experienced postnatal depression, with the effect of reducing the smiling, nurturing and loving interactions between mother and infant, this further prejudiced the baby's development. If this depression is accompanied by re-jection of the child or by harsh styles of parenting, the risks of future major difficulties are strongly intensified.

In respect of parenting factors there is a substantial body of evidence in the United Kingdom published by Murray and her associates concerning the impact of postnatal depression upon infant and toddler development. For example, Cooper & Murray (1998) have followed up the children of mothers diagnosed with this disorder, comparing their progress with that of children whose mothers did not experience postnatal depression. The evidence is that chronic maternal depressive disorder, particularly when it occurs in the con-text of general adversity, poses a significant risk for the child's subsequent cognitive, emotional and behavioural development.

Many studies from different parts of the world have shown that a harsh parenting style has seriously damaging effects upon children. Longitudinal studies have consistently shown that the experience of cruel and neglectful parenting is a major risk factor for antisocial behaviour and later offending (Farrington, 1996). Parenting style has been closely studied by Baumrind (1971) and when her work was developed by Maccoby and Martin (1983) two main dimensions of parenting style were noted, yielding four main styles of parenting (see Table 1.2).

It is the very authoritarian style which seems to lead to the worst outcomes for children. This harsh parenting style is often associated with physical abuse. Indeed data reported by Smith, Bee et al. (1995) indicated that up to 75 % of parents had smacked children in their first year of life – a response that seems to reflect irritation, anger and exasperation about what to do about crying babies. *Far more research is needed on the practical steps necessary to support parents in this field and on how to provide the help needed to relieve stress arising from the care of very young children.*

However, it has been shown that protective factors do come into play. It is during this period that Nature normally inclines mothers, fathers and those who care for babies to coo and smile at them, admiring their eyes,

Table 1.2 The two main dimensions/four main styles of parenting

		Level of affection and acceptance	
		High	Low
Level of control	High	**Authoritative** parents tend to be high in both control and in warmth, setting clear limits, expecting and reinforcing socially mature behaviour, but also aware of the child's needs. These parents are less likely to use physical punishment than more authoritarian parents. They may discipline older children by e.g. 'time out'. The children tend to be confident with high self-esteem.	**Authoritarian** parents tend to be very demanding of their children but not very nurturing. They try to control their children but give little warmth and positive attention. The children tend to respond either by being fearful or by being aggressive and out of control.
	Low	**Indulgent, permissive** parents may not exercise necessary controls over their children. If parents are permissive towards aggression, the children may also develop aggressive behaviours.	**Neglecting, uninvolved** parents tend to be psychologically 'unavailable' to their children for a range of reasons: e.g. postnatal depression or being overwhelmed by other problems. The children seem to have many difficulties in relationships with adults and other children.

Source: Adapted from Maccoby & Martin (1983). Socialisation in the context of the family: Parent – child interaction. In Mussen (ed.) *Handbook of Child Psychology, Vol. 4.* Chichester: Wiley.

smooth skin and tiny fingers ... These spontaneous, admiring interactions between caregivers and babies and young children have been found to have an optimal stimulating effect upon the children's emotional and cognitive development and upon the capacity for attachment and bonding of each to the other (Gerhardt, 2004). For example, Dawson, Groter-Klinger, Panagiotides, Hill and Spieker (1992) and Dawson, Ashman and Carver (2000) postulate that the left hemisphere of the brain is physiologically associated with feelings that tend to reach out toward the environment, such as joy and contentment, so that loving and positive interactions with tiny babies facilitate the development of this potential. Correspondingly, the right hemisphere is said to be associated with feelings leading to withdrawal, fear and sadness – responses that might unintentionally be elicited by a depressed mother.

In respect of cognitive development, stimulating interactions with babies, including exploring colours, shapes and sounds, looking at picture books with them, singing and repeating rhymes and rhythms, are all greatly enriching. They provide infants with a strong sensory, emotional, verbal and cognitive

Table 1.3 Childhood temperament: patterns among young children that tend to persist beyond infancy

The 'easy' child	These young children are adaptable and easy to manage. They move early in life into regular patterns of sleeping and waking and seem contented and flexible.
The 'difficult' child	These babies are less adaptable. It is more difficult to get them into a routine of sleeping and feeding regularly, and they seem more tense and irritable in their responses to new situations or people.
The 'slow to warm up' child	These babies fall between the two patterns shown above but it takes considerable time to settle them into a routine. Having made that adjustment, however, they are fairly easy to manage.

Source: Adapted from Thomas & Chess (1977). *Temperament and Development.* New York: Brunner/Mazel.

repertoire that holds them in good stead as they encounter other children and adults and, in due course, move into play group, reception class and infant school. Without this nurturing stimulation and the experiencing of the world 'in small doses' toddlers do not develop their potential for communication, for coping with the demands of the world and for enjoying its richness and bounty.

Turning to the contribution of the babies themselves, as it were, towards the overall outcome, it is now generally accepted that an infant's innate temperament is an important factor. Many babies can be said to be 'easy' to manage, but a substantial proportion are hard to help to settle into life, being restless and resistant in adapting to feeding and/or sleeping routines. A further proportion take a long time to make these adjustments. With consistent management, restless babies can be helped to settle, but the birth of a restless baby to an inexperienced and isolated mother can place great strains upon both parent and child.

Further, circumstances may affect how readily a given baby develops a secure attachment with his or her mother or main caregiver. It is generally thought that around 65% of babies develop a secure attachment, but about 15% seem to develop an insecure (avoidant) attachment, a further 15% develop an insecure (ambivalent) attachment and about 5% appear to develop a so-called disorganised attachment. This last group seems to have experienced a markedly inconsistent style of parenting, with affectionate interactions interspersed unpredictably with episodes of rejection or harshness. When this occurs the baby or toddler cannot be sure whether his overtures for attention will be met with warmth and cuddles or with being ignored or even with physical punishments. When these children are followed up in later life, it seems to be this last group that experiences the greatest difficulties (Main, Kaplan & Cassidy, 1985; Main & Solomon, 1990).

It is likely to be during this period that evidence will emerge of ADHD. As indicated above, this has been found in some instances to be associated with high levels of stress in the third tremester of pregnancy but there is also evidence that the condition can be inherited from father, mother or sometimes both. On other occasions, it seems to be linked with a high level of disorder in the household, where much attention is given to instances of undesired behaviour with minimal attention being shown to calm and settled behaviour.

Promising interventions during this period have not been exhaustively researched; for example, much more work needs to be done to explore the beneficial effects of baby massage. We can readily understand that apart from possible benefits in helping a baby to relax in response to soothing massage, the activity offers an ideal opportunity to promote attachment between baby and the person offering the massage, desirably the baby's parent or main caregiver. There are indications that baby massage can offset maternal depression (Onozawa, Glover, Adams, Modi & Kumar, 2001) but this is as yet a relatively unexplored field. Claims may similarly be made that baby slings worn in front of the person carrying the infant enhances attachment but further work needs to be done to test this.

Murray, Cooper, Wilson and Romaniuk (2003) found that sensitive support offered by health visitors had a positive effect upon mothers experiencing postnatal depression in the year following their baby's birth. When several models of support were investigated, including nondirective counselling and cognitive behavioural approaches, there was little difference in the impacts of the various approaches: the mothers generally benefited from this sensitive support. Similarly, in a major review of research on home visiting, Bull, McCormick, Swann and Mulvihill (2004) report that, despite the variety of models of home visiting, professional, volunteer, etc. and the varied lengths of time over which visiting takes place

> . . . home visiting programmes can be associated with improvements in parenting, reported improvements in some child behavioural problems, improved cognitive development, especially among some sub-groups of children such as those born prematurely or born with low birth weight, a reduction in accidental injury among children and improved detection and management of postnatal depression.

However they did not find that home visiting was associated with reductions in child abuse, reduced hospital admissions or maternal participation in education. It does, however, appear established that support from the start can significantly help mothers and their babies but much work remains to be done to establish the best model of help, which features of the support are experienced as most helpful, whether professionals, paraprofessionals or volunteers are most effective, and for how long the support is needed.

Table 1.4 Continuum of characteristics of three-year-old children in using play activities

Under controlled (i.e. destructive, disruptive)	Unsettled children who found it hard to settle to play	Confident children who made good use of play opportunities	Reserved children, who were timid but who did settle to play	Overcontrolled, inhibited children

Source: Adapted from Caspi et al. (1996). Behavioral observations at age three predict adult psychiatric disorders. *Archives of General Psychiatry, 53*, 1033–1039.

Age Three to Eight Years

Longitudinal studies are a particularly valuable source of information for understanding the development of children's behaviour difficulties, and two such studies in particular have been very illuminating. The first, undertaken in New Zealand, involved over a thousand children from the age of 3, who were followed up into their twenties. One of the papers from this study has the startling title, 'Behavioral observations at age 3 predict adult psychiatric disorders' (Caspi, Moffitt, Newman & Silva, 1996). The study was conducted so that assessors placed the children in one of five groups according to their responses to standard play activities when the children were three. These groups are shown in Table 1.4.

When the children were aged 21, those at the two extremes of the continuum were compared with those in the middle. It was found that the undercontrolled children, in comparison with the confident children, were twice as likely to have a diagnosis of antisocial personality disorder; were twice as likely to be repeat offenders, were twice as likely to be diagnosed with alcohol dependence (boys, not girls), were four times as likely to have been convicted for a violent offence and were much more likely to report having attempted suicide. By contrast, the overcontrolled children were, by comparison with the confident group much more likely to have been diagnosed with depression, were more likely to have difficulties with alcohol (boys, not girls) and were more likely to report having attempted suicide.

A further longitudinal study by Stevenson and Goodman (2001) in Britain, followed a sample of 828 children from a London borough from the age of 3 to the age of 23 or 24. At followup it was found that the risk of having *any adult conviction* was associated with the following characteristics in the child when he or she was 3 years old: soiling and daytime wetting, having a high level of activity and the parents having difficulty in managing the child. Further, the risk of the individual having an *adult violent conviction* was associated with the child as a 3 year old having serious temper tantrums and the parents having difficulties in managing the child. These results then appear to confirm

Table 1.5 Experiences of language across three types of family within one year

Type of family	Average no. of words experienced by children
Professional family	11 million
Working-class family	6 million
Family on welfare	3 million

Note: Three year olds extrapolated to age four (Hart & Risley, 1995).

Source: Adapted from Hart and Risley (1995). *Meaningful Differences*. London: Brooks Publishing Company.

the New Zealand findings, namely, *that children's serious behaviour problems at age 3, particularly where the parents appear to have difficulty in managing the child, are grounds for urgent support to the parent(s) or carers. These are emergency situations.*

More benignly, it is also during this period that the effects of encouragement and stimulation in the earliest years of life are typically beginning to show their effects. Children who have been fortunate enough to enjoy these early encouraging experiences may already be confident in play group, nursery school and primary school whereas those who did not have these encouraging experiences may find themselves less competent, less socially skilled, less cognitively developed than their companions. We see in Box 9 of the frontispiece that children who enter school without the fundamental skills of self-help, being able to share toys, to take turns and to care for others are at a disadvantage in terms of social skills. Others are also already at a cognitive disadvantage through not having had the experience of looking at books with their caregivers, singing simple songs and noticing colours, shapes and textures.

It is not commonly understood that language and thought develop in response to 'talk, touch and gaze', so many children in these earliest years of life do not receive the stimulation from their caregivers that is necessary for optimal language development. Hart and Risley (1995) gathered data over approximately 2.5 years from 13 professional families, 23 working-class families and 6 families receiving welfare benefits. They coded the interactions between parents and their children aged 10 to 36 months for an hour every month, examining the number of words used, the richness of vocabulary, and the types of feedback offered to children. The results are shown in Table 1.5. Other findings were startling: for example, by age 3, the spoken vocabularies recorded for the children from the professional families were larger than those recorded for the parents in the welfare families.

The children in families on welfare were not only relatively deprived linguistically but as they grew older to age three they were also severely

Table 1.6   Experiences of average encouragements and discouragements across three types of family within and year (Hart & Risley, 1995)

	Encouragements	Discouragements
Professional family	166 000	26 000
Working-class family	62 000	36 000
Family on welfare	26 000	57 000

Source: Adapted from Hart & Risley (1995). *Meaningful Differences*. London: Brooks Publishing Company.

disadvantaged with regard to the number of affirming, as opposed to discouraging, messages that they received from their parents (See Table 1.6).

Hart and Risley report that *'The amount of children's experience with encouraging feedback was strongly associated with the magnitude of their accomplishments at age 3 and at age 9–10'* (my italics).

This study is of the greatest importance because in addition to demonstrating the discrepancy between the linguistic experiences of advantaged and less advantaged children, it demonstrates the mechanisms, the underpinning *processes*, which contribute at least in part to that advantage. And of what do these underpinning processes consist? They are not all that difficult to provide for every child: they are language baths, given through conversations, stories, poems, and song; they are frequent doses of nurturance and encouragement and they are generous offerings of admiration and praise – all administered daily from infancy!

Considering now the influences in Box 10 of the frontispiece, harsh parenting is particularly damaging. Inconsistency between parents or by the same parent is almost as difficult for children to cope with. Children can typically learn to adjust to a strict parenting pattern or even to a permissive one but as we indicated on page 17, it is almost impossible for them to learn to adjust to a pattern that is sometimes harsh and sometimes indulgent: the unpredictable parent is a confusing parent. This unpredictability, however, may be a frequent characteristic of many parents who are coping with mental illness, with addiction to drugs or alcohol, or sometimes with a combination of these conditions. In such settings, young children's fundamental security may be profoundly compromised (Cleaver, Unell & Aldgate, 1999).

When we consider the experience of the child (see Box 11 of the frontispiece), additional factors come into play. For example, a child of three may have learned that by screaming, lying down in the street and threatening aggression he can come to dominate his inexperienced and agitated parents. If he is rewarded, even if only occasionally – in fact, in terms of social learning theory, *particularly* if only occasionally (see p. 58) – by getting his own way, he will repeat these actions, often over and over again. A three year old with a powerful will can readily become the dominant figure in a household: I met them repeatedly in my research work, and continue to do so.

Similarly, we are only just beginning to take note of the impact of domestic violence upon the growing child. Moffitt and Caspi (2003) have shown how growing up in a setting in which domestic violence and abuse is the norm predisposes a child to continue to abuse, either physically or verbally, those about him, parents or brothers and sisters. Further, Moffitt has shown how this pattern continues into adolescents' early intimate relationships and tends to be reproduced when the children of a violent relationship become parents themselves. There really is no great mystery here!

Dietary factors have long been suspected as being implicated in a child's susceptibility to behaviour difficulties but only fairly recently has there been firm evidence to support that suspicion. Parents were invited to take part in a study in which a coloured drink was made part of the diet of a large number of children. A 'double blind' controlled study was undertaken: that is, all the children received a coloured drink, but no one, not even the parents, knew whether the drink was one containing the substances thought to contribute to hyperactivity or whether the drink was simply coloured water. The final result astonished some researchers: the parents, 'blind' as to which drink was being given, reported more hyperactive behaviour when their children were receiving the drink with additives than when they had the placebo drink (Bateman et al., 2004). The results of this study, which was particularly well designed, have major implications for those who devise children's meals and who have influence over whether vending machines selling coloured drinks shall be made available in schools.

So much for risk factors; let us now briefly consider protective factors. One variable that is supported by strong research evidence is praise for 'good' behaviour. The evidence is unequivocal: whether the setting be the home or the school, there is extensive evidence to show that identifying specific be-haviour(s) desired by parents and/or caregivers (e.g. complying with a clear request to help put toys away) and warm praise for the child when he or she complies, has the effect of increasing the frequency of that behaviour. Indir-ectly this leads to improved relationships between adults and children. The main parenting programmes all include components that encourage parents to use warm praise and active appreciation for desired behaviours (Sutton et al., 2004). Recent research among 35 facilitators of parenting groups, drawn from 4 rigorously researched parenting programmes, indicated that helping parents to praise their children was seen as of primary importance in bringing about improvements in the children's behaviour (Sutton & Precht, unpub-lished data).

Turning now to Box 12 of the frontispiece and to specific interventions that provide firm evidence of improvement of misbehaviour in children in this age group, it is not surprising to find that the most effective interventions are those that help parents to manage their children's behaviour in clear and consistent ways. Facilitators who use these interventions guide parents to set firm boundaries for children's behaviour, to develop strategies that ensure that these boundaries are respected but, particularly important, they incorporate a strong component of praise for positive behaviour by the children. As explained, there are a number of parenting programmes that have been rigorously researched and evaluated using randomised controlled trials and which have consistently given positive outcomes: these include *Living with Children* (Patterson, 1975), from which my own material, *Parenting Positively*, has been developed; *The Incredible Years* (Webster-Stratton, 1992); *Triple P* (Sanders, 1999) and the *Parenting Partnership* approach (Davis et al., 2002). All of these parenting packages are gaining ground and popularity as families discover that life becomes pleasanter when they deal with their children and young people using the principles advocated.

Age 9 to 13

Considering now the material in Box 13 of the frontispiece, which concerns community factors placing children at risk, there is abundant evidence (e.g. Farrington & West, 1993) that in neglected and disadvantaged neighbourhoods there is even less informal supervision than in other communities. That is, if adults see children getting into mischief, shoplifting, scrawling graffiti or vandalising buildings, they are less likely to intervene than is the case in more affluent localities. In America, Sampson, Raudenbush and Earls (1997) showed that in disorganised neighbourhoods, this lack of 'informal' social controls, such as adults being prepared to intervene to control public antisocial behaviour by young people, meant that offending was not checked or, in some cases, even noticed. As we know from cognitive behavioural theory, each time a child gets away with misbehaviour, he or she is learning that misbehaviour is rewarded – so, of course, it happens again – and again, and again. It is to counter this situation of low informal social control that the present government is introducing more community-based police officers. It is intended that they will help maintain order within communities and offer an example to residents of what can be achieved when adults refuse to tolerate vandalism, racist abuse and wilful destructiveness.

Despite major efforts to tackle truancy, this issue continues to cause great concern. Thousands of children are not only failing to complete their education, so missing the opportunity of acquiring the fundamental skills of being able to read, write and calculate, but they are learning strategies of avoiding difficulties rather than coping with them, or obtaining help to cope with them. These habits are all too readily taken into adult life. Further, the temptations of shoplifting and petty vandalism are learned effortlessly when young children are spending day after day inactive and bored, and yet are seeing the products of the materialistic society literally within easy reach. However, attempts to involve young people in taking responsibilities, appropriate to their age, in maintaining and improving their communities, are demonstrating some initial positive effects. For example, some of the Communities that Care initiatives have shown that enabling young people to develop and participate in Youth Councils and in initiating pregnancy testing centres, has contributed to a reduction in offending (*Communities that Care*, 1998).

In Box 14 of the frontispiece we see that having a convicted parent at age 10 is likely to lead to subsequent offending on the part of the young person. Again, there is no mystery here: if a child grows up in a household where acquiring skills in burglary or taking and driving away cars is a topic for discussion, with children being actively taught different approaches to, say, breaking and entering, then those children will learn these skills just as they would learn skills of plumbing, carpentry or dentistry if their parents were employed in those crafts.

If parents do wish to divert children of this age group from activities likely to lead them into trouble, extensive research, as well as common sense, indicates that the children need firm supervision. The studies of Harriet Wilson (1980, 1987) are instructive here. She compared the delinquency rates of children living in either the inner city or the suburbs according to whether the degree of parental supervision exercised over them was 'strict', 'intermediate' or 'lax'. She found that, after controlling for other variables, 'strictness', defined as parents knowing where their sons were and exercising control over their activities, conferred protection against delinquency. Within the inner city, for example, the delinquency rate of 'lax' families was over two-and-a-half times that of 'strict' families. So the key protective factor was not a matter of where families lived but of how much supervision parents exercised over their children. Patterns of parental supervision are likely to be set in the early years of children's lives and are thus a very important component of prevention.

In Box 15 of the frontispiece we see reference to the evidence that 'a high proportion of young people who have committed violent or murderous offences have been the victims of childhood trauma in the form of abuse and/or loss and frequently both' (Boswell, 1995, p. 30). The abuse may be physical, sexual or emotional. The mechanism whereby they move from being victimised to becoming, in some cases, abusers themselves may again be one of social learning.

At this stage too, there is evidence that if a child has ADHD, referred to on page 6, and if this behaviour has been compounded by the child becoming aggressive, then this interaction intensifies the probability of the child's following a route into offending. His unacceptable behaviour in school, probably contributing to his becoming an unwelcome member of his class, is likely to drive him to seek companions among other equally undercontrolled children. Often, despite the best efforts of teachers, classroom assistants as well as parents, these children are in danger of social exclusion, and experience early initiation into offending.

When reading research studies to prepare the frontispiece, we were very surprised indeed to discover how few studies there were concerning both girls and black children/young people. It is known that black children are particularly vulnerable in respect of difficulties in the early years. For example, according to a report in the *Times Educational Supplement* (9 July 1999), the rate of exclusions of black pupils has fallen since 1997, but by July 1999 they were still far more likely to be expelled from school than white children. Apparently Afro-Caribbean pupils remain at the highest risk of exclusion and in 1997/8 were nearly 4.5 times more likely to be compelled to leave school than white children. A wide range of explanations for these figures has been given but it seems likely that many black children encounter far more of the risk factors discussed above in their earliest years of life and so experience a cumulative risk far higher than that for their white counterparts. Yet there continues to be a dearth of well evaluated studies concerning the circumstances of children from black and ethnic minorities and also of rigorous studies showing how best to help them and their parents or carers.

Situational and Cognitive Variables

Boxes 17 and 18 of the frontispiece refer to specific factors that are inherent in the way in which given individuals perceive stimuli and decide to take action. Criminological studies have shown that certain locations, such as those with poor lighting and with features conducive to burglary or damage, are more likely to be settings for offending than are better lit and supervised areas. Similarly, Dodge and Frame (1982) have explored differences in the ways in which children with records of aggressive behaviour and nonaggressive children process and respond to cues in the environment. These researchers found that aggressive boys were 'hypervigilant' in scanning their social environment for potential threat and that they responded to perceived hostility with aggressive responses far more readily than did nonaggressive boys. Discussing this work, Kendall (1991) writes: 'Aggressive boys have been found to be 50 % more likely than non-aggressive boys to infer that antagonists in hypothetical provocations acted with hostile rather than neutral or benign intent' (Dodge & Frame, 1982). This work has been replicated in a series of studies, all of which confirm that aggressive boys attribute hostility to others far more frequently than is in fact the case. They also underestimate their own aggressiveness (Lochman, White & Wayland, 1991).

Thus, the reasons why some children get into difficulties while others do not are in part to do with the way social and cognitive variables fall out for an individual child and how they interact with each child's innate endowment. I would reiterate that to help children we need to be alert both to structural factors, such as unemployment, poverty and poor housing, and to the circumstances of each individual family and how its members interact. In other words, we need explanations for children's difficulties which encompass *both* sociological *and* psychological perspectives.

THE EFFECTIVENESS OF INTERVENTIONS TO HELP CHILDREN

There has been a great deal of research into strategies for helping parents whose children appear to be encountering difficulties. The first edition of this book drew upon the work of Kazdin (1987, 1995) who surveyed the effectiveness of different models of intervention in children's antisocial behaviour and it is encouraging to be able to report that Kazdin's judgment that parent management training was an extremely promising approach has been borne out by many subsequent studies.

Research into Parent Education and Training

Behavioural parent training has been widely investigated in many studies carried out across the world. As indicated above, four programmes in particular have been extensively tested using randomised controlled trials (RCTs) in which participants are randomly allocated to different methods of training under experimental and controlled conditions. These are as follows:

- *Living with Children* (Patterson, 1975)
- *The Incredible Years* (Webster-Stratton, 1992)
- *Triple 'P' Positive Parenting Program* (Sanders, 1999)
- *Parenting Partnership*, formerly *Parent Advisor* (Davis et al., 2002)

There are many other programmes that claim very positive outcomes, but which have not been adequately funded so that the evidence of their effectiveness has not been rigorously evaluated. Such programmes include *Strengthening Families, Strengthening Communities* (Steele, Marigna, Tello & Johnson, 1999).

A wide range of other publications attest to the impact of programmes based on cognitive behavioural theory in enabling parents to learn to interact more effectively with their young children; for example, Richardson and Joughin (2002) concluded from their major review of a wide range of programmes that behavioural parent-training programmes are the most effective in reducing conduct disorders in young children. This conclusion is supported by Sanders, (1999), Scott (2002), and a wide array of publications by Webster-Stratton and Herbert (1994) and Webster-Stratton, Reid and Hammond (2001).

My own research: further evidence for the effectiveness of parent training

It was because of this body of evidence of what can be done to help the families of young children that I undertook a substantial research programme (Sutton, 1992, 1995, 2001) in this field, which was reported in the first edition of this book. The essentials are summarised here again because I believe that some of its lessons have not yet been learned – notably, the similarity of outcomes whether parents are met in a group, at home, or are contacted by telephone. After a pilot study with 11 families, which yielded encouraging results, I worked with 37 further families, all of whom were seeking help for their pre-school children who had previously been screened by professionals. Pre-intervention measures were taken (see Figure 1.1) and the families were sequentially allocated to one of four methods of intervention:

- my working with them in a group context
- my visiting them at home
- my offering training over the telephone without meeting them
- being on a waiting list to see if the children's behaviour improved with the passage of time – the so-called 'delayed treatment waiting list control'.

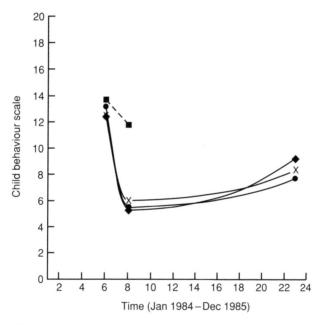

Figure 1.1   Effect of parent training during training and at followup as measured by the Child Behaviour Scale

> *Source:* Reproduced by permission of the British Association for Behavioural and Cognitive Psychotherapy from Sutton (1992) Training parents to manage difficult children: a comparison of methods. *Behavioural Psychotherapy, 20,* 115–139.

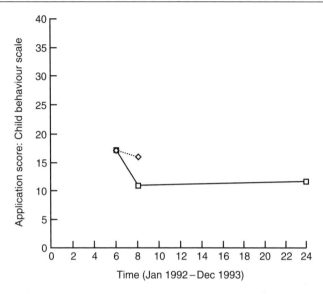

Figure 1.2   Effect of parent training at pre-training, post-training and at followup as measured by the Child Behaviour Scale

> *Source:* Reproduced by permission of the British Association for Behavioural and Cognitive Psychotherapy from Sutton (1995) Parent training by telephone: a partial replication. *Behavioural Psychotherapy, 23,* 1–24.

Each training sequence lasted 8 weeks, involving one meeting per week lasting about 2 hours for those parents meeting in a group, 1 hour for those whom I visited at home and an average of 45 minutes for those whom I trained by telephone. Each group received two follow-up 'booster' trainings. Figure 1.1 (see p. 28) shows the outcomes for the various groups on one of the main measures, both at the end of the 8 weeks of training and 12–18 months later, when independent assessors visited all the families to see how the children were faring.

From this work I developed a number of conclusions:

1. It was possible to train the parents of difficult pre-school children to manage them effectively by means of eight weekly sessions of no more than two hours per week, boosted by two follow-up sessions.
2. The children became more manageable by comparison with the children of parents who did not receive training.
3. The effects of the training persisted at 12–18 months, as reported to independent evaluators.
4. There was a falling away, however, in the extent to which effects were maintained between postintervention and followup. The telephone method showed most falling away.
5. There was little to choose between outcomes at any stage among the three methods of active training: group method, home visit method and telephone method.

Factors apparently central to success

1. *The availability of family or marital support.* I did not ask parents explicitly about marital distress but it became apparent that those mothers who had the least or no success were those who were either without marital or family support or whose husband, partner or wider family actively disapproved of the methods being taught. A number of single parents were extremely successful, including several in the telephone method and even one with twins in this method. These parents had the support of someone who appeared to approve of the practices being taught, for example the child's grandparents. Where such people did not approve, or undermined consistent management of the children, the parents were virtually doomed to failure.
2. *Competence in using time out.* Many studies, for example Forehand and MacDonough (1975), found time out (from positive reinforcement) to be an effective strategy for managing a wide variety of childhood misbehaviour, whereas Hobbs, Forehand and Murray (1978) have shown four minutes to be the most effective length of sanction. I found that parents who were able effectively to place a child in time out and to keep him there were much more likely to achieve a positive outcome than those who found this difficult or who were inconsistent in so doing.
3. *The use of training manuals.* The use of eight brief manuals, distributed one per week for each of the eight weeks, was seen as central to the successful outcome. Feedback from the parents indicated that they had found them useful as a means of developing their confidence in practising the theoretical ideas being taught. Some parents, however, particularly those who could barely read, asked for simpler materials involving 'fewer long words'.

Clinical significance of the findings from this study

A number of other important points may be made:

1. *The falling away of the effects of training is a well-established phenomenon.* Patterson (1974), for example, found that half the families in his sample began to slip back into former patterns of parenting 6 months after completing their training. It was on these grounds that he recommended 'booster' sessions to maintain treatment gains. While I did offer 'boosters' 2 weeks and 12 weeks after the completion of training, Figure 1.2 shows that additional 'boosters' should be built in at regular intervals following the completion of training.
2. *Socially disadvantaged people can be helped effectively.* There was no evidence from my study that the training methods were more successful with the more well-to-do families. It was the availability of support and the ability to implement time out that were the key variables.

3. *Parents whose children have had a difficult start in life need additional support.* This emerged from examining the data for those children referred by general practitioners or paediatricians and who had had, for example, multiple hospital admissions in the first year of life. These children were among those with the most serious behaviour disorders (perhaps associated with the anxiety that their parents felt about them) and should not be allocated to a telephone method. The families may well need many booster sessions.

Further evidence from a partial replication of this study

Because I was surprised by the evidence that it was possible to train parents without ever meeting them or setting eyes on the child, I undertook a further study (Sutton, 1995) to replicate the telephone method of training. I worked with 23 families whose preschool children had been screened by GPs or health visitors and trained with the parents entirely by telephone. Applications were randomly allocated, either to an immediate intervention group or to a delayed intervention waiting list control group, and preintervention measures were taken of the children's behaviour and of the level of depression of the mother. The programme of training as described above was replicated, but on this occasion it was carried out entirely by telephone. As before, measures were taken before and after the training. Figure 1.2 (see p. 29) shows the improvement in the children's behaviour and Figure 1.3 shows the

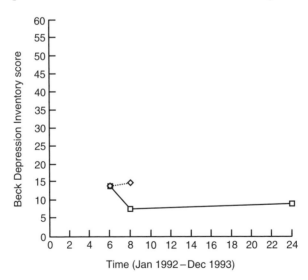

Figure 1.3 Effect of parent training on maternal depression at pre-training, post-training and at followup as measured by the Beck Depression Inventory

Source: Reproduced by permission of the British Association for Behavioural and Cognitive Psychotherapy from Sutton (1995) Parent training by telephone: a partial replication. *Behavioural Psychotherapy, 23,* 1–24.

improvement in the mothers' levels of depression as their children's behaviour improved.

The results confirmed those of the earlier study and were in line with hundreds of other studies across the world. The second study made the distinctive
contribution that such training can be successfully offered by telephone, provided an appropriate professional has screened the child for all the other
possible factors that may be contributing to the child's behaviour difficulty.

There is no space to report several factors in these studies that caught my
attention. They may, however, form the basis of another researcher's inquiry.
First, it seems that sheer inexperience of the role of the parent regarding how
to manage a child is playing a part. Second, very gentle, unassertive parents
sometimes experienced more difficulties than others – especially where their
child was demanding, high-spirited and wilful. It may just not be within your
capacity to assert yourself sufficiently to manage a headstrong two or three
year old who is defiantly refusing your quite reasonable requests. It is highly
likely that on at least some of these occasions the child 'wins the day', so
reinforcing his or her assertiveness. Third, some parents confided to me that
they longed so much for the love of their children that they feared that if they
were 'too strict' the child would not love them. They believed that indulging
the child would lead to gratitude from him or her; alas, the opposite was the
case. As we shall see, however, cognitive behavioural theory also supplied
the key to improving the situation.

SOCIAL LEARNING/
COGNITIVE-BEHAVIOURAL
THEORY

How do we begin to make sense of the complexity of the human situation? Of the many ways that social scientists have developed of conceptualising and coming to grips with this complexity, I wish briefly to consider here two: human beings as part of 'systems' and a range of 'perspectives' regarding human beings.

WAYS OF THINKING ABOUT HUMAN BEINGS

Human Beings as Part of 'Systems'

A system has two main features. First, it is an assembly of parts or components connected together in an organised way; second, the parts of the system affect each other – a change in one may well precipitate a change in another. Human beings are themselves 'systems', assemblies of closely integrated networks in which breathing, digesting food, circulating blood, reproduction and the other highly organised and integrated webs of activity together compose a living person. All the smaller systems contribute to the smooth functioning of the larger system, the body, and a significant change in one, such as catching flu, is very likely to affect the functioning of the others. Yet we ourselves are not only assemblies of systems; we also exist *within* systems: the family system, the education system, the political system, and so on. We are affected *by* others in those systems, such as our relatives and teachers, and we ourselves also affect other systems, for example other families and other organisations like schools and hospitals. We are all intimately connected in networks of relationships: no-one is an island.

Figure 2.1 shows a system, limited by a boundary, containing smaller systems in relationship. Other systems feed in and out of it. The larger system

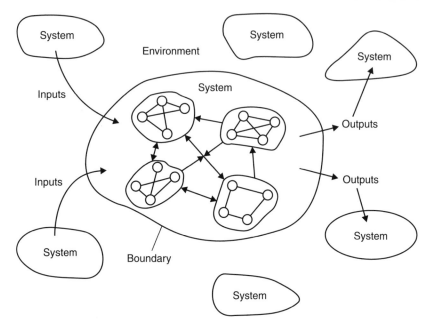

Figure 2.1 A system with subsystems, interacting with other systems

Source: Reproduced by permission of The Open University from Open University (1980) Systems Organization: The Management of Complexity. T243 Block 1: Introduction to Systems Thinking and Organization. Milton Keynes: Open University Press.

could represent either a person, composed of smaller systems and influenced by forces acting upon him or her, such as the events of family life, or it could represent a health authority or social services department, both affected by central government policy and consumer groups and influenced in turn by decisions by voters and by letters to MPs.

As I have written elsewhere (Sutton, 1994):

> Human beings, then, are inextricably linked with other human beings, since our deepest needs can only be met by other people. We are, however, also very different from one another. So we have this tension: human beings are at one and the same time both intimately bound up with each other and yet highly individual.

Figure 2.2 shows, in a schematic way, a child called Amrit Patel who, as a member of both an immediate and an extended family, is affected by the influences of people within those families, which are in turn affected by influences brought to bear, directly and indirectly, upon them.

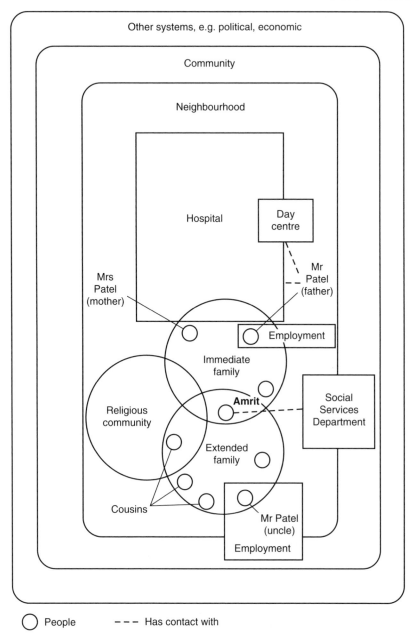

Figure 2.2 A child as part of many systems

Source: Reproduced by permission of Sutton & Herbert (1992) from *Mental Health: A Client Support Resource Pack*. Windsor: National Foundation for Educational Research. Nelson.

A RANGE OF PERSPECTIVES ON HUMAN BEINGS

Psychology is a discipline whose focus is primarily upon individuals, families and small groups and their interactions – as distinct from sociology, which usually focuses upon larger groups and processes. In order to grapple with complexity, psychology has often taken different *perspectives* upon systems and upon human nature. The ideal, of course, is an 'holistic' approach, in which each person is perceived in his or her entirety, encompassing the physical body, development and learning, human experience, creativity, potential and so forth, but in order to keep things manageable, five perspectives upon the human being (Figure 2.3), often called 'models', have been developed. These are:

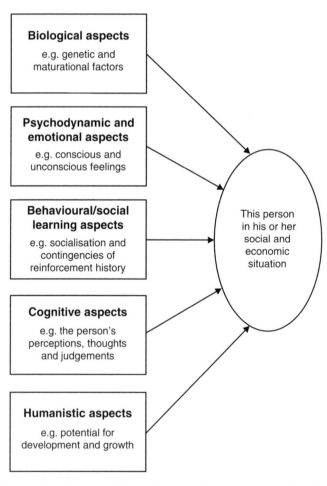

Figure 2.3   Five psychological perspectives on the human being

A. The *biological* perspective, this focuses upon the person as a biological phenomenon.
B. The *psychodynamic/emotional* perspective, including feelings, conscious and unconscious.
C. The *behavioural and social learning* perspective, including learning in a social context.
D. The *cognitive* perspective, including individual perceptions, thoughts and judgements.
E. The *humanistic* perspective, including the potential for development and growth.

I shall briefly consider these perspectives, each of which overlaps and interacts with the others, before focusing upon the behavioural and cognitive perspectives, as research in these areas has been found particularly valuable in understanding and helping troubled children.

The Biological Perspective

This perspective focuses upon human beings as biological phenomena. It takes account of genetic influences and such processes as maturation and ageing. Genes govern the processes of growth and maturation and make a contribution to some of our psychological characteristics; they determine our biological sex and physical characteristics such as our eye, skin and hair colouring; and they may be implicated in some aspects of our health and mental health, such as sickle-cell anaemia and schizophrenia.

The study of how innate factors affect development is a very complex field indeed. One particular method is to investigate characteristics of identical twins, called monozygotic or MZ twins, meaning that they were born from a single egg, as distinct from dizygotic or DZ twins, born from two separate eggs and therefore not identical. In the past, identical twins were sometimes separated at birth and grew up in different environments; this allowed rare opportunities to distinguish innate effects from those acquired from the environment. As I have written elsewhere (Sutton, 1994):

> Major studies, such as that of Tellegen and colleagues (1988), who examined 44 pairs of identical twins separated in early infancy and subsequently brought together at an average age of 34 years, showed major similarities between the pairs of twins. The highest similarities were found on measures of sociability, intelligence and measures of stability or instability. These findings, which are in line with other studies, suggest that we inherit about 50% of our potential for these characteristics.

Other fields of human experience that seem to be underpinned by biological factors include the attachment of infants to their mothers or other caretakers, bonding between mothers and their infants and children, introversion or extraversion, as well as responses to threat, such as aggressiveness and anxiety.

The Psychodynamic and Emotional Perspectives

Sigmund Freud and his early followers, Jung and Adler, were among those who made the earliest attempts to ground the study of human experience upon a scientific, as distinct from a philosophical, basis. Freud (1856–1939) was a doctor and neurologist who developed his theories as part of his research for a treatment for people who came to him in Vienna with disorders whose origin was inexplicable, such as sudden paralysis of limbs or the onset of blindness. In some instances, the opportunity to speak freely, expressing feelings of anger, resentment, bitterness or sexual desire, which were often kept hidden especially in late nineteenth-century Vienna, seemed to relieve the problem.

Freud developed a complex theory of psychosexual stages of human development. This has been very influential in its time and in the past provided the main theoretical framework for trying to help troubled children but it has many critics, particularly among those who are aware of the multifactorial underpinnings of human distress. Atkinson, Atkinson, Smith , Bern and Hilgard (1990) have offered an objective appraisal of Freud's theories, pointing out that rigorously designed studies provide little empirical data in support of Freud's psychosexual stages; moreover, the sample of people upon whom he based his theories was far from representative. They consider, however, that he and his daughter Anna made at least three major contributions towards the understanding of human experience: first, devising the method of free association – speaking whatever comes into one's mind in an uncensored way; second, elucidating the principle that much human behaviour is a compromise between our wishes and our fears and anxieties; and third, showing that much of our behaviour is influenced by processes that are nonconscious.

The Behavioural and Cognitive-behavioural Perspectives

Behaviourism

In reaction to the claims of Freud and his followers that they had established a scientific basis for the study of human development, there arose a number of challengers. Many were concerned to place the study of human experience upon as firm an empirical foundation as the physical sciences had achieved, and J. B. Watson (1930), for example, in an attempt to employ a means of gathering information and evidence in such a way that it could be tested and verified, proposed *behaviour* as a phenomenon which could be observed, measured and recorded by observers. Building upon the work of Pavlov, he was able to demonstrate that a great deal of learning takes place via a process known as 'conditioning'. The term was used because it referred to the learning of a behaviour *on condition that* it was associated with another event. Two main forms of conditioning have been distinguished: classical conditioning and operant conditioning:

- *Classical conditioning* is the learning of a behaviour because it is associated in time with a specific stimulus with which it was not formerly associated. An example of this is the child who has had a hospital admission, who subsequently shows fear when he encounters someone in a white coat – say, when going to the butcher's shop. The white coat, formerly a neutral object, has become associated with distress and thus elicits the fear response in the child.
- *Operant conditioning* is the learning of a behaviour because it *operates upon* and is affected by the environment. In essence, if a behaviour is followed by an outcome or response that is pleasurable or rewarding to the person or animal concerned, the behaviour is likely to be repeated: if it is followed by an outcome that is not pleasurable, it is less likely to be repeated. If, for example, a shy student contributes in class and what is said is acknowledged constructively by the tutor, that person is likely to contribute again; if what is said is ridiculed, the student is less likely to contribute again.

Cognitive-behavioural theory – a development of social learning theory

Behavioural theory seems to present the person as the passive recipient of the conditioning process: cognitive-behavioural theory (deriving from social learning theory) incorporates what is known about the laws of how patterns of behaviour are learned but also places far more emphasis upon the context of that learning and the specific beliefs that are part of that learning. Herbert (1981) emphasised that learning takes place *within a social context*; for example, Billy may come to understand the subtleties of the systems of which he is part and in the light of these think through various strategies for getting what he wants. Thus, while he may have learned that when he asks his Mum for sweets she usually ignores him unless it is Sunday, he may also have noticed that if he asks on weekdays in a way that makes her laugh, he is more likely to get them. In these circumstances, Billy may learn to be a bit of a clown because the attention and rewards he gets from his joking teach him to go on trying to make people laugh.

I shall consider very briefly three important concepts within social learning/cognitive-behavioural theory:

- learning via reinforcement and feedback
- learning by imitation and modelling
- learning through cognitive processes.

Learning via reinforcement and feedback

There is no doubt that parents and carers, childminders, teachers and all who have the care of children and young people do their jobs within a framework of social learning theory and employ principles of reinforcing certain patterns of behaviour and sanctioning others whether they are aware of it or not. When Danny drinks up his milk and his mother tells him, 'You *have* done well!' she is rewarding his drinking up his milk and giving him positive feedback. When Jenny shows her mother a painting she has done at playgroup and her Mum says 'We can't take messy paper home: you must leave it here', she may in effect be 'punishing' Jenny. She will certainly be discouraging Jenny from painting pictures 'to show Mummy'. These little scenes capture the processes of feedback that parents and all those who have the care of children and young people offer to those in their charge throughout the day. *The carers may or may not be aware of the consequences of their reactions and they may or may not intend those consequences but they happen whether they are aware of them or intend them or not.* The meanings of the terms are as follows:

1. *A reinforcer.* This is anything that has the effect of increasing the probability of the behaviour which preceded it occurring again. It can be positive or negative.
2. *Positive reinforcement.* This is any event that has the effect of increasing the probability of the behaviour which preceded it occurring again; for example, appreciation, praise, thanks, promotion and salaries. A child commended for trying hard at her school work is likely to continue to try hard; a social worker thanked by her team manager for her supportive behaviour to other team members is likely to continue to behave supportively to others in the team.
3. *Negative reinforcement/feedback.* This may be hard to understand. Technically, it is any happening that, because it is unpleasant (e.g. the sound of a pneumatic drill), has a rewarding effect when it stops. It may therefore increase a behaviour. For example, if a toddler is whining and crying and, when her father shouts at her, she stops, this stopping crying is likely to increase the frequency of the father shouting at her. The stopping crying acts as a 'negative reinforcer' to the father's shouting. In popular parlance, the expression 'negative reinforcement' is often, mistakenly, confused with and used instead of the more accurate expression 'punishment' or 'penalty'.
4. *Punishment, penalty or sanction.* This is any event which has the effect of decreasing the probability of recurrence of the behaviour that preceded it. There are two types of punishment: one is the occurrence of an unpleasant event following a behaviour; the other is the loss of a pleasant event following a behaviour.

Watson and Tharp (1981) clarify the distinctions between negative reinforcement and the two types of punishment as shown in Box 2.1.

Box 2.1: The distinction between negative reinforcement and two types of punishment (Watson & Tharp, 1981)

- *Negative reinforcement*. 'Behaviour...escapes or avoids a (usually un-pleasant) consequence; this strengthens the behaviour.' Another example is that studying may be increased in school children by removing threats of loss of pocket money, contingent upon behaviour.
- *Punishment, type 1*. 'Behaviour...leads to some unpleasant event; this makes the behaviour less probable.' For example, a child's hitting other children may be reduced by its being consistently followed by the child's being excluded from play with other children.
- *Punishment, type 2*. 'Behaviour...leads to the loss of something pleasant; this also makes the behaviour less probable.' For example, a child's swearing may be reduced by people walking away whenever it occurs.

Both 'rewards' and 'punishments', however, are highly individual, so that whereas for many children a smack may be a powerful punishment and discourage the behaviour that preceded it, for others, the smacks may be actively rewarding – because *for them, any attention is better than none*. This is a very important theoretical point. Box 2.2 illustrates the ways in which different patterns of response to a given pattern of behaviour often act to increase or decrease the probability of that pattern of behaviour occurring again.

Box 2.2: Behaviours, consequences and their probable outcomes

(Reproduced with permission from Herbert, 1987.)

Desirable behaviour	+	reinforcement (reward)	⟶	more desirable behaviour
Desirable behaviour	+	no reinforcement	⟶	less desirable behaviour
Undesirable behaviour	+	reinforcement (reward)	⟶	more undesirable behaviour
Undesirable behaviour	+	no reinforcement	⟶	less undesirable behaviour

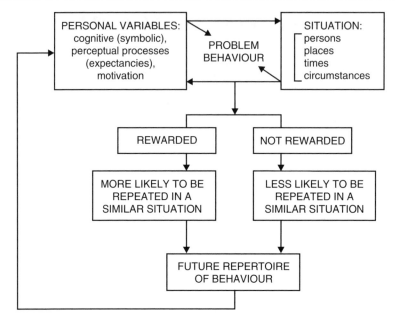

Figure 2.4   A feedback loop suggested by cognitive-behavioural theory

> *Source:* Reproduced from Emmett (1987) A feedback loop suggested by social learning theory. In Sutton (Ed.) *A Handbook of Research for the Helping Professions.* London: Routledge & Kegan Paul.

Much learning seems to occur via a series of feedback loops, as shown in Figure 2.4 (Emmet, 1987). For example, learning the language of one's community, although underpinned by genetically based factors, is obviously acquired by the feedback a child receives.

Other behaviours, including problem behaviour, may be learned in similar ways. If, for example, a child is rude to a teacher, the teacher tolerates this and the young person's friends admire him for it, then being rude to the teacher is likely to happen again. Such sequences can escalate into full confrontations and even violence.

Learning by observation, imitation and modelling

Cognitive behavioural theory also takes account of 'modelling' – that is, the way in which people imitate others, particularly those with status and with influence over them. Parents or caregivers are likely to be the first models whom young children imitate – their language, their accents, their choice of words, as well as their customary ways of behaving and their attitudes. Children learn specific roles at least partly through imitation; for example, children tend to imitate the parent or caregiver of the same sex, particularly if the parent is seen as nurturant and influential. If girls see mostly men in positions of influence and authority, such as doctors, business executives, judges and politicians, they have little opportunity to imitate women in such roles and are more likely to take subordinate roles for themselves.

There is evidence that much prosocial and antisocial behaviour is learned by imitation. The power of peer group pressure upon young people is well established and many young offenders have learned their behaviour by taking influential members of their peer groups as models. There are good reasons for calling institutions for young offenders 'universities of crime'. Bandura (1986) has written extensively about these processes of modelling.

Learning through cognitive processes

Mischel (1973) has considered some of the individual differences in thinking, judging and valuing that contribute to the very personal ways in which we perceive and behave in day-to-day life. He also emphasised the multi-dimensional interactions that are implicit in human affairs and incorporated this awareness into social learning theory. For example, although people are much influenced by their upbringing and socialisation experiences they may become very aware and critical of them, and actively choose not to follow similar approaches in bringing up their own children. For example, one mother with whom I worked felt she had been given little attention as a child: she resolved never to ignore her own small son, with the result that he followed her around every minute of the day, wanting this and demanding that, and never giving her a moment to herself. The mum, still bent on never ignoring her child, had made a rod for her own back but was grateful to hear that it was in her child's best interests, and certainly in hers, that he should sometimes be ignored. This cognitive understanding soon helped to release her from the well intentioned but misguided rule that she had imposed on herself.

The Cognitive Perspective

This perspective focuses upon the perceptual, thinking, judging and intellectual processes of human beings. It takes account of the evidence that we are not simply driven by unconscious forces or reacting to stimuli in the environment: on the contrary, we form opinions, we judge others' actions and attitudes, we consider other alternatives, we plan strategies and are creative in our efforts to make sense of the experience of being alive. According to this perspective, human beings gather and process information and take action on their view of this information. Piaget (1896–1980), the renowned child psychologist, monitored the growth of children's cognitive capacities as they passed through various stages of development. These stages appear to correspond with stages of brain development, following a predictable sequence in all children – although some children will pass through them more swiftly than others. There is no space here to consider the detail of Piaget's work but it is important that health visitors, nurses, social workers, counsellors and all those who work with people in distress are familiar with the concepts. For example, *that people really do see the world and things that happen in it differently*: they attend to different things, they remember different things and they put different interpretations upon what they have perceived; reality is, as I have already indicated, akin to 'seeing pictures in the fire'.

Further, because of their immaturity and inexperience or the ways in which they may have been told to interpret events, children make judgements about events that may be inaccurate and in some instances completely wrong. A child whose parent, in a moment of exasperation, says, 'you are a bad/horrible/wicked child', may believe what has been said into adulthood and beyond; another may witness sexual intercourse and believe that the people concerned are fighting and that someone is being hurt; while a third, who has been abused, may have been threatened that if she tells anyone about what has occurred she will get ill or will be 'sent away'. Young children are trapped in their perceptions and their interpretations of those perceptions. The same is, of course, true of adults.

The Humanistic Perspective

This view of humanity is concerned with positive and optimistic features of human experience. Two psychologists who have redressed the tendency of researchers to focus upon human pathology and have reasserted a constructive view of people and their potential for growth and development are Abraham Maslow (1908–70) and Carl Rogers (1902–87). Maslow's (1970) hierarchy of human needs is familiar to many students. Rogers, his contemporary, believed that human beings demonstrate one basic 'tendency and striving – to actualise, maintain and enhance the experiencing organism'. He therefore sought to identify the circumstances and conditions that other people could provide, which would help them reach such potential. Rogers, together with those

---

Box 2.3: Components of helpful and effective counselling (after Truax & Carkhuff, 1967)

- *Unconditional positive regard* by the therapist or worker for the client.
- *An attitude of personal warmth* towards him or her.
- *The capacity for empathy*, so that the person feels deeply understood.
- *Congruence*: the notion of being genuine, of not playing a part.

who have subjected his theories to detailed investigation, such as Truax and Carkhuff (1967), identified several features that seem reliably to contribute to helping people in distress (see Box 2.3).

These concepts have emerged from repeated studies as key components of helpful counselling and are cornerstones of 'client-centred counselling'. This same sensitive regard for people in distress, and especially for troubled children, is taken for granted in what I am advocating. Our efforts to help children and their families will usually go beyond counselling, but they are underpinned by the same attitudes of respect and concern for people in distress that have proved so beneficial within counselling.

EXPLORING PRINCIPLES OF COGNITIVE-BEHAVIOURAL THEORY

Having briefly introduced five main perspectives within psychology, I wish now to explore cognitive-behavioural theory more fully. This rather clumsy term refers to a body of concepts and principles that incorporates both cognitive perspectives and those deriving from behavioural principles. As indicated, an earlier name for this body of concepts and principles was social learning theory, which emphasised that behaviours are learned in a social context, but the expression 'cognitive-behavioural theory' has emerged as the preferred term because it incorporates cognitive perspectives.

We saw on p. 42 that much behaviour is *learned*, both by imitation or modelling and in accordance with certain contingencies of reward and sanction. This understanding is extremely important: it provides us with the means of analysing undesirable patterns of behaviour to see if they are being maintained by the rewards that are, often unwittingly, being provided by parents or caregivers; alternatively, we can see whether desired patterns of behaviour, which occur only occasionally, are 'extinguishing' or fading away because, unintentionally, parents are punishing them or failing to reward them (see Box 2.1). Practitioners find that this is happening very frequently indeed.

Perceptions of Children: Cognitive Distortions

There seem to be four main areas of difficulty experienced by parents. These are shown in Box 2.4. Let us consider examples of each in turn.

1. Incomplete or faulty knowledge of child development

How can parents know what is typical or atypical in their children's behaviour? Every child has a different genetic inheritance and while children

Box 2.4: Parents' concerns about children calling for cognitive approaches

1. Their knowledge base about normal child development may be incomplete/inaccurate.
2. They may have deep feelings about the child, which affect their responses.
3. The way they perceive their child's behaviour may be skewed: e.g. they may focus primarily upon aspects of misbehaviour, neglecting positive behaviours.
4. They may have negative beliefs or feelings about themselves or the child that lead to unhappy outcomes.

pass through developmental stages in the same sequence, they pass through them at different rates – a wide range of which are completely normal. It is easy, then, for parents to come to believe, for example, that their tiny child is deliberately behaving in ways that upset them rather than displaying behaviours which are completely normal for a child of that age. For example, when a toddler soils his nappy just after he has been changed, some inexperienced parents may assume that this has been done deliberately to provoke them. Box 2.5 shows further examples of misinformation about child development.

2. Deep feelings about the child which affect their responses

Other parents may have very powerful feelings towards their child which are entirely understandable in the light of their experiences, but which get in the way of their being able to express loving and positive feelings towards him or her. See Table 2.1.

Box 2.5: Inaccurate beliefs about child development

1. At 12 months, a child should be able to use a potty reliably and cleanly.
2. If children have plenty of toys, they should be able to amuse themselves for an hour.
3. It is OK for toddlers to be sat in front of the TV for two hours at a time.
4. As babies haven't learned to talk, there's no need to talk to them.
5. Toddlers understand most of what we say to them.

Table 2.1 Feelings towards child that affect reactions to him or her

Feelings towards child	Beliefs about the child
I never wanted this child.	I'll never be able to love him.
These are my new partner's children, not mine.	We just don't like each other. We never shall.
This child is exactly like my ex.	He'll grow up to knock me about, like my ex did.
Giving birth to this child was such torture: it's affected my feelings about him forever.	Every time I look at him, I think of the suffering he caused me.

3. The way they perceive their child's vehaviour may be skewed

Other difficulties may arise because the parent has been taught, or has arrived at, mistaken assumptions about herself or about the child. Table 2.2 shows examples of skewed or mistaken beliefs about a child can lead to mistaken conclusions and a focus upon his or her negative characteristics with the result that the child's positive features are neglected or downplayed.

4. How negative beliefs or feelings about themselves or the child can lead to unhappy outcomes

Table 2.3 developed by Iwaniec (1995) illustrates how parents' beliefs can lead to negative feelings and frustration, which in turn can contribute to a chain of counterproductive behaviours and distressing long-term outcomes. Each group or type of misconceptions needs, of course, a separate approach. Table 2.4 shows some possible ways in which cognitive behavioural approaches can help to counter inaccurate misconceptions or other beliefs.

Table 2.2 Examples of skewed or mistaken beliefs about self or child

Parental perception	Mistaken conclusion
I grew up in care . . .	. . . so I'll never be able to care properly for a child.
I can't cope with this child when I'm tired . . .	. . . and I don't think I'll ever be able to cope with her.
Whatever I try, Josh doesn't eat food I make for him . . .	He doesn't like me . . .

Table 2.3   Chains of parents' beliefs, negative feelings and unhappy outcomes

Event	Belief	Feeling	Behaviour	Outcome
Child fails to gain weight	I can't cope. He deliberately behaves like that to spite me	Inadequacy, helplessness, despair	Force feeding, screaming, shouting	Food avoidance behaviour, losing weight
Developmental delays	He/she dislikes being picked up; dislikes me	Depression, frustration, uselessness	Does nothing	Child is under stimulated; emotional neglect
Child does not respond to parental requests	I am inadequate as a parent. I can't cope	Frustration, anger, depression	Smacks, shouts, criticises	Distorted relationship, emotional abuse

Source: Adapted from Iwaniec (1995) *The Emotionally Abused and Neglected Child*. Chichester: Wiley.

Table 2.4   Illustrative ways of responding to parents' beliefs and concerns using cognitive behavioural approaches

Parents' area of difficulty	Workers' ways of helping
Misinformation about child development	*Gradually* giving more accurate information about e.g. feeding, toileting
Feelings towards and beliefs about a child that affect reactions to him/her	1 Active, nonjudgmental listening. 2 Over time, eliciting any positive feelings towards child and helping parents enhance these. 3 If necessary, structuring, e.g. play, situations so that the child can gradually experience nurturing attention from parent.
Focus upon negative aspects of the child's behaviour	1 Active listening and accepting parents' resentment... 2 *Gradually* redirecting parents' attention to positive features of child's behaviour
Parents caught in a chain of negative feelings, actions and outcomes	1 Active listening and accepting parents' resentment... 2 Introducing a supportive and structured strategy for reducing tension e.g. relaxation ... 3 Introducing a reduction of critical interactions and an increase of positive ones.

Meeting Children's Needs for Attention

First things first. Children need attention. Children need a great deal of individualised attention and nothing in this book should be interpreted as suggesting otherwise. Light may be thrown upon the behaviour of troubled children in an important paper on autism by Howlin (1998), in which the author discusses how this condition makes it very difficult for affected children to have any clear impact upon their environment. Howlin cites the work of Durand and Carr (1991) and suggests that 'the five main functions of aggressive, self-injurious, stereotyped or other disruptive behaviours' are as follows:

1. To indicate the need for help or attention.
2. To escape from stressful situations or activities.
3. To obtain desired objects.
4. To protest against unwanted events/activities.
5. To obtain stimulation.

These five functions of troubled behaviour have been distinguished in the context of the study of autism but I suggest that they are relevant to *all* children. In other words, many children with serious behaviour difficulties are seeking to meet one or other of the above needs. It follows that although it may well be impossible and inappropriate to try to avoid frustrating them or to give them desired objects whenever they demand them, this way of looking at children's behaviour does suggest that children need and seek extensive attention. *Adults are responsible for responding to those needs but in ways and at times that help children learn prosocial behaviour.* Thus, to attend extensively to Darren when he has just bitten another child at playgroup will teach him that this is an effective way of gaining attention from adults; to ignore him or reprimand him briefly at that time but to give him individual attention at another available time is likely both to meet his needs and to help him learn to live acceptably with other children.

The importance of shared play

Many of the needs of children for this individual attention will be met via play (Box 2.6). Bee (1992) has suggested that although children show several different kinds of play at any one time, there are often regular patterns of play that are noticeable as children develop. Bee makes the point that:

> ... in some very real ways, play is children's 'work'. Opportunities to manipulate and experiment with objects, pretend with them, play parts and roles, all seem to be important ingredients in the child's cognitive and social development ... The key point is that children need to have *time* for play – time when they are not watching TV, not organized, not required to do anything 'constructive'.

Box 2.6: Patterns of young children's play (after Bee, 1992)

1. *Sensorimotor play*. Children of about 12 months explore and manipulate objects, mouthing them, shaking them and moving them along the floor.
2. *Constructive play*. By the age of two, children are building towers, making patterns with shapes, using blocks that fit together, twist and so on.
3. *First pretend play*. Young children begin to 'feed Teddy' and 'put dolly to bed'. They experiment with roles by putting on hats or Mummy's shoes.
4. *Substitute pretend play*. Around two or three years, children begin to let one thing stand for another: boxes become boats or cars; clay can stand for food; and imagination, given rein, can invent rich fantasy games.
5. *Sociodramatic play*. Children begin to take on roles: Mummy and Daddy; farmer and farmer's wife; astronaut; teacher and child. Bee suggests that this play helps them relinquish their egocentric way of understanding the world.
6. *Awareness of roles*. Around six years, children plan their play ahead and give out roles: 'You be the teacher and I'll be the child and then we'll swap.'
7. *Games with rules*. As children enter primary or elementary school, pretend play declines and is replaced by more and more games with specific rules.

Moreover, these stages will all be enriched if the child's parents, grandparents or other caregivers can make time, even if only for a few minutes daily, to share the child's developing world of play. These times can be low-key, involving no expensive bought games, but short periods when the child is allowed to lead the play. So, children may choose whether to look at a story book together with a caregiver, to sit on the floor with bricks, to use homemade playdough or to wash up together with an adult. Not only do these short individualised times foster the cognitive and language development of the child, but also this nurturing attention builds trust and attachment: its importance cannot be over-estimated.

Behaviour Analysis

Parents typically make very general complaints about their troubled children. 'Henry is a bad boy'; 'Winston is aggressive'; 'Joanne's been nothing but trouble since she was born'; 'Sanjay is naughty'. It is sometimes startling for them when I ask 'Exactly what does Henry/Winston/Joanne/Sanjay *do* that upsets you so?' They usually find it very difficult to specify *exactly what their child does* but this is a crucial step in using this body of theory. We need to know precisely which *behaviours* the child displays that so upset his parents, his brothers and sisters, his teachers and sometimes himself. With help, parents can eventually identify and work out a 'problem profile' for their child. These often include some of the following:

- he hits other children or parents
- he bites other children or adults
- he tips over furniture
- he does not stay in bed; or demands unnecessary attention in the night
- he does not do what parents ask
- he throws food
- he does not settle to anything for more than a few minutes: short attention span
- he demands mother's attention so that she cannot talk to anyone else
- he swears at mother or visitors to the house
- he spits at family members.

I also ask them if they can identify positive or pleasing aspects of their child's behaviour, aspects that they would like to see more of. This is sometimes even more difficult for them. Sometimes they can suggest two or three things: bringing home for them things made at playgroup; Dean's readiness to come for a cuddle; or the way Poppy, a terror while awake, sleeps all night through. Sometimes, very sadly, there is nothing that parents can think of that they like about their child; they have already written him off at the age of three and 'can't wait until he goes to school'. Eventually, however, we are usually able to develop a 'positive profile', which may include an acknowledgement that the child:

- occasionally carries out a request
- finds something which is lost
- feeds the dog
- eats well
- looks at picture/story books calmly.

This way of analysing what often seems to parents to be a blur of continuous misbehaviour by distinguishing its component behaviours at first mystifies parents but gradually they come to see the advantages of identifying specific behaviours and addressing them separately.

In my work it was necessary to ask the parents to collect two sets of behaviour counts, known as 'data' or evidence. The first record showed, on a day-by-day basis, the instances of one negative behaviour, typically the child's refusal to follow instructions or requests, whereas the second showed the instances of positive behaviour, carrying out requests (see Table 2.5). These records are necessary for a minimum of one week, to provide a 'baseline' or benchmark against which to measure subsequent change. They also provide the means of judging, over the weeks that follow, whether the behaviour is

Table 2.5 Positive and negative forms of some specific behaviours

Negative behaviour	Positive behaviour
Does not follow requests within 1 minute	Begins to follow requests within 1 minute
Hits or bites others	Shares or lends toys
Comes downstairs after being put to bed	Settles after being put to bed
Refuses to eat/throws food	Eats a small amount of a meal
Disrupts other children's activities	Plays quietly with other children
Speaks rudely to or shouts at parents	Speaks calmly and quietly to parents

changing in the desired direction: that is, with negative forms of the behaviour decreasing and positive ones increasing.

Analysing the Antecedents–Behaviour–Consequence Sequence

The relationship between a behaviour and the events in the environment associated with it is called a *contingency* and it includes three components: the behaviour itself, antecedent events, both distant and immediate, and consequent events. It has proved easy to remember these important terms by referring to them as the A–B–C sequence, standing for 'Antecedents', 'Behaviour' and 'Consequences'. The term 'activator' is sometimes clearer to use than 'antecedent', and is useful in that it has connotations of being a cue or a trigger to behaviour. Since practice using principles of cognitive-behavioural theory involves analysing how behaviour may be affected by its antecedents, by its consequences, or by both together, let us consider some examples of each situation.

Examples of antecedents/activators triggering behaviour

It is possible to analyse many sequences of behaviour, focusing upon antecedents or consequences. One or other will often throw light upon difficult behaviour. Similarly it is possible to analyse other situations showing how the consequences are rewarding the very behaviour complained about. See Table 2.7.

You will see that, in all the examples in Table 2.6, the child's undesired behaviour followed directly from what went before, the *antecedent*. In effect, the child was cued to behave in the very way that the parents did not want. This is no-one's fault, or at least it was certainly not done with the intention

Table 2.6 Analysis of behaviour with a focus upon activators

Antecedent/activator	Behaviour	Consequence
1 Dad and Jack come in from playgroup... Mum says 'Well Jack, who did you upset today?'	1 Jack goes up to his Mum and hits her...	1 Mum phones the health visitor and says she must call at once!
2 The health visitor asks Tom to add a brick. Mum says 'He won't do it'.	2 Tom checks his movement towards the brick. He does not do as asked.	2 Mum says, 'I told you so!'
3 Chris is going back to school after illness. Dad says, 'Are you sure you feel OK?'	3 The child does not go back to school.	3 Mum and Dad have a row about whether Chris was well enough to go back.
4 Mum says 'Now just you eat all this up!'	4 Jane puts down her spoon.	4 Jane does not eat the food prepared for her.

of cueing the child, but it nevertheless had that effect. So there is no point in blaming people for being unaware of something that is extremely subtle. It is, however, how learning takes place, so it is helpful if parents and other people who look after children can come to see that sometimes we unintentionally and unwittingly *teach* children to behave in undesirable ways.

In the examples in Table 2.7 the children have learned from the *consequences* of their behaviour that if they persist long enough and unpleasantly enough in demanding their own way the adults will eventually give in! We may not be aware of what we are teaching children when we give in to their threats or

Table 2.7 Analysis of behaviour with a focus upon consequences

Antecedent or activator	Behaviour	Consequence
1 Dad told Danny to put the TV off.	He kept putting it on.	Eventually it was left on to give people a bit of peace.
2 Grandma told Janet to wear her blue jersey.	Janet said she wanted to wear her new red one.	Eventually Grandma gave way because she wanted Janet to like her.
1 Paul was out shopping with Mum.	He demanded an ice cream. Mum refused.	Paul began to scream. Mum gave way because she didn't want people to stare at her.

Box 2.7: Cognitive-behavioural procedures (after Martin & Pear, 1992)

1. Taking account of principles of classical conditioning.
2. Getting a behaviour to occur more often with positive reinforcement or reward.
3. Encouraging perseverence through intermittent reinforcement: pitfalls of this approach.
4. Getting a behaviour to occur less often by avoiding rewarding it so that it extinguishes or fades away.
5. Getting a behaviour to occur less often by actively penalising it.
6. Getting a behaviour to occur less often by 'response cost'.
7. Using modelling and rehearsal to affect behaviour.
8. Helping an individual child or young person to develop self-control.
9. Helping children and parents to come to understand their own beliefs and concerns so that misinformation and flawed assumptions can be corrected (e.g. Box 2.5).
10. Using problem-solving approaches.

---

their rudeness *but we are ourselves teaching them to be rude and threatening just as if we told them in a classroom 'it is right to be rude and threatening to people'.*

MAKING USE OF PRINCIPLES OF COGNITIVE-BEHAVIOURAL THEORY

Cognitive-behavioural theory is emerging from extensive research as a valuable resource for helping people. Box 2.7 draws on the work by Martin and Pear (1992) on cognitive-behavioural approaches and also includes principles which I have found helpful in my own research. I shall consider each one.

1. Taking Account of Principles of Classical Conditioning

The earliest formal account of this is still an excellent illustration. In 1920 two researchers, Watson and Rayner, sought to establish whether fears could be acquired simply by association. They worked with a little boy, Albert, aged 11 months, who showed no fear of a variety of objects placed on the floor near him; these included a white rat. Then, as part of the study, while Albert was watching the rat closely, one of the researchers banged a steel bar with a hammer just behind Albert's head, causing him to be startled and to cry. During two separate sessions, a week apart, the researchers linked the loud noise to the sight of the rat on seven occasions – causing Albert to show signs of great fear. Subsequently, whenever the rat appeared, Albert became very upset, trembled and cried and these fears also spread or 'generalised' to other animals, including a dog and a rabbit.

The principle here, then, is that a neutral stimulus, in this case the rat, has acquired the capacity to elicit fear by being presented at the same time as a fear-provoking event.

An everyday example of this was suggested by a participant at one of my training events. A little girl, who never objected to going to bed and who loved bedtime stories, one evening was read a story which she found very frightening; thereafter, for many evenings, she became very fearful when she went to bed. Her bed, and the bedtime routine, which formerly had had neutral associations, had now acquired very frightening associations.

The means of reducing such an acquired fear is, happily, also based upon cognitive-behavioural principles. If we were seeking to help Albert overcome his fear of rats, a structured programme might be developed, as shown in Box 2.8.

Box 2.8: A programme to help a child frightened of rats – little Albert

1. Albert sees other children looking at picture books of children, the seaside, farmyards and so on, while sitting on his mother's lap.
2. Albert joins other children looking at picture books.
3. Picture books containing photographs of animals are included among the books over the next few days.
4. Albert joins other children enjoying looking at photographs of animals, while with his mother who shows interest and pleasure in the photographs.
5. Over several days, Albert is taken for walks in the park where there are birds and perhaps squirrels in the distance.
6. Albert's walks include going closer to the birds and squirrels in a very calm, easy way.
7. Albert is taken past a pet shop where there are hamsters and other small animals in cages.
8. This walk is taken very frequently, in the presence of loving and unconcerned adults, who do not hurry him to overcome his fears. Rather, the fears are allowed to subside.
9. Albert and his mother look in the window of the pet shop where hamsters and rats are kept. They do this for several days.
10. Albert and his mother go into the pet shop and look briefly at the animals, including hamsters and rats in their cages. Everything is done lightheartedly and pleasurably.

This procedure is called *desensitisation*. We shall see the research evidence of its helpfulness in the chapter on helping children with sleeping difficulties (see Chapter 7). Similarly, in the case of the little girl who was frightened by the bedtime story, it was possible to ensure that once the origins of her fear were understood her bedtime routine was kept calm and enjoyable but without too much overanxious reassurance and with only amusing and lighthearted stories when she wished for them.

2. Getting a Behaviour to Occur More Often by Means of 'Reward'

Human beings are motivated to a very great extent by what they, individually, find rewarding. This statement may make people sound very unpleasant and selfish but this is not intended. Sometimes the rewards are *tangible* or *material*: most people want money in the form of a salary or payment of some kind as a means to attaining both the essential and inessentials of life. How many of us, if our salaries were completely withdrawn, would continue to do the same work, or the same amount of work, for more than a few days? Many people also want certain possessions, a car, a house and things to go in it. Advertisers are constantly attempting to stimulate our readiness to want possessions by offering inducements to purchase furniture, clothing, jewellery or household goods. Children too seek tangible rewards – although, as we shall see, they are less motivated by these when they are little: they are *taught* to want material possessions as they grow older. We have *learned* to give presents at Christmas and our materialist society seeks to teach us to place a value upon these things according to their cost.

People are also motivated by *social* rewards: by the friendliness of other people, by concern and by affection. Many are also motivated by seeing the values that they hold advanced or disseminated. Some act as volunteers in activities that are important to them for years on end; others give generously to charitable causes where they will never meet the recipients. In such situations it is the success of the projects that they support and the feeling that they are contributing towards the *furtherance of their aims and values* that is rewarding. Rewards are highly individual, even idiosyncratic, but they are nevertheless absolutely central to understanding human behaviour.

Other rewards are only available from other human beings: *we cannot be ourselves by ourselves*. We need friends and companions and contact with supportive people: these are profoundly important to our emotional well-being. To receive a letter or telephone call from a friend or an invitation from someone we like makes us feel valued and appreciated. Having people in whom we can confide has been shown to be one of the necessities for good mental health

Box 2.9: Different adult responses to Danny's fighting – what Danny learns.

1. If both parents and all the other adults in Danny's world prohibit fighting by disapproving reactions and by sanctions against it he is likely gradually to learn to inhibit fighting.
2. If both parents and others approve it, by saying to him 'you're a real boy, aren't you!' he will soon learn to develop his fighting ability.
3. If his parents approve of his fighting but his teachers disapprove he is likely to learn to inhibit fighting at school; but because of the tendency of behaviours to generalise from one situation to another – that is, from home to school – it will not be easy for the teachers to inhibit the fighting.
4. If one parent approves and one parent disapproves, Danny will be very confused. He is likely to react erratically to this inconsistency and to resort to fighting when situations become frustrating for him.

(Brown & Harris, 1978). Thus, to receive acknowledgement of our contribution towards some success or to be thanked for a kindness is a very rewarding experience: indeed, we often feel undervalued or underappreciated if our efforts are not acknowledged in this way. These needs are particularly acute for young children: the affection and attention of their parents or dependable caregivers are absolutely essential to their psychological wellbeing. It follows that nurturing attention and approval are powerful emotional and social rewards for children.

As we have seen in Box 2.2, a behaviour that is followed by a reward, whether tangible or social, is likely to increase. This suggests that commendation or 'positive feedback' from people who are important in the child's world, parents, caregivers, teachers, is, whether they are aware of it or not, making it more or less likely that certain behaviours will occur again. If we attend positively to a child's learning to feed herself, to use a potty or to dress herself, and commend her for her achievement, she is likely to continue to practise these skills. If, however, we attend positively (and rewardingly) to a child's provocation, her swearing or her smearing and throwing food, then she is likely to continue to practise *these* activities too. A close analysis of the exact antecedents and consequences of an aspect of behaviour is often extremely informative and illuminating.

Consider an example. Children learn and work out *from their experiences* whether fighting other children is permitted or not. Suppose that Danny, a well-built three year old and tall for his age, has discovered that children give up their toys to him when he fights with them. If we want a behaviour such as fighting to change, we have to do at least three things:

1. Get Danny's parents and *all* the people who care for him to agree that they will stop him fighting and will not let him hit other children or take their toys away.
2. Explain to Danny that fighting is not allowed either at home or at school.
3. Find opportunities to help Danny manage mini-situations (laying a table, giving out the crayons, putting away the Lego) without fighting and then commend him warmly for this.

In theoretical terms, Danny will need the following:

- First, every instance of this success should be commended (*continuous reinforcement*).
- Later, he will need commending only occasionally (*intermittent reinforcement*).

This example is valid for the promotion of all new learning, whether for children or adults. In all cases the new learning will be acquired most effectively and most enjoyably if early instances of the newly acquired behaviour are noticed, appreciated and commended by the teacher or instructor. If you doubt this, think back to your own learning in childhood: to read, to swim, or to ride a bicycle. Or think of learning a new skill as an adult: to drive a car or to use a word processor. Try to recall whether this learning was accompanied by encouragement or criticism or perhaps by no feedback at all, so that you didn't know whether you had done well or poorly. Finally, remember what the effect of these various responses was upon your learning.

3. Getting a Behaviour to Persist through Occasional Reward, but Noting Pitfalls

As children learn new skills, such as how to dress themselves or use cutlery or chopsticks they are typically commended on most occasions at the outset by the smiles and praise of those who care for them: as indicated, this is called *continuous* reinforcement. This is as true for adults as for children. As learners become more proficient, however, teachers either consciously or unconsciously realise that only an occasional reassurance is necessary – 'You're getting on well with that, Jane', or 'You're doing fine, Winston; keep going'. This is called *intermittent* or *occasional* reinforcement.

This principle operates, however, for good or ill. Children need much encouragement as they learn the skills required of them in the educational system and adults need much encouragement from their spouses, partners and relatives to continue with the demanding tasks of bringing up children to be constructive members of society. But the principle also operates in ordinary, day-to-day life. Indeed, thousands, millions of people regularly buy tickets in the National Lottery because they anticipate that one day they will win a substantial reward. Although their better judgement may tell them that this is unlikely, the pay-out of small £10 rewards on an occasional basis keeps them buying lottery tickets week by week.

It is known from laboratory studies and from everyday life that behaviours which have been rewarded only occasionally tend to persist and are very hard to change. An everyday example of this is a child, Johnny, who has acquired the habit of coming to his parents' bed at least twice a night. Sometimes they let him into their bed and sometimes they don't. His parents, short of space and weary, decide to encourage him to sleep in his own bed. They agree to return him to his own bed every single time he appears at their bedside and to commend him every morning for remaining in his own bed. They are eventually successful by using *continuous* reward. Perhaps, however, after several weeks of successfully following this plan, Johnny, awakened by chance, once again appears at their bedside at 2.00 a.m.; on this occasion the parents, being particularly tired, again allow him to get in and sleep with them. It is highly likely that Johnny will reappear the following night, for he has effectively been taught to do so on an *intermittent* basis – that is, he has been occasionally rewarded for coming to his parents' bed. To repeat, behaviours that are occasionally rewarded are very hard to change.

This theoretical issue is extremely important. *It is operating whether we are aware of it or not* and it underpins the importance of parents, teachers and care-givers attempting to be as consistent as possible in their ways of responding to children's behaviours. If they say one thing one day and another the next the child does not know where he stands: similarly, if one parent or family member reacts angrily to being sworn at one day but lets the child get away with it the next, the child will persist in swearing.

4. Reducing the Frequency of a Behaviour by Not Rewarding It

If a behaviour is not rewarded it will tend to fade away; the technical name for this fading away is 'extinguishing'. This, too, will happen whether people intend it or not or whether they are aware of it or not. For example, when I worked in a child and family centre, a mother told me that her daughter's teacher was very upset by the behaviour of the little girl, aged seven years. The child was much distressed by the death of her father and was very unsettled both at home and at school; she constantly left her seat to go to the teacher's desk seeking help with her work. The teacher, aware of the little girl's distress and anxious not to reject her, attended to her every time she went to her desk, *unintentionally making this behaviour more likely to recur.* This situation was, however, both intruding upon the rights of other children to the teacher's time and causing the teacher acute conflict. Using cognitive-behavioural theory we can see that the teacher was unwittingly reinforcing the very behaviour she wanted to discourage. The solution would have been to give the little girl the absolute minimum of attention each time she went to the teacher's desk so that this behaviour gradually extinguished and to give her individualised attention when the teacher was in a position to give her time – for example, at the end of the lesson.

Here the principle for reducing the frequency of a behaviour is: first undertake an A–B–C analysis and then, when you have established which rewards are maintaining the undesired behaviour, withdraw those rewards altogether. If this is inappropriate then one should gradually reduce them so that the behaviour slowly fades away. This last is particularly relevant if the reward that is maintaining a behaviour is attention.

Many petty misbehaviours can be reduced and even eliminated in this way. Children's whining and demanding are particularly stressful to adults but can be reduced by showing the child that you are not attending to them. Getting out a Hoover and actively attending to the dust on the carpet gives an extremely clear message to a grizzling child and can be done every time the whining starts!

5. Reducing the Frequency of a Behaviour by Actively Penalising It

Some behaviours are too serious to be ignored. One cannot ignore a child's biting or hitting another child, or deliberate disobedience, or disruption of other people's or children's activities. Sometimes clear penalties are necessary. Consider the issue of smacking, still advocated by many parents as the best means of chastising children, but clearly contrary to the Children Act 1989. The advantages and disadvantages are outlined in Box 2.10.

Box 2.10: Advantages and disadvantages of smacking

Advantages: It is quick and the effects are usually immediate.
                It tells the child 'don't do that!'
                It relieves the parent's feelings.
Disadvantages: It provides the child with a model of aggression to imitate.
                It does not tell the child what he/she should do instead of the unwanted behaviour.
                It loses its effect if frequently used.
                It may become a reward if it is virtually the only attention a child gets.

Table 2.8 Different levels of time out

Level of time out	Management
1 Activity time out	The child is simply barred from joining in an enjoyable activity, but still allowed to observe it; i.e. having misbehaved, she is made to sit out of the game
2 Room time out	He or she is not allowed to take part in the activity but is not totally isolated: i.e. having misbehaved, he is seated at the far end of the playroom.
3 Exclusion time out	The last resort. The child is briefly isolated in a situation away from rewarding contingencies, e.g. in a hallway or empty room (unlocked). The place must be *boring* and safe.

Source: Reproduced from Webster-Stratton & Herbert (1994). *Troubled Families: Problem Children.* Chichester: Wiley.

Using Time Out/Calm Down

A *far* more effective penalty than smacking is to use the principle of withdrawing attention by placing misbehaving children in a location where they are not receiving any rewarding attention at all. This is called placing them in time out, although the term 'calm down time' is increasingly favoured as explaining more clearly what is meant to happen during the period of being ignored. Webster-Stratton and Herbert (1994) have distinguished three forms of time out, of increasing effectiveness (Table 2.8).

Young children can be placed on a cushion or chair in the corner of the room; older children can be placed in a safe hallway, or on the stairs. I myself recall being stood in the corner after some small misdemeanour; I was mystified and bored. I don't recall having it explained to me why I was being stood in the corner or what I should do to avoid this boredom on another occasion. It is now known that such an explanation helps a child understand what is happening and is now built into this work at the planning stage of work with families. Other strategies that work to the same ends and which have been reported to me as effective during training sessions include:

- Holding a child who struggles against being placed in time out *very* firmly by the hand or wrist so that he cannot run off, but offering 'no speech, no eye contact'. The time period is two to three minutes. This is said to be effective for a young but obstreperous child in understaffed classrooms!
- Other children in a family or small class are asked actively to ignore the misbehaving child for the time out interval each time he misbehaves.
- The mother herself leaves the child without an audience and goes to the bathroom for the time out interval – having checked the room where the child is for safety.

Box 2.11: Guidelines for using time out/calm down

1. If you decide to use time out, explain it to the child or young person beforehand.
2. Give one warning only before carrying it through.
3. Keep as calm as you possibly can when placing a child in time out. Avoid shouting and threatening, as this will invite the child to shout back. No speech, no eye contact.
4. Never threaten to use time out and then fail to follow through.
5. Never use a frightening place for time out; use a place that is safe, unrewarding and dull: see Webster-Stratton and Herbert (1994) and Table 2.8.
6. Always check for safety.
7. Never lock a child in a room. Just keep returning him or her to the time out/calm down place, insisting that he or she stays until the 'penny drops' with the child that you really mean it.
8. A useful rule of thumb for how long a child should remain in time out/calm down is the number of minutes corresponding to the child's age. Thus:
   A two or three year old remains two minutes on each occasion.
   A four–nine year old remains four minutes on each occasion.
   A 10 year old remains 10 minutes on each occasion, and so on.
9. There is no point in making the time out period very long. We are trying to help a child learn a new association between misbehaving and the inevitability of the penalty. He or she will learn this link best from having every instance of misbehaving consistently followed by a brief time out period.
10. If the child who has been placed in time out repeats the misbehaviour on emerging, he or she goes straight back into time out/calm down. If need be, repeat this as many as 15 (or more) times a day so that a new association is learned as soon as possible.
11. The person who puts the child in time out/calm down takes him or her out.
12. Keep a simple record of how often you have had to use time out/calm down day by day. This will show if instances of the misbehaviour are increasing or decreasing.
13. *Things may get worse before they get better.* This is important. Having 'ruled the roost' for so long the child will work hard and misbehave all the more to keep his or her dominant and controlling position. If you persist, however, the message will eventually be learned: *you* are in charge now.

One warning should always be given to the child so that he or she can anticipate what may happen but if the misbehaviour persists then the warning *must* be acted upon. In settings where a special chair is used for the child who has misbehaved, the term 'naughty chair' is increasingly frowned upon in educational circles: the 'thinking chair' (as providing an opportunity for reflection upon transgression) is apparently acceptable.

The optimum time out period for primary-school children is 4 minutes Hobbs et al. (1978); a 2 or 3 year old responds to 2-minute exclusions, a 4 to 9 year old to 4-minute ones and thereafter according to age. A kitchen timer is very useful here. The procedure should be explained to the child (see Planning, p. 106) who should be told that he cannot rejoin the other members of the family or group until the bell has rung and he has stopped shouting or crying. Whoever puts the child into time out takes him out. If the child will not stay where he is put, the parent can either be very assertive and insist that he stays until fetched or, if he cannot be stopped from rejoining the family, they should totally ignore him until the time interval has elapsed. Alternatively, a mother alone may explain to the child that she will go into the bathroom with a magazine for the specified number of minutes – this having the required effect of ensuring that the child does not receive gratifying attention. Guidelines for using time out/calm down are shown in Box 2.11.

6. Reducing the Frequency of a Behaviour by 'Response Cost'

This is a variant of the above methods for reducing the frequency of a behaviour. The essence is that a person, child or adult, is awarded the full potential reward *before* the problematic situation occurs. For example, a child is given his/her pocket money on a Saturday for the forthcoming week. It is made clear, by negotiation with the youngster concerned, that certain infringements of rules will lead to a fine; for example, 5 pence for leaving a coat on the floor; 10 pence for not putting dirty clothes in the laundry basket, and so on. The point is that each undesirable behaviour, clearly discussed and written down beforehand, has a cost – which should be exacted immediately. This practice is obviously more suitable for older rather than younger children but the principle can be used at all ages, particularly if the adults are fined too. It can be a very effective approach: the same rules can be negotiated for adults as well as young people within a family, and it is helpful if someone in a supportive but neutral role can act as arbiter. Further, there needs to be agreement that the money so gathered will be sent to a cause agreed by all the family – not to take them all on a family outing!

7. Using Modelling and Rehearsal to Influence Behaviour

Young children are natural imitators, as we have explored above. They copy the patterns of behaviour of the adults around them, whether they or the adults are aware of it or not. Despite its problems and its embarrassments, this predisposition to imitate allows us to use it to help children who are experiencing difficulties. For example, a child who is afraid of the sea can be encouraged to watch how his more confident sister sits at the edge and allows the water to touch first her toes, then her ankles and finally to wash over her legs. Very shy children or those who find it hard to make friends can be guided to watch how more confident children approach other children and make friends.

Role play and rehearsal have much to offer as strategies to help children who lack confidence. I have spent many sessions helping students practise skills of speaking up in a classroom situation and discussing with them how, by first making simple comments and then, as the weeks pass, by making longer or more detailed contributions, they can gain confidence in speaking in public settings. Exactly the same principles can be used to help children who are withdrawn or who lack confidence. Similarly, I have worked with many parents, all mothers, who needed to rehearse giving their child a clear and forthright instruction. I play the child while the mother is herself. If Mum gives an unclear instruction in an uncertain voice, I say 'no, I won't …!', but If it sounds as though 'Mum means business this time' I say 'oh, all right then …' This is fun to do and typically accompanied by a lot of laughter.

8. Helping a Child or Young Person to Develop Self-control

Although this approach may only seem relevant for adults who seek, for example, to lose weight or to take exercise, it can also be appropriate for quite young children. They can be encouraged to develop a routine to increase the amount of time spent on a desirable but demanding skill, such as learning to read or play a musical instrument. In such a case, a 'baseline' of minutes daily spent in practice can be kept for one week and then the parents or a teacher of the child can help her to decide for herself how long daily she wishes to practise – advising modest and attainable goals! The point is that their approval should be secondary to that of the child herself; the child is the one who decides, for example, to do her practice or homework before watching television: the adult is there not to nag but to support and commend the child's self-management.

9. Helping Children and Parents to Understand their Own Beliefs and Concerns so that Misinformation and Flawed Assumptions can be Corrected

We saw earlier (p. 48) that parents often have inaccurate information about child development, as well as powerful feelings and beliefs concerning their children, which affect how they respond to them (see Table 2.1). Iwaniec

(1995, 2004) in particular has illustrated extremely lucidly how a parent may be caught up in a vicious spiral of negative beliefs and feelings, leading to counterproductive management of the child. A practitioner who can give accurate information about, for example, child development, or who can help a parent acknowledge her current dislike of her child and make sense of it, can sometimes free her to learn more positive ways of handling him. Such skills are of a very high order and need specialised training, but a worker able to use cognitive behavioural theory in this way can literally change people's lives.

We saw earlier in the work of Hart and Risley (1995) that some children receive a strong diet of positive feedback from their parents: encouragement, appreciation and guidance as to how to behave and develop; by contrast other children receive the opposite diet: blame, rejection, criticism and fault finding. These patterns of responses are often internalised by children. For all of us, to some extent, 'we are what we think'. People are often unwittingly rehearsing thoughts about and views of themselves, many of which, as discussed earlier, were heard in childhood and adolescence: 'I'm no good'; 'I'll never amount to anything'; 'I am not lovable'; 'I'll never be a good mother'. Young children may hear the refrain, 'you are so naughty; there must be something wrong with you', or 'I've got two children, one good and one bad – and you're the bad one'. Such beliefs, frequently rehearsed, consciously or not, can undermine a child's confidence and self-esteem for life. Sometimes they may surface in discussion with, say, an empathic counsellor, but more often they fester inside, their origin and their effects unrecognised.

Box 2.12: Steps of the problem-solving process (after Spivack, Platt & Shure, 1976)

1. Pinpoint the problem.
2. Gather all the relevant facts about the problem.
3. Formulate the difficulty in terms of a problem to be solved.
4. Generate potential solutions by means of a 'brainstorm'. Any ideas may be put forward: criticism is deliberately withheld.
5. Examine the potential consequences of each solution. How well does each one solve the problem?
6. Agree on the best strategy/solution.
7. Plan how to implement the strategy.
8. Put the plan into action.
9. Review and evaluate the effectiveness of the plan. If unsuccessful, adapt it or try another strategy from the list which was generated. Repeat as necessary.

Practitioners can use cognitive approaches to help both adults and children. We can ask them, in a simple way and not necessarily as part of a major counselling or therapeutic approach, what ideas and beliefs about themselves they can identify within their thought patterns. If, as is so often the case, a mother, say, can recognise her thought pattern, 'I'm a bad mother' or 'he'll never do what I say – I'm no good', understanding help can be given both in questioning such thoughts and in considering more helpful ones, for example:

I am *not* a bad mother; I've got a lively three year old but I'm learning to manage him.

He often does what I say now. I am getting better at managing him.

I was unhappy as a child; my child seems much happier than I was. *I* achieved that!

No-one gets training to be a parent; I am doing a pretty good job, all considered.

Similarly, it is possible to help children practise to take control of their beliefs and substitute more constructive ones. A recent video by Professor Carolyn Webster-Stratton showed her coaching three young children about to be excluded from school for unacceptable language to say to themselves, 'I don't have to talk rudely; I can talk nicely to the teacher and then I won't be put out of school'. Teaching such self-talk is certain to become more common as its effects enable unruly children to control themselves.

10. Problem-solving Skills

This strategy is surprisingly little known in view of its usefulness in a number of different situations, including ordinary, day-to-day difficulties. There is substantial evidence of its helpfulness in working with people with mental health problems, such as schizophrenia (Falloon, Boyd & McGill, 1984) and depression (Nezu & Perri, 1989). I believe it can be readily adapted to working with troubled children and their families.

According to Spivack, Platt and Shure (1976), problem solving can be divided into a number of steps (see Box 2.12). This approach could readily be adapted to many of the difficulties experienced by families seeking to maintain good relaionships with their adolescents but could also be used to deal with disagreements between family members about how to deal with the troubles of younger children.

Box 2.13: Recapitulation of principles of cognitive-behavioural theory (after Martin & Pear, 1992)

Principle 1 A behaviour that is rewarded is more likely to be repeated.

Principle 2 A behaviour that is penalised is less likely to be repeated.

Principle 3 A behaviour that is consistently ignored or penalised is likely to fade away.

Principle 4 A behaviour that has been established, then ignored, but then rewarded again, is likely to start all over again.

Principle 5 A behaviour may be learned because it occurs in association with another behaviour.

Principle 6 A behaviour may be learned by imitating another's behaviour.

Principle 7 A behaviour may be acquired by thinking it through and practising it beforehand.

Principle 8 A belief can be examined to see if it is based upon sound evidence.

Principle 9 Beliefs can be tested out to see if they are accurate or not.

Principle 10 People can be helped to use problem-solving skills rather than 'rehearsing the problem'.

SUMMARY OF SOME KEY PRINCIPLES
OF COGNITIVE-BEHAVIOURAL THEORY

Box 2.13 shows well tested principles arising from this body of theory. Reference will be made to those principles in later parts of this book.

3

ENGAGING AND SUPPORTING PARENTS AND FAMILIES

No matter how sound the theoretical base for one's work and no matter how great the enthusiasm of the practitioner to help families in this way, it is essential that there should be a number of supportive structures in place before work can begin. It is no good expecting hard-pressed professionals, already carrying large caseloads, to take on the necessary work without additional time and resources. This is skilled work, requiring training for practitioners and time for them to do the extra work; if it is attempted without such resources it will fail and matters will be worse than before. 'We've tried that', parents will say, 'and it doesn't work'.

Once these support mechanisms are in place, there are a number of principles for engaging and supporting families. Thus, this chapter will first consider the statutory context provided by the Children Acts 1989 and 2004 and the organisational support necessary for working with children in preventive ways; second, what the evidence suggests concerning the best methods for giving support; third, the difficulties of getting alongside families and collaborating with them; fourth, the importance of being aware of and responsive to cultural factors; and finally, the importance of developing a positive focus for the work.

CHILDREN WITHIN A STATUTORY AND ORGANISATIONAL CONTEXT

An extremely important group of troubled children falls directly within the scope of the Children Acts. Under Section 17 of the Act of 1989, local authorities have a duty to safeguard and promote the welfare of 'children in need' or, if they do not make direct provision themselves, they have to ensure that their welfare is provided for. They are responsible for supporting families in bringing up their children and must provide services, including accommodation, for them. The Act states:

> For the purposes of this Part a child shall be taken to be in need if:
>
> (a) -he [sic] is unlikely to achieve or maintain, or have the opportunity of achieving or maintaining, a reasonable standard of health and development without the provision of services by a local authority under this Part;
> (b) -his health or development is likely to be significantly impaired, or further impaired, without the provision for him of such services; or,
> (c) -he is disabled.

Since the first edition of this book was published the major Green Paper, *Every Child Matters* (Department of Health, 2003) has been published, stimulated in part by the events surrounding the death of Victoria Climbié. This report has required that services organise themselves so as to facilitate a number of positive outcomes for children and young people:

- being healthy
- staying safe
- enjoying and achieving
- making a positive contribution
- achieving economic wellbeing.

Organisationally, it is intended that in order to enable children to attain these outcomes, the former local authority services, together with the Child and Adolescent Mental Health Services (CAMHS) and some services provided by the health authorities, will all be brought together under an overarching body focused upon children: the Children's Services Authority. So in respect of children with mental health needs, CAMHS will be required to liaise closely with other practitioners in multidisciplinary teams, with a named worker having key coordinating responsibility for a given child.

HOW CAN WE BEST SUPPORT FAMILIES?

In a unique study on the effects of poverty on parenting in Britain, Ghate and Hazel (2002) in their book *Parenting in Poor Environments, Stress, Support and Coping*, asked 1,750 parents living in especially poor circumstances what they thought of the resources available and how practice in family support services could be improved. Their responses are shown in Box 3.1.

Box 3.1: The main areas of desired improvement in services identified by parents (Ghate & Hazel, 2002)

- improved accessibility (for example, extending opening hours, reducing waiting lists and charges for use)
- expansion of services (for example, increased range of activities, improvements to facilities, increased numbers of staff)
- improvements in the quality of training of staff (have more understanding staff, have better training for staff)
- expanding the social profile of users
- supplying written information for parents to read at home.

This book focuses less on the provision of formal services and more on the detail of how to support parents who are dealing with troubled children. Its focus is therefore linked with the request for 'improvements in the quality of training of staff – have more understanding staff, have better training for staff'.

As a fundamental principle, when working with families, parents or carers, it is essential to offer them that understanding by conveying the unconditional positive regard that Rogers (1951) and his fellow researchers have shown to be central in the field of helpful counselling. Showing empathy, concern and respect underpins the work of parent education and training. As the Bullock Report (Department of Health, 1995b) stated concerning child protection:

> The most important condition for success is the quality of the relationship between a child's family and the professionals responsible. Terms used in the research publications vary: alliance, empowerment, support and information all occur, but each implies a conscious attempt to incorporate the family into the investigation and protection plan . . .

This is precisely the approach that effective practitioners adopt when working to engage families with troubled children. Some of its components are considered below.

Using Active Listening Skills: Enabling Parents to Vent Their Feelings

As in any distressing situation, it will almost certainly help those with whom we work if we *listen* to them – often at length. Some parents will need only the opportunity to express their anxiety, depression or distress but others may need longer as they test us out for understanding or trustworthiness.

Wherever possible it seems desirable to devote much of one's first meeting with a mother or father simply to being there and accepting the bitterness, anger, despair, fear or the sea of other emotions that parents experience when they have done their best to cope with troubled and often troublesome children.

This stage must not be rushed. If people are tense with anxiety and anger they are physiologically very 'aroused' and defensive: their adrenalin levels are high and this is experienced subjectively as very uncomfortable. If we are to help we must give time for this level of tension to subside, typically by offering an opportunity to express or pour out the feelings and frustrations formerly held in check. Our response must be empathic and nonjudgmental and must convey our active wish to be supportive. This response on our part often helps the parents to become open to considering their child's behaviour more objectively – a step that may be almost impossible if we do not allow the time for parents' agitation to subside.

Often, of course, the feelings that are expressed do not relate solely to the child or children: they concern the parent's partner, parents, in-laws or even neighbours. Readers may reasonably ask where one draws the line between becoming overinvolved in the many interlocking strands of history or current circumstances that together seem to contribute to the child's difficulties. I can only report my own experience in the research which I described above: because it was necessary for practical reasons to focus primarily upon the day-to-day interactions between parents and child, I listened as long as time permitted to the many difficulties described but then gently brought the speaker back to the practicalities of managing the aggressiveness, destructiveness or other behaviour difficulties. This was in part because the work was a research study, with a tight structure and only limited time, but also partly because I could easily have lost my own sense of direction had I tried to address the many, many problem areas, practical and in terms of relationships, which the parents described.

Field social workers may have particular difficulties in this respect in that many of them will visit families because of a referral in respect of a child and will come to realise, in the course of their assessment, that the child is experiencing either harsh or seriously inconsistent parenting or that he or she is being neglected. In other words, there are issues of child protection involved. I know from my own experience that there is no space within the caseload of a mainstream field social worker to incorporate time-consuming sessions on parenting in such situations. In these circumstances, social workers who have attended my training sessions on 'Parenting Positively' have proposed two ways forward: first, that the 'regular' social worker continues to deal with, for example, the statutory aspects of the work while a colleague undertakes a circumscribed piece of work with the parents – typically eight weekly one-hour sessions with two follow-up sessions; or second, for a specialist worker whose work is primarily related to parent education and training to be appointed by the Social Services/Social Care Department. Both strategies take a preventive rather than a reactive approach and are said to be working well.

Getting Alongside Families

We need to show families that we are, or wish to be, alongside them in their efforts to help their children. Although the legislation does not actually use the expression 'partnership with parents', this phrase has come to be seen as one of its cornerstones as workers seek to empower parents to care for their children effectively and to avoid removing them unless there are the gravest of circumstances. This is easier said than done, for the fear of losing their children is so great among some families that there is an almost immediate negative reaction to those of us with statutory powers.

Experienced practitioners confirm that almost the only way forward with families who are hostile to us and to their children is deep empathy. This may well be inappropriate if there are serious issues of child protection but if this is not so then sincere empathy can sometimes reach the most rejecting and defensive parents. A highly skilled colleague of mine has described how she can say, genuinely, 'How have you coped with this situation for all these years? I could not have done so', as she hears of parents who have regularly spent five and six hours a night awake with their apparently tireless toddler, or 'You feel you've done your very best for your child, and all he can do is to call you foul names – how have you borne it?' This demonstration of understanding and empathy can act as balm to a parent who has given up all hope of gaining help for her child or for herself. As has been found in a counselling context, this non-blaming understanding and acceptance lays an essential foundation for subsequent work and opens the way to enabling people to unburden themselves of sometimes years of pent-up emotion.

With a strong relationship as a foundation, we can draw upon a range of strategies to support families. We can sometimes help parents who are having current difficulties by involving other parents who have successfully learned skills of parenting positively; other parents often have greater credibility than professionals. Sometimes the word gets round that the health visitors or social workers who run groups for parents really do have a lot to offer. Sometimes, however, we can only continue to show reliability, honesty and goodwill and hope that this will eventually win families' confidence. In my own case, I speak briefly of my personal difficulties as a mother as I find that this helps other mothers to accept that I am speaking from experience!

It will be important during this early stage to find out what other forms of help families have already sought or received in connection with their child's difficulties. If they have met with a worker whom you know, and report that he or she was unhelpful, it is tempting to collude with the parent's view of the worker but professional standards should prevail; one needs to note

Table 3.1 REST: the essentials of an approach in helping stressed parents

	Key component	Examples
R	Reassurance	• that the worker is not seeking to remove the child • that the situation in which the family finds itself is not uncommon • that the practitioner is experienced in giving help with the issue in question
E	Empathy	• conveyed by sensitive listening and reflecting feelings • with all family members for the stresses they are coping with
S	Structure	• by using a clearly understood approach to difficulties which makes sense to parents: e.g. the ASPIRE process. (see p. 84).
T	Time out for parents	• by trying to arrange respite for parents, for example from community resources or support.

the parent's perception but to avoid reinforcing it. Other families may report similar views of our own practice on another occasion! Useful and important information may be forthcoming, however, concerning the types of help that parents have sought and from whom it has been received: medication in the form of sedatives or other drugs; various forms of therapy; counselling, as offered by general practitioners, psychiatrists or paediatricians, social workers, health visitors, school nurses and counsellors. This information should all be noted in order to facilitate inter-professional practice.

I am sometimes asked what language to use when families employ words local to their neighbourhood to describe their children or some aspect of family life. I try to use the same terms, for example 'pissed off' for feeling depressed or upset, 'a mardy child' for one who grizzles or cries a lot, or 'getting caught' for becoming pregnant. If we are meeting in a group, I tend to use the family word alongside one that other group members would recognise. The whole point is to put people at their ease but also to promote clear communication.

Working in the context of research into children's sleeping difficulties, Keefe (1996) has developed a useful mnemonic, REST, as a means of summarising the essence of her research-based approach to working with highly stressed parents. See Table 3.1. It is relevant to practice in many contexts.

Emphasising a Collaborative Approach with Parents

It is vital when working with families to avoid giving the impression that we are the 'experts' in bringing up children. Each parent will know more about his or her child than we can ever hope or wish to know; they are the experts but we have gathered some useful knowledge and skills through experience and training. The approach that has been found useful is essentially a collaborative one. Indeed, Patterson (1975) calls this empowering of parents the 'Golden Rule', and O'Dell (1985) advocates interventions that 'heavily involve the parent, seek his or her advice and treat him or her more like a co-therapist than a patient . . . ' We can acknowledge that we have received some relevant training or have had particular experience but in essence we are seeking to collaborate with families, to empower them, to pass on what we have learned but also to learn from their experience in bringing up their children. The same point is made by Webster-Stratton and Herbert (1994) in their excellent book, *Troubled Families: Problem Children*.

DEVELOPING AWARENESS OF CULTURAL ISSUES

If we are to engage parents to work with us, then we need to develop our awareness of the cultural diversity of families in Britain. Here I am referring both to issues which affect families belonging to ethnic minorities and to those belonging to cultural minorities.

Awareness of the Wider Family Context

Each culture has its own ways of dealing with family difficulties: in some, it is the convention to seek help from outsiders to manage domestic tensions, so to go to a GP or to a family counselling organisation is natural and totally acceptable; in others such a step is outrageous, deeply disloyal to the family and a cause of additional stress. The professional or counsellor cannot ordinarily know whether seeking help for an unhappy child is acceptable or not to the family of the child concerned but we must be alert to every possibility. Increasingly I have come to the view that as British society grows ever more diverse, we can make very few generalisations indeed: every single family is special, with its own culture and conventions. I have also concluded, however, that each person within each family seeks *respect* from others, both for him or herself and for the family of which he or she is part.

This attempt to be sensitive to individual families and to individual sets of parents places major responsibilities upon workers, for it means that we must make no assumptions. We must attempt to rid ourselves of preconceptions and, in particular, those that pertain to people who are often marginalised: lone parents, families where the sexual orientation of the parents is gay or lesbian, families in which fathers are the main carers for their children, families belonging to ethnic minorities. Forehand and Kotchik (1996) have published

Box 3.2: Questions to alert practitioners to parents' needs in a diversity of cultures (after Forehand & Kotchik, 1996)

1. How do you feel about going to a professional to help you deal with your children's difficulties?
2. What behaviours do you most like in your child?
3. What child behaviours are most difficult for you as a parent?
4. What parenting behaviours work best in changing your child's behaviour?
5. What parenting skills do not work so well in changing your child's behaviour?
6. What would be some of the things that might keep you from taking part in a parenting programme?
7. What would make it more likely that you would take part in parent training?
8. Are there any really important things that we ought to bear in mind in trying to help you deal with your child?
9. How do family members feel about your seeking help in dealing with your child?
10. What is the best way to teach parenting skills to you?
11. What are the stresses that keep you from doing your best as a parent?
12. What are the most important characteristics that you would like in someone who helps you deal with your child's problem?

an important paper entitled 'Cultural diversity: a wake-up call for parent training'. This draws further attention to the fact that parent education and training must be sensitive to the beliefs and norms of an ever-widening range of community groups and cultures in the United States: the same is exactly true of the United Kingdom. Parents in all communities appear to need help, but unless there is sensitivity to the way in which such 'help' is perceived by parents and by community members, then it may not prove to be helpful at all. These authors suggest a number of questions (see Box 3.2) which can be usefully explored with parents in order to make practitioners more sensitive to the finer details of the work.

Further, it would not be good antidiscriminatory practice to assume that there will be a female figure or a male figure in the life of a given child. As children are increasingly brought up by lone parents or by lesbian or gay couples, there may not be caregivers of both genders available. We are reminded by the Children Act 1989, however, that many different people can contribute helpfully to the child's development: grandparents, aunts, uncles, cousins and distant relatives. In any case, as we shall see, it is essential that as many people as possible among those who make a significant contribution to a child's development are involved in cooperating to care for the child.

Gathering Information to Make an Assessment

As we shall see in the next chapter, and as professionals already know, it is necessary to gather extensive information about a child and his or her background to inform the assessment. According to the child's age, this information may well come from the child as well as from the child's caregivers or parents. Yet, as already indicated, it may be totally against family conventions to divulge information to outsiders: the children are not necessarily being stubborn if they choose not to talk to a social worker or other practitioner, and their silence may not necessarily indicate that there are secrets that must be investigated: it may rather mean that children have been instructed that he or she should not talk about private family matters to non-family members. If issues of child protection are involved, then enquiries may have to go ahead without the full cooperation of the family; if they are not then it may still be a considerable time before we can gain parental cooperation in giving us a fuller understanding of the child's difficulties.

Working with Cultural and Religious Diversity

As the United Kingdom becomes ever more racially, culturally and religiously diverse, so it is extremely challenging for professional workers to familiarise themselves with this diversity. My discussions with students and practitioners from a wide range of community groups have led us to conclude that any kind of stereotype is inappropriate and, as it is almost impossible for any one individual to become familiar with the diversity within one estate let alone one city, the most appropriate approach may be to convey one's wish to help, one's unfamiliarity with the background of the family or parents concerned, and to ask if they would tell you what their expectations are of their child. Sometimes these may be inappropriate in terms of the child's age or developmental stage and in such cases we have an important educational role, but often we can note that many parents' expectations are quite reasonable – 'if only he'd do as I say!' – and we can confirm that this is indeed a reasonable expectation.

Building Credibility and Rewardingness

Skills in forming positive relationships and in developing active helping roles are essential here. Sometimes it will be our listening skills and empathy that will enable a hostile person to move from being defensive and resentful to being ready to collaborate with us; sometimes we may be able to demonstrate goodwill by showing the individuals concerned that they are entitled to more welfare benefits than they had realised. Sometimes only the passing of time will reassure them that we seek to enable them to care for their child themselves – not to remove the child.

It is right, however, to have confidence that one has knowledge and skills to offer and referring to the fact that we have helped other families with similar difficulties to a successful outcome may raise our credibility. One very skilled health visitor known to me has compiled a folder of 'success stories'. These are testimonials from families, identified only by initials, with whom he has been successful in resolving complex and longstanding sleeping difficulties: he has the permission of these satisfied customers to show the testimonials to newly referred families. This is a way of building one's credibility that can prove very persuasive.

DEVELOPING A POSITIVE FOCUS

With the foundations laid for a constructive relationship, we move towards making an assessment. The detail of this will be considered in more detail in Chapter 4; here I am concerned with the importance of adopting from the outset an approach that 'places the parents in the driving seat', so to speak. This can best be achieved by structuring our work so that the families set the direction and pace of the work. In the past there tended to have been a focus, in work with families, upon the difficulties that the families are experiencing and upon, say, their shortcomings in coping with their children. We are now appreciating that to focus upon *family strengths*, upon the parents' achievements in bringing their child to the point where he is, say, fairly healthy, can dress himself, can amuse himself for a while, are all matters to be proud of. To focus primarily, sometimes exclusively, upon difficulties is counterproductive: demoralised or angry parents need the reassurance of the practitioner that their strengths and those of their child are actively recognised and appreciated. Building upon strengths is a core approach when working with parents and children in distress.

Focusing Upon What the Parents Want to Achieve

Professor Martin Herbert, the leading psychologist in Britain in helping families with troubled children, suggests that we invite parents to set the goals for the work that they and the practitioner are undertaking together. He suggests saying words to the effect of 'If I had a magic wand, and if I were able to help you, how would you want your child to be behaving in a few months' time?' This approach has a number of advantages:

1. It encourages parents to look forward rather than backward.
2. It helps them to begin to think in terms of specific behaviour.

3. It empowers them to identify their own hopes for their child – as distinct from those of some external expert.
4. Yet it does not guarantee change – as we shall see, the parents are the change agents.

Depending on the age of the child the answers might be:

1. I want him to do what I say without constantly arguing.
2. I want him to go to school.
3. I want him to speak to me politely – not call me horrible names.

Each of these is a distinct *behaviour* – one that can be written down; it is also possible to monitor progress towards each one.

At this point I wish to emphasise that this book focuses upon children rather than adolescents and it is my intention to illustrate the concepts by reference to preschool and primary school-age children rather than to those in secondary school. This is because of my commitment to preventive work and because one short book cannot cover all ages of children and young people. However, once an assessment has been made, this same strategy of focusing upon desired patterns of behaviour is equally relevant to work with adolescents.

We shall see in Chapter 5 how this strategy of goal setting can enable parents and workers to be clear about the ends to which they are working – rather than becoming involved in nonspecific 'therapy' without any clear idea of what they are trying to achieve. As we shall discuss, it is often difficult to enable parents to orientate themselves towards a more hopeful future as their past has been so full of difficulty and hopelessness and their present remains so. Such a forward-looking orientation, however, is both appropriate and constructive.

Recognising Positive Features of the Current Situation

One step that is often helpful is to acknowledge those features of the present situation that do give grounds for hope and optimism. Parents who have experienced years of tantrums and arguments with their young child, or who have decided that their only course of action, if they are not to harm their child, is to ask for him to be accommodated by the local authority, may experience astonishment and relief on hearing a worker actively acknowledge their ongoing care and concern for their child. Skilled and sensitive practitioners are able to say, genuinely and honestly, 'if you didn't really care about your child, you wouldn't have come to us' or 'it shows that you still care about him, despite all that has happened, if you are willing to talk to us about very personal and private things that have happened in your family'.

I am not suggesting that workers should give false hope or offer spurious reassurances that things will improve; I am suggesting, however, that when we recognise that underneath the outward anger with and rejection of the child there is still the hope that the relationship can be rebuilt, then it is fitting to build upon this hope in a firm but realistic way. This is not based upon vague optimism, but upon a confident familiarity with the research literature, which reports, as I have already explained, 'the successful treatment of thousands of children with a wide variety of problems'.

PRACTICE ISSUES: THE IMPORTANCE OF STRUCTURE

A number of important points arise when seeking to engage parents, particularly in complex situations:

Keeping a Very Clear Focus for Oneself

In order to build confidence and trust in the parents, it is important to be extremely clear and focused in one's work with them and open to questions from them. I am not referring here to high standards of professional behaviour concerning punctuality and accountability – these I take for granted – but to setting very modest goals for our work together at each meeting and explaining these to the parent(s). 'Yes, as I said, I want this week to talk with you about Johnnie's bad behaviour and his good behaviour, and to give you a way of noting how often these happen. Are there any particular things you would like to talk about?' ... 'Right. You'd like to talk about whether we should tell Johnnie's teacher about my being in touch with you: fine ... Let's write these topics down so that we don't forget them. Anything else?' To have very specific goals for the session gives confidence to parents and provides everyone concerned with a clear structure for progress.

Another means of engaging families that depends upon openness involves devising a shared service contract. This is considered further in Chapter 12. In essence, the worker undertakes to offer a family structured support to help a troubled child by means of, say, a series of eight weekly meetings. The focus upon parenting may well be part of a much larger intervention involving alcohol abuse by the father, mental ill health in the mother and concern about the wellbeing of a preschool child, but a clear statement about the specific focus upon support in parenting the preschooler can clarify both the timing and boundaries of this work.

Being Honest with Parents

Nothing is to be gained by a dishonest emphasis upon the positive features of a situation. Indeed, the more worrying the situation, the more important it is to be straight, but not blunt, with the family. One example offered by a very experienced practitioner was, in appropriate circumstances, to say, truthfully but in a constructive tone, for example, 'your child is on the Child Protection Register and unless we work together to improve the situation, he will stay on it'. This can have the effect of motivating some families to work hard to have this stigma removed.

Giving Ongoing Supportive Encouragement to Parents

Given that many families with whom we work will have had deeply disadvantaged childhoods themselves, and given that nurturing children is largely a learned behaviour, we ourselves have the opportunity to offer the parents who now seek our help something of the encouragement and warmth that so many of them missed in early life. We can show empathy for their difficulties, appreciation of the problems they encounter in being positive to children whom they have come to dislike or even fear, and a sense of humour when everything goes wrong. In essence, we have to make the meetings with parents very rewarding events whether they are in the privacy of someone's home or whether they are group meetings where everyone has his or her own personal agenda. Remember that each person is carrying out an implicit cost–benefit analysis (Sutton, 1994); each is estimating whether it is more advantageous to meet with the worker or to pretend to be out when she calls – or whether it is more advantageous to come to a particular group meeting or to stay away. Part of our job is to make the meetings as genuinely rewarding as we can, partly by helpfully offering skills to help parents cope with their children but also by providing opportunities for laughing and for sharing the ups and downs of family life in a lighthearted way. You could say that we are offering some parents a mini-experience of being nurtured and parented all over again.

I have been asked whether there are not dangers of encouraging dependency in taking such a role. I have not found so. The time that I typically spend with the parents, eight weekly sessions of between one and two hours and then two followup meetings, is usually devoted primarily to discussing how to get a child up in the morning and off to school or to getting him or her to take notice of a parent's requests. We do not have long to spend on reflecting upon the parent's own childhood experiences. If anything, the difficulties I encounter are more linked with maintaining contact when the structured sessions are over, so that support is ongoing, rather than in dealing with dependency.

Table 3.2 Common problems in engaging parents – and possible solutions

Common problem	Possible solution
Getting started	Promise, and give, regular support Offer deep empathy Boost mother's self-esteem Show reports from other parents
Keeping going	'Buddy'/support group of other parents Encouragement from practitioners
I tried that and it didn't work	Checking exactly what they tried and for how long. Exactly what happened?
Parents say 'he'll grow out of it'	Emphasise that research does not support this view
Getting parents to take responsibility	Working out a written agreement with them

Handling Difficulties Along the Way

Sometimes, despite our best efforts, parents are unmotivated to improve their child's misbehaviour or, having made some initial progress, lose momentum. These objections are very hard to deal with, but Table 3.2 shows some of the difficulties that health visitors whom I have encountered in my work have experienced and the range of solutions which they have tried.

INTERAGENCY WORK

Finally, quite apart from the statutory requirement, there are many advantages in working with other agencies to support families. For example, if a child's circumstances have already been considered by a case conference it is likely that a 'core group' has been identified to coordinate the child's welfare. The members of that core group, representing many different agencies, may well be able to provide encouraging and positive information concerning the child, which can stimulate optimism about the future. For example, a nursery nurse may be able to report that a child has seemed calmer, more settled and more able to play for a longer period of time after a parent has been trying to be more positive in her management of the child; this can provide crucial encouragement to the parent herself and can motivate her to continue her efforts.

From the point of view of management, group work appears to have advantages in that it is not only more cost effective than individualised home visiting but it may be possible for, say, a community worker to respond to the interests of a group of isolated young parents: first via a focus on, for example, health, sport and leisure activities, so establishing trust and involvement in the group, then, at the request of group members, for a health visitor, social worker or other practitioner to focus upon issues of parenting. A range of ways of working is required, allowing families choice in their preferred way of gaining support.

METHODS OF GIVING HELP: EVIDENCE FROM RESEARCH

I have already described, on page 28, the three different methods I have used in my work for dealing with preschool children having serious behaviour difficulties – working with parents in a group, visiting them at home and supporting and training parents by telephone. They were found to be equally effective. Other researchers have investigated other strategies of support for parents. An important study by Puckering, Rogers, Mills, Cox and Mattsson-Graf (1994) focused upon 21 mothers with severe parenting difficulties. The study was group based, lasting 4 months. Psychotherapy was available 'to allow mothers to come to terms with past and present stressors'. This work had positive results, with 10 of 12 children whose names were on the Child Protection Register having their names removed – which compared well with figures in a control area. It will be noted that this admirable work involved at least five practitioners, by contrast with my own work in which I met with parents for 2 hours weekly over 8 weeks and worked alone.

The point I am making is that despite a flurry of publications in this area, it is still a relatively new research field and we do not yet know all the details of the best ways of working to support families reporting serious problems in their children; only further research will provide this. The parents themselves will have had hugely varying experiences of being parented: some will have had positive experiences and need only minimal guidance and support before they can employ new strategies for managing their children; others will have had deeply unhappy experiences, deprived of the affection that brings security and cared for by people who rejected and punished them. Yet with so many children in difficulties, research into the optimal ways of helping their parents to help them is urgently needed. So my own position is that while counselling or psychotherapy for parents may be highly desirable, only a tiny fraction of them are going to receive it. We need to find a way of undertaking preventive work with families that is both effective and cost effective and the research programme towards this goal is only just beginning.

We see, then, that engaging and maintaining engagement with families who have troubled children is no easy matter. Only a small proportion of those who come to our attention are strongly motivated: many are reluctant participants and readily lose heart. Yet, as these ways of helping families become better known, so their positive features will also become better known; and as we practise positive methods of interacting with the parents, emphasising their strengths and their concern for their children, so a benign circle of constructive relationships can be established.

4

ASPIRE – ASSESSMENT

I am happy to confirm that the process for practice that was discussed in the first edition of this book is proving helpful to students and practitioners. It was originally devised in a book written with Professor Martin Herbert (Sutton & Herbert, 1992) and it is proving its usefulness to health visitors, counsellors, social workers, group workers, community workers and a range of others.

ASPIRE: A PROCESS FOR PRACTICE

ASPIRE is a mnemonic composed of the first letters of other words. It is chosen because these letters represent stages in working with people, which offer a useful reminder of the process at times when we may feel overwhelmed by information or events and need to find our bearings again. Box 4.1 shows the four stages of the ASPIRE process. These stages are particularly relevant in working with parents with troubled children – and indeed with anyone who is experiencing life difficulties or challenges whether as an individual, as a member of a group or as members of a community

The first and most important stage is that of assessment, and this chapter will be devoted to it. The later stages will be considered in Chapter 5. The way in which the ASPIRE process is set out in Box 4.1 implies a simple, linear series of steps and of course life and practice are never as simple as that: the process is more likely to be cyclical (see Figure 4.1).

Box 4.1: The ASPIRE process (after Sutton & Herbert, 1992)

AS	Assessment
P	Planning
I	Implementation
RE	Review and Evaluation

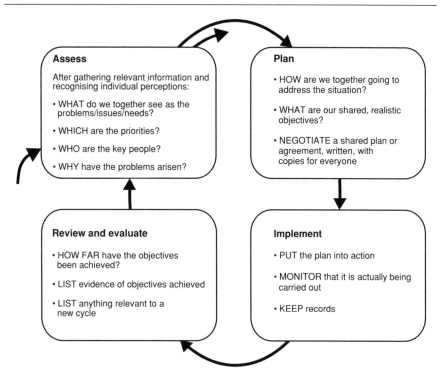

Figure 4.1 The ASPIRE process as a cycle

WHAT IS ASSESSMENT?

To 'assess' means to judge or estimate something; the comparable word in a medical context is to 'diagnose'. There are, however, major differences between 'assessment' and 'diagnosis'. As I have written elsewhere, in a medical context a doctor typically judges what is amiss with systems internal to the person's body; a person trying to help a family with a troubled child typically tries to understand the child's difficulties directly but also via the systems of which he or she is a part: family, school, friendship, cultural and others (Sutton, 1994).

Accurate assessment is the key to effective intervention. As Herbert (1978) has written: '. . . difficulties and failures in treatment of children's behaviour problems can be frequently traced back to lack of precision during the crucial assessment (or diagnostic) phase of a therapeutic contact.'

Assessment in this context is the activity of gathering information concerning the circumstances of a troubled child and of making a judgment about possible links between those circumstances and his or her difficulties. It is not a once-and-for-all judgement but a *process* so that the assessment can be changed or adjusted as new information comes to light. Thus, we aim to understand the child's own development, her history, the key people who have featured in her experience and how the life events of those people or of the child may have played a part in the child's troubles. The people will include the immediate caregivers as well as others who may be geographically distant. They may even be dead but still continue to be of profound importance.

It is a requirement now that practitioners should work in multidisciplinary teams. People trained in the context of one particular profession, be it medical, psychological, psychiatric, health visiting or social work, are likely to perceive a child's difficulties initially through the spectacles of their own professional group, so this move to multidisciplinary teams is facilitating a broad-based view of children's difficulties. Where teams are working well and there is respect among the members for the knowledge and skills that each profession can offer, there can be highly integrated approaches to assessment.

Aspects of Assessment

It is also a requirement that any person who comes into contact with children in a professional capacity and who has to make an assessment of a given child, shall use the Common Assessment Framework (see Figure 4.2). This provides a template for any worker to structure their report upon and, as is apparent, it has three key dimensions: the child's developmental needs, family and environmental factors and parenting capacity. Accordingly, this chapter will take this framework as the primary model for assessment.

Box 4.2 shows questions that practitioners and managers might pose when considering the material gathered via the assessment framework. They are framed in the context of child protection work, but have relevance for all families where an assessment is called for.

It is now useful to show how to locate the framework within the ASPIRE process for practice: a schematic outline for this is shown in Box 4.3.

Aspects of Assessment

The worker's responsibility is primarily to the child so, as the framework makes clear, his or her developmental needs are fundamental. That is, a psychologist, psychiatrist, social worker, health visitor or other professional must be sufficiently familiar with the research literature on the main developmental features for the majority of children to be able to judge when, for a given child, there is a significant departure from normal. For example, it is known (Ollendick & King, 1991) that children aged five and six show characteristic fears, particularly of animals, ghosts and monsters, and that these typically

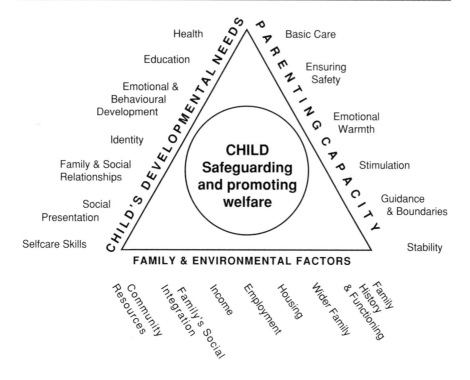

Figure 4.2   The Common Assessment Framework

Source: Reproduced from Department of Health (2000). *Framework for the Assessment of Children in Need and their Families.* London: HMSO.

fade as the child grows older. Similarly, workers of all professions need to be familiar with the evidence that severe misbehaviour in young children is a very worrying sign indeed, particularly if it occurs both at home and in settings outside the home.

The process of information-gathering and formulating an assessment will be ongoing throughout one's contact with a child or family. If I am to work with a family in a group or by telephone, I visit them at home at least once (and if possible twice) beforehand so that they are likely to feel more comfortable and secure, but even a meeting of up to an hour is seldom sufficient to enable me to believe that I have enough information to proceed. Of course, during the initial meeting one is doing much more than gather information: one is developing relationships, meeting other family members who come in part-way through, winning confidence, recognising risk factors and establishing confidentiality or its boundaries. More specifically, one is enabling some of the anxiety of the parent to subside – anxiety underpinned by increased adrenalin secretion, leading to physiological arousal, raised heart rate, increased

Box 4.2: Questions to assist practitioners and managers to make decisions and plans for children and families (after Adcock, 2000)

1. Developmental needs of the child
   What are the developmental needs of the child?
   How are these needs being met by the parent/carer?
   Are other people meeting any of these child's needs?
   Which needs are not being met?
   What is the likely outcome for the child if these needs remain unmet?
2. Parenting capacity
   What are the parenting strengths and weaknesses in terms of the dimensions of parenting capacity?
   What parenting issues impinge on parenting capacity?
   What is the attitude of the carers to the concerns expressed by the referrer and/or other professionals?
3. Family and environmental factors
   Are there members of the extended family or other people who could meet the child's needs?
   Are there members of the community network who can meet the unmet needs of the child?

stomach secretions and emotional agitation. Yet I also know that, for overworked health visitors or social workers, to give this amount of time is a luxury and is often found at the expense not of other needy people but of the workers themselves or their families.

I have said that assessment is a process. As such, it is provisional, tentative and couched in such a way that it can be easily adjusted. When we meet families with troubled children it is wise to convey this tentativeness, this provisionality, partly in order to avoid being invested with the mantle of 'expert' and the expectation that we can solve huge and longstanding difficulties at a stroke, but also partly to engage families on as equal a footing as possible in what is essentially a problem-solving exercise. Our shared task is to engage in understanding answers to the question, 'How has this situation come about?' and the parent(s) will have crucially important information, ideas and hunches that we inevitably lack. An advantage of working in this open way is that it permits new information or new perspectives to be taken into account in our attempts to understand a child's difficulties; so the process of assessment is gradual and cumulative, not fixed and final. The aim, then, is to arrive at a *provisional but shared view* of the situation, so that all those concerned are broadly in agreement about the nature of the difficulties. In my experience family members are likely in these early stages still to be seeing the difficult behaviour of a child, his or her anxiety or disruptiveness, primarily as located *within* the child – the 'there's something wrong with him' perspective.

Box 4.3: The 10 steps of the ASPIRE process

Step 1 Introduce yourself: build supportive and empathic relationships.

Step 2 *ASSESS* (AS of ASPIRE process):
- Gather information according to framework for assessment: i.e. child's developmental needs
    parenting capacity
    family/environmental factors

Step 3 Identify problem behaviours: i.e. problem profile:
- What are the difficulties?   ⎫ Use scales to
- Which are the priority problems?   ⎪ identify behaviour
- When do they occur?   ⎬ problems if
- Who is involved?   ⎪ appropriate
- Why do parents think they happen? ⎭

Step 4 Identify positive profile:
- What are the child's strengths/positive behaviours?
- Which behaviours would parents like to see more?

Step 5 Discover desired outcomes; write them down for future reference.

Step 6 Explore tentative rationale for child's/family's difficulties:
- stressful events in child's/parents' earlier experiences
- factors intrinsic to the child; e.g. hearing impairment
- day-to-day difficulties: suggest you can offer useful skills to help parents manage these.

Step 7 Ask for one week's counts of one negative ⎫ Introduce
behaviour and one positive behaviour.   ⎭ A–B–C

Step 8 *PLAN* (P of ASPIRE process).
Empower parents by exploring plans:
- to relieve any specific stressor for child/parent
- to practise skills for managing day-to-day difficulties
Teach A-B-C sequence; lots of examples; no blaming parents. Explain which skill to use when negative behaviours happen and when positive behaviours happen.

Step 9 *IMPLEMENT PLAN* (I of ASPIRE process):
- Put plan into action: much encouragement for parents. Reward rewarders!
- Ask parents/caregivers to continue to keep records.
- Troubleshoot difficulties.

Step 10 *REVIEW* and *EVALUATE* (RE of ASPIRE process).
Provide much support and boosters to maintain progress.

THE STEPS OF ASSESSMENT – AND BEYOND

Box 4.3 shows an outline of the steps for undertaking an assessment. For clarity, the steps to be undertaken under planning, implementation, review and evaluation are also included in Box 4.3, although steps 8–10 will be discussed in Chapter 5. Let us look at these steps in more detail.

Step 1 – Building Supportive and Empathic Relationships

As already discussed, the first steps in making contact with the parent(s) of a child with difficulties, after introducing oneself, are to show warmth and respect, a readiness to listen, concern for their distress and a capacity to offer empathy. Readers will recognise the features and approaches identified by Truax and Carkhuff (1967) from their detailed examination of 'thousands of research studies' as characteristic of effective counsellors and therapists: empathy, warmth and congruence – that is, the counsellor is all-of-a piece. Together, these characteristics convey an absence of threat, an unmistakable valuing of the person concerned and a readiness to attempt to understand the person's experience from his or her standpoint. This can be deeply reassuring to anxious families, who typically want to help a troubled child but do not know how to do so.

Practitioners are increasingly recognising the urgent necessity of active efforts to enhance the self-esteem of parents who are experiencing difficulties with their children. Often the needs of the parents are as great as those of the children, as their troubled and troublesome children bring increasing criticism from neighbours, teachers and relatives. If we, too, join the ranks of the critics, we are adding to their difficulties. We must remain nonjudgmental, actively recognising parents' achievements and strengths by pointing them out and adding our own encouragement and support to strengthen their wilting motivation. Explicitly 'giving positive feedback' seems to be a very important variable in work with parents. Indeed the approach known as 'solution-focused' directly recommends giving parents 'compliments' so that they are aware that the practitioner has noticed their efforts and strengths. Care must be taken not to sound insincere or condescending but this 'giving of compliments' can bring about hope and renewed effort among people who may have received few enough compliments in their lives.

On the other hand, community workers on deeply disadvantaged housing estates have told me that it sometimes takes them weeks or months of contact with families who have previously been bruised by their contact with the statutory services to begin to establish trust in anyone in any role of authority. The premature giving of compliments or an offer of training in parenting skills would lead to the worker being shown the door!

This can be draining work for practitioners. In a sense, we are attempting to offer nurture and encouragement to people who may themselves have experienced little of either and it can be very exhausting. We must avoid fostering dependency, and having very specific goals agreed with parents assists in this. Yet we, too, need our support systems and means of recharging our own batteries. Regular supportive supervision for practitioners is essential.

If possible and acceptable, it is helpful to meet as many people who have contact with the child as possible, as well, of course, as the child in question. In this way one can gain an impression of the difficulties as perceived by a number of family members. Moreover, I always try to avoid situations in which a young child hears one or both parents talking about his misbehaviour or his unhappiness to me – a complete stranger. This is likely to cause an already difficult situation to get worse.

It is important to clarify the expectations of those we are seeking to help. In the various settings in which I have worked, some people are very frightened that their child will be accommodated or removed from them while, at the other extreme, some actively *want* their child to be accommodated or removed from them! In either case, it is helpful to try to find out their hopes and fears, to correct the inaccurate and confirm the well-founded.

Step 2 – Gathering Information to Inform the Assessment

An early step will be to ask 'How can I help you?' or words to that effect. There is likely to be an outpouring of complaints and/or distress about the child or young person, which may seem intense, exaggerated or, by contrast, very mild. It is here that an empathic response, albeit of a general kind, is most helpful – along the lines of 'this experience has upset you very much, hasn't it?' It is a good idea to request permission to write down key information at this stage, undertaking to show the information given to the person concerned at the end. One can sit side by side with the person so that each can see the questions and complete them together, rather than across a desk or in such a way that he/she cannot see the questions or what we are writing down. I have found that showing what one has written both imposes a discipline upon the notes I take, and contributes to the development of trust between myself and the people I am meeting.

The child's developmental needs

This dimension of the framework for assessment is of primary importance and the practitioner will have these developmental needs in the forefront of her mind when gathering information from parents. For example, when did they first notice that their child appeared to be tense or worried – indeed, what did they notice about the child as a baby and toddler: was he or she tense then or did this tendency develop later? If the complaint concerns the child's overt behaviour, how early did the parents note his or her increasing wilfulness or disruptiveness? There is a good deal of evidence that such behaviour often stems from age two or even earlier (Rose, Rose & Feldman, 1989). When did family members begin to notice the child's difficulties and distress? Were these occasions linked with family factors such as a separation or divorce among parents or the bereavement of a family member. Such details as these should be written down, in chronological order.

Under this heading, too, will be noted all those factors that make it intrinsically more likely that the child will experience stress. Here will be recorded the developmental factors that may be playing into the situation: hearing or visual impairment, developmental delay, as well as being taller or shorter, fatter or thinner than most of the children in the neighbourhood or classroom. Here too will be recorded a child's medical difficulties, epilepsy, heart problems, as well as eczema, asthma and all the other conditions which make life hard for children. In my own work, I require that parents ask a GP, a school nurse or a health visitor to examine the child, not only to rule out organic factors but to talk to the child about things that he or she may worry about, such as protruding ears, skin blemishes or being overweight; the significance of these may be dismissed by parents but they can be a cause of acute distress to a child. Often much can be done to help.

It is increasingly understood that a child may suffer from racism or bullying because of the colour of his or her skin or other features linked with ethnicity. In such circumstances, which may not have been disclosed to the parents, permission will be necessary from the parents both to approach the child's playgroup or school so that the bullying and name calling stops and to help the child take pride in his or her ethnic identity.

An area that is attracting much attention from speech and language therapists is the extent to which a child's poor receptive language abilities – the ability to understand and make sense of messages – may underpin slowness in, for example, complying with requests. A recent paper by Cross (1997) makes this point clearly: she writes:

> It is significant that children with previously unsuspected language problems might be perceived as more 'difficult'. [Cohen, Davine, Hordezky, Lipseu & Isaacson, 1993] found that those with unsuspected language deficits were more likely to have externalising behaviour problems; for example, oppositional behaviour, hyperactivity and aggression . . . Generally expressive problems are relatively easy to spot, but parents and medical professionals tends to underestimate receptive problems . . .

In addition, there is the whole array of difficulties that fall on the spectrum of hyperactivity: those at one end may be extremely apparent but milder forms may be harder to spot and a child who has substantial difficulties in sustaining attention or in controlling restlessness or impetuosity may simply be labelled as 'naughty'. Similarly, many children suffer from serious impairments in respect of their social interaction skills: for example, their difficulties in making and maintaining eye contact. These crucial abilities have their roots in the earliest years of life when the exchanges with caretakers of 'gaze, touch and talk', by which attachment and all that goes with it are established, have not taken place adequately, if at all. Skilled and detailed assessment is essential if the deep-rooted difficulties of these children are to be identified and help given. Appendix 1 includes a form that permits the gathering of details additional to those required in the assessment framework.

Family and environmental factors

As may be seen from the Common Assessment Framework, there is a range of potential contributory factors to be considered under this heading, but there are two particular sets of 'life events' to be considered here: those affecting the child and those affecting the parents. The latter also indirectly affect the child, although parents may be unaware of this. In respect of major events in the child's life, parents can sometimes pinpoint a date or an event that they think contributed significantly to the child's difficulties: an accident, an admission to hospital, a move to a new school, a bereavement or the separation of the child's parents. Some children, however, may be reacting to a life event whose significance is either not recognised by the parent or about which nothing can be done. Appendix 2, concerning life events, may be useful here and can form the basis of a useful discussion with parents about important happenings in their own and their children's lives: experiences at school, the loss of a close friend, being bullied or being the target of racism or name calling. Older children can report the events themselves; parents may or may not know about them. The practitioner will have to seek the child's permission to tell the parents what he or she is coping with but a skilled worker who follows the child's wishes faithfully and so maintains trust can often be of enormous help in such situations. The point is that this greater understanding can facilitate nonblaming communication between the child and parent: it opens the eyes of each to the emotional experiences of the other.

One approach to understanding major events in the experience of the parent(s) is to invite them to complete the Life Events Scale devised by Holmes and Rahe (1967) (see Appendix 3). This gives parents 'permission' to understand the extent of the difficulties with which they themselves are dealing and to appreciate the level of stress they have dealt with or are dealing with: serious illness in themselves or in another family member, a marital separation, a relationship breakdown, or bereavement. A total score of 340 or more indicates a high level of risk to one's health. Talking of these events in a sensitive and supportive relationship may give much relief, which in turn relieves the pressure upon the child. In some cases it may be necessary to discuss whether the parent(s) would welcome referral to a counselling organisation for individual supportive help.

Parenting capacity

Assessments on these topics are likely to turn upon the observations and judgments of the assessor rather than upon discussion with the parent(s). Few caregivers are likely to discuss calmly whether or not they 'emotionally warm', or indeed whether they adequately stimulate, their child. Yet these variables are important, and any practitioner who did not consider them would be neglecting her responsibilities towards the child in question. Skill is of course needed in how such observations are worded in any assessment, but addressed they must be. Similarly, the matter of 'guidance and boundaries' must be addressed. Are parents of a toddler unwittingly allowing him to make decisions that are rightly the responsibility of his parents, for example in matters of hygiene or when they come in from play or go to bed? A father who actively declines to control his toddler's aggressiveness, on the grounds that he does not wish to 'break the child's spirit' could be seen as neglecting his welfare as directly as if he neglected to give him adequate food.

A next step is to identify some of the main behaviours that are causing problems. This leads to an analysis in terms of antecedents–behaviours–consequences (sometimes called a 'functional analysis' because it shows what *function* the behaviour is serving for the child). This includes:

● Pinpointing the specific problem behaviours.
● Identifying possible antecedents that may be triggering the behaviour problems.
● Identifying the consequences that may be rewarding the behaviour prob-lems. Appendix 5 may be useful for this analysis, enabling the details of a child's behaviour to be identified, together with the antecedents to and consequences of that behaviour, which may be contributing to it. This im-portant issue will be examined in greater depth in later chapters. Table 4.1 shows an example of the way in which information to inform an assessment might be set out.

A summary of key information relevant to an assessment

Table 4.1 provides a very simple summary framework which one can bear in mind when compiling information to understand the child's difficulty. It is included as Appendix 4. Knowledge of the child's developmental needs, including awareness of organic or developmental variables, together with a recognition of the stresses placed upon parents from their personal circum-stances and an analysis of the child's day-to-day behaviour are together likely

Table 4.1 Summary of aspects of assessment

Child's developmental needs	Parenting capacity	Environment/family factors
What are this family's strengths? 1 2		
Communication. Are clear messages being given? i.e. does the child understand what he is being asked to do?		

Activator	Behaviour	Consequences
1		
2		
3		

Priorities for action agreed with parents
1
2
Other professionals involved
1
2

to throw considerable light upon the behaviour of a troubled child. Table 4.2 is a completed example of such information.

Step 3 – Identifying the Problem Behaviours: Developing a Problem Profile

As shown in Tables 4.1 and 4.2 the next step is to develop a 'problem profile' (Herbert, 1991). This is a statement of the specific things a child does – so an appropriate enquiry might be: 'What exactly does Chris *do* which is so

Table 4.2 An example of information gathered to contribute to an assessment

Child's developmental needs	Parenting capacity	Environment/family factors
(a) Child has a mild hearing impairment. (b) He is rather overweight.	(a) Mother is depressed. (b) Child makes many demands of mother. (c) Mother gives in to keep the child quiet.	(a) Parents separated when the child was three. (b) No contact between father and child, who asks 'where's Daddy?'

What are this family's strengths?

1 The mother loves the child dearly. She has sought help from many professionals, but none has seemed able to help.

2 She is willing for child to see his daddy. She wants what is best for the child.

Communication. Are clear messages being given – i.e. does the child understand what he is being asked to do?
Not really. Mother gives many instructions; does not see them through.

Antecedent	Behaviour	Consequences
1 Child demands only chocolate biscuits for dinner and tea. Mum refuses.	Child says, 'I shan't love you if you don't give them me'.	Mum tries to resist, but eventually gives way.
2 Child is asked to put his toys in the toy basket.	He takes no notice.	Mum says, 'Do what I say or there'll be no TV'.
3 Child looks at her.	He grins at her, and says 'I love you'.	Mum laughs and puts TV on. Later she puts toys away.

upsetting?' The replies are likely to be very general: 'He's so difficult', 'She's impossible . . . ', 'We think there's something wrong with him', or 'I can't get a civil word out of her . . . ' We need a more precise description of the behaviour. We might say, 'You say, "He's so difficult . . . " Can you give me some idea of what Chris actually *does* when he's being difficult? What would I *see happening* if I were there?' People need help in describing their child's difficulties in terms of *behaviour* but eventually a mother or father might specify:

1. When I ask him to do something, he never does it.
2. He hits and kicks his sister and sometimes me.
3. He is very rude to my mother and sister when they come to the house; they say they won't come any more.
4. He demands things; he's always pestering me for biscuits, sweets or TV.

For a withdrawn child, they might be:

1. She hardly ever goes out to play with the other children.
2. She sits for long spells staring into space.
3. She bursts into tears a lot – even though we try to comfort her.

The priority issues as seen by the parent(s) or carer(s) should then be negotiated, but remember that everyone needs to succeed in these early days, so a simple behaviour that might be allowed to fade away (extinguish) is probably the one to start with, rather than longstanding difficulties involving several members of a family. So the above lists might be reordered. For the aggressive child:

1. He demands things – biscuits, sweets or TV.
2. When I ask him to do something, he never does it.
3. He hits and kicks his sister and sometimes me.
4. He is very rude to my mother and sister when they come to the house.

For the withdrawn child:

1. She bursts into tears a lot – even though we try to comfort her.
2. She sits for long spells, staring into space.
3. She seldom goes out to play with the other children on the street.

It will be apparent that each of the above behaviours can be recorded and counted – whether it be instances of biting or hitting other children or of bursting into tears. Families will need suitably designed charts upon which to record their child's behaviour – see Appendix 6, which is a recording sheet on which one behaviour should be entered. Practitioners will need to clarify carefully exactly what is to be recorded; they should also anticipate some puzzlement or resistance on the part of parents as this will probably be a novel way of thinking of their child's behaviour.

This step of targeting specific behaviours corresponds to the *immediate factors* (see Tables 4.1 and 4.2). In the past, a great deal of time has often been spent in discussing any predisposing variables in the belief that by exploring their impact an improvement in the child's difficulties will follow. There is very little evidence indeed to support this formulation. There is much more evidence that although it is important to understand any predisposing factors, it is often by understanding and intervening in respect of the *immediate* variables that one can really begin to help children (Herbert, 1991). As we shall see, many interventions will begin by helping parents try to transfer their attention from the child's misbehaviour to his or her good behaviour.

In some situations the behaviour is apparently antecedent to or follows certain situations which the child finds hard to cope with. If, for example, a child is always difficult after returning from a visit to his father and step-mother, this suggests that an exploration of how these visits affect him is likely to be helpful. Many children hide, or attempt to hide, fear, anxiety, confusion or hurt from their parents but an opportunity to confide in someone they trust can lead to misunderstandings being resolved and fears subsiding. I remember, for example, one boy, the child of a lone parent, who became increasingly reluctant to go to school. He was labelled 'school phobic'. A careful enquiry by a skilled school nurse gradually revealed, however, that he was not school phobic in the usual sense of the term: rather, he had heard his mother complaining of feeling unwell and his fear was not of going to school but of leaving home lest he lose his sole remaining parent.

Older children, once their confidence has been won, may be able to convey the causes of their unhappiness, either directly in conversation or indirectly through painting, drawing or story work; younger children are likely to be unable to articulate the causes of their distress as clearly.

Using a standardised scale for assessing behaviour

The practice of using a standardised scale for the assessment of a child's behaviour, in both its negative and positive forms, is gaining ground. A scale, the Strengths and Difficulties Questionnaire, has been published by Goodman (1997) and it is being adopted as the key measure by a range of organisations working with children and young people. The scale can be used by parents, teachers and young people themselves to identify both problem behaviours and positive behaviours. It is suitable for children from 4 to 16 years. The particular value of such validated questionnaires is that they can be used, if appropriate, as measures before and after a programme of intervention and, indeed, at followup some months or years later. This demonstrates whether there have been any effects of training the parents or caregivers to manage the child's difficulties and whether any improvement has persisted.

A number of subscales are incorporated in the questionnaire:

1. Emotional symptoms score.
2. Conduct problems score.
3. Hyperactivity score.
4. Peer problems score.

These, added, produce a Total difficulties score. A Prosocial behaviour score is also incorporated. Goodman has also prepared a number of associated materials for use with particular groups of children: three year-olds, and children from a diversity of minority groups. Paper versions of the SDQ can be downloaded direct from the Internet at http://www.sdqinfo.com/.

Step 4 – Identifying a Positive Profile

At this stage it is extremely important to gain a picture of some feature(s) of the child or the child's behaviour that the parents actively value and appreciate. So the question, 'Now that you've told me about some of your child's shortcomings, is there anything that he does that you really like?' is important. Some parents, surprised, will say, 'Oh yes, he has days when he's wonderful – he'll do anything to help and he's really nice to be with', but others will say sadly 'I can't think of anything I like about the child . . .' This is an emergency – one where all our efforts are needed in an attempt to prevent the hostility between parents and children spiralling down into total rejection. So it may be helpful to say something appreciative about the child, which values and validates the contribution that the parent has made to the child's development, which we, as members of the outside world, have noticed. Without sounding patronising, we can say something like, 'I noticed he was polite when he came in . . .', or 'His teachers told you that, when he's on his own, he's a very thoughtful child, didn't they?' – something, almost anything, is needed to 'prime the pump' of enabling parents to consider their child positively! I cannot overemphasise the importance of this – although clearly one should avoid getting into an argument about whether the child has or has not any redeeming features or behaviours. The point of this is that we need gently to redirect the parents' attention towards the child's remaining positive behaviours so that he or she may receive the nurturance and positive attention that are absolute essentials for any child. Typically, these few remaining positive behaviours have been all but overwhelmed by the attention paid to the misbehaviour.

Step 5 – Discovering Parents' Desired Outcomes:
Targeting Hoped-for Behaviours

Now is the time to attempt to confirm the desired outcomes as perceived by the parents or caregivers and as perceived by oneself in one's professional role. I have learned that most parents of children who have a sleeping difficulty are likely to say that this takes precedence over all other concerns, and indeed, once a pattern of sleeping regularly has been established, many other difficulties of irritability, low attention span and general fractiousness are likely to diminish.

So one urgently desired outcome may be:

1. I want him to sleep through the night – or at least until 5.00 a.m.

The threat of exclusion from nursery or school is likely to be seen as an urgent priority by many families because this may also threaten the capacity of a parent to continue in employment. Social workers and health visitors may have different priorities from parents, however, and any pattern of behaviour that angers the parent to the point where they may perpetrate some form of child abuse, such as attacking the child, is likely to be *their* focus for concern. A mother said to me, 'I'll swing for him . . .', while others have said to social workers, 'what do I have to do to get help – punch him or beat him up?' In this case an urgently desired outcome may be:

2. I want him to stop hitting other children; or, phrased positively, I want him to play calmly with other children.

Other parents know that they are at breaking point if their child is persistently rude to them or to other adults. This 'shows them up' in a humiliating and embarrassing way and causes intense family stress. In these circumstances a desired outcome might be:

3. I want him to speak quietly to me and to people who come to the house, using no swear words.

Other target outcomes which parents have frequently identified are:

4. I want him to do what I ask him – simple things, like coming when I call.
5. I want him to eat his meals without throwing food or deliberately messing with it.
6. I want him to settle to play alone for at least five minutes at a time.

Box 4.4 shows the actual list of positive behaviours, phrased as goals, which one mother worked out in discussion with me concerning her little boy, Paul.

> **Box 4.4:** Positive behaviours targeted for Paul
>
> 1. That Paul will do as he is told, whether by his Mum or his Dad, almost every time he is asked.
> 2. That Paul will not have more than one temper tantrum, lasting 3 minutes or less, each week.
> 3. That Paul will accept his Mum's saying 'no' when out shopping without having a temper tantrum.
> 4. That Paul will sit on his potty when his Mum asks him.
> 5. That Paul will leave his Mum and Dad alone and play by himself for three spells of 10 minutes daily when told, 'leave me alone – I'm busy'.
> 6. That Paul will not hit or bite other children, or his Mum or Dad, more than once a week.
> 7. That Paul will not interfere with, or disrupt the games of, other children more than once a week.
> 8. That Paul will not tip things over in the lounge.

Now this was a fairly wild little boy, aged two-and-a-half at the time of referral, living in a maisonette with no garden or outdoor play space on an inner city council estate and driving his mother frantic. She had 'tried everything' and, as she said, 'Hitting doesn't work. I've been hitting him for two years and I know it doesn't work'. The lengthy list in Box 4.4 reflects his behaviour and her exasperation.

Readers may protest that it is relatively easy to improve a two year old's behaviour and that in any case there are too many goals. My answer is that it is *not* so easy to improve these young children's behaviour without a structure – a set of principles for doing so. A great many parents are dealing with so many difficulties that, as Paul's Mum did, they 'try everything' and then, when nothing seems to work, they give up, living in despair from day to day. We included a lot of targeted behaviours partly because I am very confident that these principles are effective and partly because I have found that when parents begin to have success in one area this often generalises into other areas. People new to the field, however, may find it more manageable to focus upon about three behaviours to be improved – or even one!

Step 6 – Attempting a Formulation: Making Sense of the Child's Troubles

This is the most demanding step of the assessment. It is the time when all the information is brought together and an attempt is made to make sense of the child's troubles. It is our responsibility to compose this preliminary assessment in such a way that it is *shared* with the people concerned and that it makes some kind of sense to them. If we are fortunate and the situation is not too complex they may arrive at a similar understanding themselves but it is more probable that we shall need to go extremely slowly at this point, explaining that we are speaking provisionally and tentatively. We should express ourselves in ways that attempt to engage people, not to alienate them – even if, as may happen, we feel angry at some aspect of their behaviour.

So to say to a mother, Stephanie, something along the lines of

> From what you have told me, it sounds as though you have all been coping with a lot of stress for a long time. You've mentioned your loss of your sister in a road accident just before David was born, and how things got off to a difficult start for you both ... And then you've told me that he was a baby who never slept, so that you wondered how you would keep going ... And you've told me that David's Dad said he couldn't stand all these crying kids and walked out when David was still a toddler. All these things must have been very difficult for you – but you kept going because you cared about David and Joanne. So now, when David cheeks you, you see red and feel you might lose your temper and hit him quite seriously ...

This sort of approach shows the practitioner's empathy with Stephanie, and so is likely to win her cooperation in any plan to help her and David.

There are often three components in this formulation:

1. Locating the child's and family's difficulties in the context of the stresses that they have all been experiencing, both in the past and in the more immediate period before encountering the practitioner. Exploring these in a supportive way allows for the release of tension and for the parents to feel understood, not criticised. *This in turn avoids triggering the 'fight' component of the 'fight–flight–freeze' response to threat, which lies deep within the brain.*
2. Acknowledging any organic difficulty the child is experiencing and if necessary making plans for referring the child for further checks or active treatment. So, if you are unsure that a child understands what he is being asked to do it might be possible for a speech and language therapist to assess the child in this respect. Similarly, medical and other checks may be the best means of providing appropriate treatment for a wide range of conditions.
3. Conveying to the parents that there are some skills of managing children's behaviour difficulties that are known to be helpful, that these principles can be taught to parents, and that research shows that they can help bring about marked improvement in children's behaviour.

So, in respect of the little child considered on page 102, we might:

- acknowledge the impact of several upsetting life events upon the child, such as his Dad walking out, leaving his Mum unsupported
- highlight the necessity of having the child's hearing rechecked and of ensuring that people who speak to him gain his attention by saying his name, placing their hands on his shoulders and giving a short and clear instruction (see p. 208)
- explain to his mother that it is vital that once a reasonable request has been made he should be required to comply.

At this stage we are being very tentative and considering possibilities (hypotheses) only. At this stage too, however, it is fitting lightly to introduce the A–B–C sequence of analysing children's behaviour, corresponding broadly to the more technical term, the 'functional analysis'. As we have seen, this terminology refers to the attempt to understand *what functions the difficult behaviour serves* for the child. For example, in the example of a child who ignores his mother's instructions – say to find his school bag before leaving for school:

1. He is able to continue watching one of his favourite television programmes for a few more minutes.
2. He avoids the chore of searching for his bag.
3. His mother does the work of finding the bag and giving it to him – again.

Early in our contact with them, however, parents may well find it very difficult to accept that they themselves play any part at all in their child's difficult behaviour; typically, they have located all the problems *in* the child and any suggestion on our part that they are implicated in any way may be totally unacceptable. It is important, therefore, that we are sensitive to their reaction when we introduce the idea that the consequences of a child's behaviour may make a crucial contribution to the probability of that behaviour's being repeated or not.

This has to be *very* tactfully done. A very skilled health visitor known to me asks parents if they have noticed mothers in the supermarket buying children sweets or chocolate if they demand it – so as to keep them quiet? She asks them what they think of this practice. Sometimes the mother says how silly it is to reward children for behaving badly! The health visitor then wonders if there could be anything similar going on with the child in question ...? Often 'the penny drops' at this point. If not, it is best not to make an issue of it at this stage: there will be opportunities to return to it later.

Step 7 – Gathering 'Baseline Data' for One Negative and One Positive Behaviour

In order to test any of the above ideas we need a 'baseline', a benchmark, against which to measure the present situation and change in the future. To that end we need to provide families with a means of recording the number of instances of that behaviour over a number of weeks. How otherwise are we to know whether there is evidence to support any given hypothesis or not?

In my own work I often ask parents to collect records, counts of whether a child does or does not follow a request. 'Obedience' and 'disobedience', to use old-fashioned terms, are major preoccupations of parents and they are often ready to follow my suggestion that we start with them. Appendix 6 is a blank recording sheet upon which to enter counts of behaviour, and Appendix 7 provides a means of logging the weekly records. This is an essential step. If parents are uncomfortable with written record sheets then they can put buttons in two jars, one positive and one negative, matches in two boxes or stickers on the fridge – anything so long as at the end of this first week there are two counts of the child's behaviour, one positive and one negative.

If no specific behaviour presents itself that can have both a positive and negative form, as does 'compliance' and 'non-compliance', then two other behaviours, one positive and one negative, must be selected. Families known to me have chosen:

Negative	*Positive*
Hitting or biting other children.	Comforting a hurt child.
Restless, impulsive behaviour for 5-minute intervals.	Sitting quietly with a book or game for a few minutes.
Rude, cheeky behaviour to a child or adult.	Speaking quietly to a child/adult.

When this baseline information is available we can begin systematically to test the ideas that have been derived from the formulation and in collaboration with the parents to explore which one(s) most accurately help us understand the child's unhappiness or troublesomeness.

We now move to the stages of planning our intervention, implementing the plan and reviewing and evaluating its effectiveness.

5

ASPIRE: PLANNING, IMPLEMENTATION, REVIEW AND EVALUATION

Planning takes place on the basis of the formulation and the ideas or hypotheses that have flowed from it. I have found in my own practice that at this stage parents can grasp only a few key ideas of those I am trying to share with them; they are still too emotionally involved in the distressing events associated with their child's difficult behaviour: broken nights, family rows, threats from neighbours and sometimes the threat of a major relationship breakup. However, we should clarify what we are doing at every stage in the hope that, as the child becomes less troubled, there will be a logic and coherence about what happens and that things will 'make sense'.

THE STAGE OF PLANNING – WITH PARENTS OR CAREGIVERS

The practitioner at this stage is probably trying to plan an intervention on three 'fronts':

1. Dealing with issues arising from specific dimensions of the assessment framework. For instance, within the dimension of 'child's developmental needs', taking steps to arrange a hearing test for a toddler who pays little attention to instructions, and liaising with other agencies.
2. Similarly, within the 'family situations' dimension, taking account of conflict between separated parents about access to the child.
3. Developing a response to the upsetting day-to-day behaviours.

All three require the parent(s) to be kept involved.

Step 8 – Planning (P of the ASPIRE Process)

Planning: responding to the developmental needs of a given child

For some children it will be apparent that they have experienced many stresses in their short lives and that these are still causing distress. In some instances, the practitioner may consider that the child concerned has developed an in-secure attachment with the parent or main caregiver: he or she shows signs of anxiety, uncertainty and/or ambivalence towards the parent(s). Other children may have had repeated experiences of separation because of, say, hospital admissions, leading to acute anxiety with unsettled behaviour in the child and an undermining of the parents' capacity to manage the child calmly and firmly. Yet other children may have special needs and be unable to interpret the instructions and guidance of parents and caregivers as readily as children without disabilities.

The life experiences of some children may call for specialised therapy. Children who have been abused, emotionally, physically or sexually, or children who have witnessed a parent or sibling being raped, assaulted or murdered and children who have been traumatised in a range of other ways are all likely to manifest their distress through behaviour difficulties, either of the anti-social or the withdrawn form. The book by Oaklander (1988), *Windows to Our Children*, may offer practitioners much assistance in helping these children.

Many children will have particular needs in respect of help with language and communication. Some receive such lengthy and complicated instructions from their caregivers that they simply cannot understand what they are being asked to do. These parents – indeed almost all parents – need help in giving very simple and clear messages to their children. For ideas on how to do this, see Box 9.4, p. 208.

A Few Minutes' Daily Play with Each Child

In order to ensure that each child receives the individualised, nurturing attention for which many of them are clamouring, I explore with each parent if it is possible for him or her to spend about 10–15 minutes every day with each preschool child – and indeed with older children too, if possible. For young children, the natural medium for this special time is play – with toys, games, clay, paint, dressing-up clothes, but it may be a time just to look at something growing in a pot or in the garden; together: The child will usually know what the activity should be. This time is *not* meant to be educational in the narrow sense: it is nourishing the child with nurturing, loving attention. It makes the child's spirit grow. Some parents find this hard to agree to: they say they do not know how to play or feel silly playing. If so, to look at a story book together and talk about the pictures offers the same opportunity for individual attention. Alternatively, they might feel able to spend 10 minutes daily with the child talking about everyday events in the child's life: a visit to the park, a ride on a bus, going to the supermarket. These activities offer time for closeness and intimacy and for extending the child's self esteem and language confidence.

For some children, our hypothesis may be simpler: the child is proving troublesome because he or she is not experiencing sufficient physical activity on a day-to-day basis to employ high levels of energy. Some young children are exceedingly lively – without falling into the 'hyperactive' category (see Chapter 8) – and become frantic if cooped up indoors in very cold or wet weather. Here the plan will include the child being given an opportunity for physical activity, for spending, say, 15 minutes daily at a park where running, climbing and chasing will use surplus energy. Some families may enjoy testing out a hypothesis, for example:

> A daily visit of 30 minutes to the park over four weeks will help Stephen's behaviour to calm down – this change to be measured by the number of incidents in one week of him throwing himself on the floor or jumping off the furniture before and after the visits to the park began.

Involving Parents in Dealing with Family and Environmental Factors

In some families the children may be the focus of intense competition for their loyalty among contending partners or families in a divorce or separation; they may find it hard to know what is expected of them and may have learned to play one parent off against another. Many others live in profound disadvantage, with multiple demands made upon their parents, who are so stressed that their children's needs for consistent management come very low on their agenda.

Liaison with Other Agencies in a Multidisciplinary Approach

As emphasised in a raft of publications from central government, it is essential that we not only liaise with other agencies in trying to help a given family but that we all understand the areas of responsibility which fall to us. As family aides and other support workers assume increasing responsibility for work with parents it is easy to relax our grip on details. Many aides are providing highly committed and effective services to parents, but the ultimate responsibilities rest with the professionals.

Here supervision comes to the fore. Experienced practitioners with a professional background and sometimes years of service to families behind them can offer support and encouragement to newly appointed workers but they also need to offer the discipline of exacting standards with a focus upon professionalism and upon a sound knowledge of cognitive behavioural theory.

So we try to respond to these stressors with every resource available to us. We shall be drawing upon community resources such as family centres and day nurseries to give parents respite from the full-time care of their children, referring families to welfare rights agencies to ensure that they are receiving their full financial entitilements and enlisting the support of community agencies such as Homestart, which can introduce befrienders to families in need.

Some children's troubles can be helped by having worrying events or circumstances that they do not understand explained and discussed with them *as far as they concern themselves and their security*. Four and five year-olds cannot grasp why marriages or relationships of great importance to them come to an end, nor why they have only one parent while their friends at playgroup have two. They cannot understand why they have to live with grandparents when someone whom they have been told is their sister lives with the mother or father. They may not understand their colour: why they are of darker or lighter skin colour than other children within the family and what their relationships are to these other children. They can, however, benefit greatly from adults being open with them and answering their questions without overloading them with too much, or too emotional, information. Many children worry acutely, and the open-ended questions suggested by Herbert (1991) can help them deal with these worries (see Chapter 6, p. 137.

Helping Parents to Strengthen their Parenting Capacity

Not all children's behaviour difficulties should be seen as stemming from major earlier life events, or from circumstances intrinsic to the child. *In many cases, it is rather that the day-to-day interactions between parents and children have become increasingly negative so that a vicious downward spiral of misbehaviour, argument, criticism and rejection has developed. In any case, helping parents develop more positive styles of interaction with their children can only improve relationships.* In these circumstances, we need to teach skills of parenting positively.

Teaching the A–B–C Sequence

We saw in Chapter 2 how behaviour is embedded within a network of antecedents and consequences. If we have not already clarified this process with parents or family members, now is the time to do so. In essence, because consequences of behaviours are so powerful, we are trying to help them understand Tables 2.1 and 2.2 (see Chapter 2) We may need to spend considerable time in helping parents think through their interactions with their children in the light of these principles. It may be that they can grasp readily that they are often rewarding the very behaviour of which they are complaining: if not, we need supportively to help them grasp it. It must *not* be a matter of confrontation.

Teaching Step-by-Step or Teaching Principles?

There is great debate among researchers about whether we should be teaching in a step-by-step way – 'when he does that, you do this' – or whether we should be teaching principles, that is, the key concepts of the importance of rewarding and penalising behaviour, of being consistent and of knowing when to ignore. After discussing this issue with many practitioners I have come to the conclusion that this is a sterile debate: the consensus seems to be that we shall almost certainly need to start by giving some direct guidance to demoralised and depressed parents but that we *should work towards* their understanding the principles and making them their own. If they can understand the principles they have them for the rest of the child's life and for the lives of their other children.

Key Ideas for Parents

Sometimes, however, the detail of the A–B–C sequence is too complicated for families to grasp amid the confusion of their child's constant misbehaviour. Many families prefer a simple statement of key ideas. Some of the main ones are given in Box 5.1.

Box 5.1: Some key ideas for parents

1. Children learn to repeat behaviours that are rewarded.
2. They learn not to repeat behaviours that are not rewarded.
3. Attention is a powerful reward for children: being ignored is a powerful penalty.
4. Even attention that seems unpleasant ('negative attention') can be rewarding.
5. It is very important to be consistent. Try to keep all promises and threats.
6. Children learn by copying behaviour – our own and that of other children.

Examples for Teaching these Key Ideas

Children learn to repeat behaviours that are rewarded

1. Ask parents to recall the familiar scene of children screaming for sweets in the supermarket. Ask them to recall or imagine the children being bought sweets to keep them quiet. Do they think it likely that these children will scream for sweets the next time they go to the supermarket? Most parents say that they will. We can then ask if they see anything similar in the fact that their own child screams and constantly interrupts when visitors come, when the mother is talking to neighbours or when she is watching television? Often 'the penny will drop' at this point, but if not we can ask: if the child is not screaming for sweets, for what might he be screaming? The child is probably screaming for attention and while it is right that he should receive attention at suitable times he must learn not to demand attention by interrupting visitors or parents speaking on the telephone.

2. Ask parents about their experience of being taught a skill: for example, driving, swimming, painting or using a word processor. Did they have teachers who encouraged them or who criticised them? How did they react to the teacher who encouraged them and how to the teacher who criticised them? Parents may need support in accepting that they play any part in their child's behaviour, good or ill; this may be a difficult and unwelcome realisation. It is important to emphasise two things at this point: first, that children come into the world differently, with differing temperaments and predispositions; second, that parents cannot be expected to know how these principles work – that attending to a behaviour, good or bad, rewards it – because scientists are only just beginning to tease out these details just as they are unravelling the story of how genes contribute to our overall makeup and development.

Children learn not to repeat behaviours that are not rewarded

1. Ask parents how they would go about teaching a child who had constantly been 'bought off' with sweets in the supermarket that his mum couldn't afford to do this any more. Their replies will probably be sound and in line with behavioural theory. For example:
   - they would explain beforehand that Mum had no pennies for sweeties
   - they would ask the child to help with the shopping by looking out for the cornflakes or the apples and telling her when he saw them
   - they would ask the child to behave quietly in the public place
   - they would take along a toy or dolly to amuse the child
   - they would tell the child they were pleased if he behaved quietly

It is sensible to encourage all the ideas that would indeed offer solutions but avoid encouraging very threatening reactions.

2. Ask parents what sanction or punishment does seem to be effective with their children. Typically, they will say, 'not being allowed television', or 'being kept in when the other children are playing outside'. If the sanction is in line with principles of behavioural theory encourage them to explain to their child that this will be the standard penalty for misbehaviour and then to use it absolutely consistently when the circumstances arise. Helping parents to find their own solutions will of course enhance their problem-solving abilities in the future and build self-esteem.

Attention is a very powerful reward for children; being ignored is a powerful penalty

1. Ask parents what they think keeps actors or pop stars performing on stage. They will probably at some point say, 'the money', 'the applause' or 'the attention they get'. Then say something to the effect of, 'so what do you think keeps your Darren always wanting to be centre stage?'

2. If the child is present at the time of this discussion and if, as often happens, keeps interrupting or pestering for attention, consistently ignore the child yourself and ask the parent consistently to ignore him. Eventually the child will lose interest and wander off to do something else. Explain that this is one of the main ideas you are talking about. One very skilled health visitor known to me explains to the parent that she is going to carry out a little experiment: she is going to persist in carrying out her interview with the mother however much the child is interrupting. She then does as she has said and manages to avoid speaking or even looking at him; invariably he eventually wanders away.

3. Ask parents about their own experience of being attended to when they were little. Did they feel they received the attention they needed? Build on their replies to illustrate how children all need and seek attention but there are certain times when it is fitting to give it them and other times when all it does is to reward misbehaviour.

Even attention that seems unpleasant ('negative attention') can be rewarding

To illustrate this idea I usually describe the mother mentioned previously who said of her little boy, Paul, 'hitting doesn't work: I've been hitting him for two years and I know it doesn't work'. I explain how this little boy had learned that the only way to get attention was to misbehave; his mother, who still loved him dearly, did what she believed was the right thing to do: she smacked him. *This is 'negative attention' – that is, gaining attention even*

Box 5.2: Practical guidelines for parents

1. Work out some house or family guidelines: for example, 'all toys must be put away before bedtime'. Everyone helps everyone else to carry out the guidelines.
2. Find three behaviours each day for which you can praise a child. Catch them behaving well!
3. Reward behaviour you want to encourage by attending to it and showing how pleased you are with it.
4. Ignore small misbehaviours: whining, pestering tantrums. Turn your back on the child.
5. Try to be consistent. Only make threats or promises that you can carry out. Then, having made them, carry them out without fail.
6. Speak directly and firmly to your child when giving instructions.
7. Encourage others who care for your child to use these same guidelines.
8. Take a day at a time. Put yesterday behind you.
9. You'll have some bad days. Try to commend yourself for what you have already achieved.
10. Try to find someone you can confide in when it all seems to be falling apart. Don't give up.

though it is of a negative kind. Happily, it was a fairly straightforward matter to guide her to ignore or briefly penalise the child's misbehaviour and to attend warmly but consistently to the few instances of positive behaviour that he did display. In line with the theory, these gradually increased while the instances of misbehaviour decreased. These principles are brought together in Box 5.2.

It is very important to be consistent: keep promises and threats

1. An approach that seems to register with many parents and caregivers is to enquire if they had ever had the experience of being promised something and then of that promise being broken. Most *have* had that experience and remember the confusion, anger and deep disappointment that accompanied it. It is then fitting to say that this is the same sort of confusion that their own child probably feels if parents make promises that are then not kept. We all do this on occasion as sometimes circumstances are beyond our control but children learn from this inconsistency; they learn to take no notice of what their parents say. Worse, they learn not to trust them.

2. We can also discuss the serious learning which occurs when parents make threats which they do not keep. 'Do that again, Jimmy, and we shan't be going to the park'. 'If you speak to me like that again, you won't be going out after tea'. The child does it again, or speaks rudely again, yet still goes to the park or out after tea. He learns that threats are meaningless, are never carried out and can be completely ignored.

Children learn by copying behaviour – their parents' and that of other children

Here we can illustrate how children learn their own main language – English, Welsh, Chinese, Urdu – largely by using skills of imitation. If they can learn a complicated skill like speaking a language by imitation they can easily learn patterns of behaviour by imitation. We can then ask parents if they have noticed their child copying them in any way, for example, by the way they talk to their dolls or teddies. Much tact is needed in exploring these areas.

Making Use of Examples of Record Keeping

Some parents want to see examples of how these principles have been helpful to other families. I am therefore including Figure 5.1, which was drawn up in a research study for a little boy who was driving his mother frantic. It may look rather 'clinical' but it illustrates how, in a determined family, children's misbehaviour can reduce and their desirable behaviour increase.

This little boy's misbehaviour, shown by the solid line, initially intensified in accord with the common finding that *behaviour frequently gets worse before it gets better*, but then began markedly to improve. Correspondingly, his positive behaviour also improved as his mother began to commend and praise him for doing as she asked. It must be acknowledged that the improvement is seldom as simple or as clear cut as this; there are often many ups and downs as parents, relatives and teachers try to learn and practise a new style of child management.

I also tell parents about the little girl who, for so-called 'eating problems', gained a great deal of attention in the form of discussion of her behaviour with other adults while she was present. She had learned a very effective method of manipulating the anxiety of her mother by toying with her meals, demanding different dishes and then not eating them – and all the while 'holding centre stage' among her family and relatives. Happily, here too, after due assessment, it was possible to plan with the parents to ignore the inappropriate attention-seeking behaviour, to give her nurturing and affectionate attention at other times and to give her reasonably balanced and varied meals alongside her mother's and father's. Her plate was removed when theirs were and no

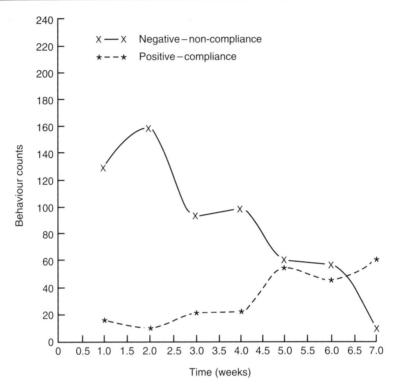

Figure 5.1 Plot of behaviour counts for R.B. over the period of the study. A record of one little boy's pattern of compliance and noncompliance

further food at all was available until the next meal-time. She was also quietly commended when she did eat but the attention was low key and calm. This longstanding difficulty resolved in less than a week.

Identifying and Working with One Pair of Behaviours

This has already been touched upon in Chapter 4, when pinpointing the behaviours whose frequency should be recorded. It is here that inexperienced practitioners should seek support and guidance from their supervisors or practice teachers. Practitioners need to establish their credibility quickly with parents or teachers; hence the need for choosing a difficulty known to extinguish fairly readily such as whining or grizzling behaviour. I recommend attempting to work with only one pair of behaviours at the outset, when everyone may be new to one another and to this way of working. Another pair can be added later while continuing to reward and penalise consistently the original behaviours.

Recall that ideally we need at least a week's counts of one negative behaviour and of one positive behaviour to act as the 'baselines' against which to measure subsequent change – and that while the parents are recording this they should not try to make any changes at all in their ways of responding to the child. If this is a fairly straightforward task, easily accomplished, then in the following week the parents can begin to collect baseline information for the second pair of behaviours – say, those associated with sleeping. If the family insist that they want help with sleeping difficulties before anything else then if you are inexperienced it is very important indeed that you should be supervised by a colleague with experience in this field. This is *absolutely essential*. Beware, too, of being pressurised to give guidance before you have firm baseline data against which to measure subsequent change.

Let us suppose that a pair of behaviours has been identified:

Negative: Samantha whines and grizzles if she does not get what she wants.
Positive: Samantha sometimes accepts quietly that she cannot have something she wants.

Or, if a misbehaviour has been chosen that does not have a simple counterpart,

Negative: Stephanie pinches her mother when she will not do what she wants.
Positive: Stephanie occasionally helps her mum clear up the living room.

Having obtained the baseline for one of the pairs of behaviours and having ensured that you have introduced family members to the A–B–C analysis for understanding behaviour, discuss how in the next week they can avoid rewarding the child's negative behaviour while ensuring that positive behaviour is attended to and reinforced. Some people understand the point immediately and offer very relevant solutions; others may need supportive guidance.

Negative: Samantha whines and grizzles if she does not get what she wants. (Probable appropriate response: parents should turn away and ignore the whining, giving 'no speech, no eye contact'.)
Positive: Samantha sometimes accepts quietly that she cannot have something she wants. (Probable appropriate response: parents should warmly praise her for accepting 'no'.)

As parents begin to understand the theoretical concepts in the light of their experience, they themselves can often suggest what steps to take with a given difficulty. It is then possible to move from the 'when he does that, try doing this...' approach to one based upon cognitive-behavioural *principles*. Typically, given that a minor misbehaviour has been chosen as the target misbehaviour and either its mirror image or some other instance of desirable behaviour has been identified as the positive behaviour, they should:

1. Attempt to pay no attention at all to the misbehaviour – or give the least possible attention to it.
2. Notice each instance of the positive behaviour, for example behaviour not accompanied by whining, and praise the child for it ('I like it very much when you talk to me so nicely, Jane; well done', or words to that effect).
3. Continue to keep records of counts of each behaviour, positive and negative.

Involving Children in the Plan

When planning a clear change in the manner of handling a situation, it will be helpful to explain this to the child or young person concerned. This prepares him or her cognitively for what is to follow and enables him or her swiftly to make sense of the changes in the parents' behaviour. For example, a mother might explain to her four year old that:

1. From now on, Mum and Dad are not going to keep on saying 'no' to requests for sweets when they are out. Mum (or Dad) will say 'no' once, and after that they will not even answer. Sweets will be available only at home on Saturdays – or whatever other arrangement the family chooses.
2. Even if Lucy's friend's Mummy allows her daughter to see a lot of television, Lucy will be allowed to see only specific programmes at home.
3. Meal times have become unhappy for everyone. From now on, Mum will not ask James what he wants to eat; she will prepare one meal for everyone and if James does not want this he can have bread and butter (or some other simple food, familiar to the family) or go without.

Primary school-age children may need a more 'thought-through' clarification at this planning stage. If a practitioner has discussed with parents the strategy of using time out (see Chapter 2, p. 62) to manage endless bickering between her children, aged five and seven, and this has appealed to the parents, then the rules for time out should be explained calmly and quietly to the children concerned so that when the new approach is used they recognise what is happening. They will still object but at least they will understand. If they refuse to go to time out then their television viewing time will be reduced – and so on. The parents *must* see through what they have said.

It is very helpful to write down the key ideas which have been discussed and the key steps that will be taken (see Appendix 8). This is supportive to the family when the practitioner is not immediately available. For older children,

---

Box 5.3: A plan that a parent might negotiate with her son

1. Mum will have a talk with Stephen about:
   (a) how much pocket money she can afford to let him have each week
      - what will have to be bought from this sum
      - When he would like her to give it to him.
   (b) what, in return, he will do to help out in the household, for example:
      - emptying the rubbish daily
      - taking the dog out each evening.
2. She will explain that once she has given him his pocket money she will not be able to afford to give him any more, however often he asks and whatever he calls her.
3. She will thank him for small things he does around the house: e.g. hoovering.
4. Stephen can earn money for additional jobs that his mother wants done; she will work out a tariff: so much for . . . and so much for . . .
5. She will go on keeping records of targeted positive and negative behaviours.

---

more in need of explanations, it may be necessary to show parents how to write an agreement in order that there shall be minimal disagreement at the stage of implementing the plan. Agreements are discussed in Chapter 12, page 272 and forms for writing agreements are included as Appendices 12 and 13. For example, a parent, supported by a practitioner, might plan as shown in Box 5.3.

Devising the Plan: a More Complex Situation

In more complex situations, where there has been a substantial period of assessment by several practitioners leading to a number of hypotheses to be tested, a fuller plan may be necessary. For example, a number of key points arise from the assessment of the difficulties of Ben Morris, a troubled 6 year old.

Child's developmental needs

1. Ben has been much upset by the loss of contact with his dad, Dave, who left six months ago.
2. His mother, Emily, says she is depressed.
3. Ben may be feeling very much on his own; he does not seem to have friends.
4. Ben does not like going to school; he says he is being called names.
5. Ben is very tall and strong for his age. People may think he is much older.

Family and situation factors

1. It seems likely that Emily experienced domestic abuse (violence) at the hands of Dave. She did say Dave had hit her to one practitioner, but when this is referred to later, Emily is reluctant to discuss it further.
2. Emily is very isolated. Her dad has died and her mum and one sister live over 100 miles away.

Parenting capacity

1. Because Emily feels so depressed she does not feel up to coping with Ben's aggressiveness and bad temper.
2. Emily loves Ben dearly but because she is beginning to be afraid of him, she doesn't like to argue with him. She tends to give in to his demands.

Immediate behaviours causing difficulty

Negative:

1. Ben throws and breaks things when he is fed up, e.g. ornaments.
2. He refuses to help at all in the house, and expects to be waited on.
3. He sometimes kicks his mother when frustrated.

Positive: Ben can be helpful: for example he sometimes makes Emily a cup of tea.

Ms Morris and the key worker agree to start with a week of recording one negative and one positive behaviour. They choose kicking his mother for the negative behaviour and clearing the table for the positive behaviour (Table 5.1).

Table 5.1   Number of instances of Ben's positive and negative behaviours over one week

CHARTING BEHAVIOURS Name:				Week beginning: 17 October Week 1			
Behaviour	*Sunday*	*Monday*	*Tuesday*	*Wednesday*	*Thursday*	*Friday*	*Saturday*	*Total*
Behaviours to encourage and praise – Clearing table							
Morning							
Afternoon							
Evening			√		√			2
Behaviours to discourage – Kicking mother							
Morning					√	√√	
Afternoon							
Evening	√	√√	√	√				8

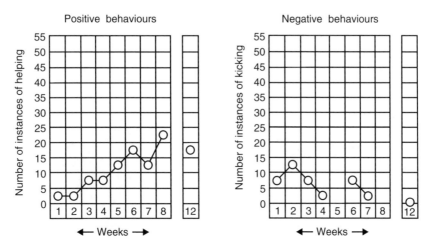

Figure 5.2 Ben's positive and negative behaviours over eight weeks and at three months' followup

Negative: Ben kicks his mother (baseline of eight instances in the first week).

Positive: Ben helps clear the table (baseline of two instances in the first week).

Thereafter, a plan to help the Morris family is drawn up (Box 5.4) with the following goals:

1. To put an end to Ben's kicking his mother.
2. To increase the number of times when Ben helps in the house.
3. To enable Ben and his mother to spend enjoyable time together.

The positive and negative behaviours are charted for the next eight weeks (Figure 5.2).

IMPLEMENTING THE PLAN

During this stage, which can follow directly from the baseline stage of at least one week, the agreed, written plan, as set out in Box 5.4, is put into action.

Box 5.4: A plan to help the Morris family

Agreement between Ms Morris, Ben Morris and Mike Cox (key worker)

Mother Ms Morris, 49 Hampton Street, Colchester. Tel. 980-876-583
Son Ben Morris, as above. Attends Southfields School.
Worker: Mike Cox, James Street Family Centre, Colchester.
Tel. 980-376-241

Our overall aim: To enable Ms Morris and Ben to live together enjoyably without arguing.
Our first goals: To increase the number of times that Ben helps in the home.
To decrease the number of times that Ben kicks his mother.

Ms Morris agrees to:

1. Spend 20 minutes daily with Ben in a way chosen by him: e.g. looking at a catalogue of cars, footballers, etc. cooking.
2. Praise Ben whenever he does as he is asked within one minute.
3. Thank Ben for helping in the house: hoovering, making a pot of tea, etc.
4. Ignore small misbehaviours: e.g. whining, pestering.
5. Fine Ben 10 % of his weekly pocket money each time he kicks her.

Ben agrees to:

1. Go outside whenever he does not get what he wants from his mother – and **not** kick her.
2. Accept that each time he kicks his mother he will forfeit 10 % of his pocket money.
3. Decide how he would like to spend the 20 minutes each day with his Mum.
4. Undertake household jobs which his mother asks: e.g. 10 minutes hoovering, tidying his room.

For his part, Mike agrees to:

1. Visit the family weekly and phone midweek to give encouragement.
2. Explore whether there is a branch of the Positive Parents group available locally.
3. Discuss with Ms Morris her wishes in respect of further contact with Dave, Ben's dad, as this may be an issue for Ben.

Other points to note

The above agreement is to be reviewed each week.
The details of the agreement can be changed if everyone agrees.
Things may get worse before they get better.
  Signed . . . . Emily Morris
  Signed . . . . Ben Morris
  Signed . . . . Mike Cox   Date . . . .

Step 9 – Implementation of the Plan: Principles to be Observed

1. Parents should be supplied with standardised charts on which to collect counts of children's behaviour.
2. They should be actively encouraged to attend to the features of their children's behaviour that they want to increase and, as far as possible, pay as little attention as they can to small misbehaviours. In terms of the theoretical principles, they should attempt to reinforce existing positive behaviours while ignoring or penalising existing negative behaviours. Thus, Ms Morris is asked to thank Ben for hoovering in the house, expressing her pleasure warmly, while penalising his kicking her by instantly reducing his pocket money by 10 %.
3. Parents must be warned that 'things may get worse before they get better'. In my own research about 50 % of the children did show this deteriorating behaviour before there was evidence of improvement. This period can be extremely difficult for hard-pressed parents to accept but it is better that they should be alerted to what may happen and find it does not than that they should not be alerted and find that it does! To be able to anticipate this possible deterioration also raises the credibility of the practitioner very agreeably.
4. The practitioner should telephone or make contact part way through this second week to encourage the family to persist with their new strategy. Part of the task of the professional at this stage is to troubleshoot, encourage and exhort the parents not to give up now!
5. The practitioner should meet with the family at the end of the week and consider the records with them. If, as already discussed, the child's misbehaviour *has* got worse, parents can be commiserated with but also reminded that this was anticipated. If the behaviour improved parents can be commended for their persistence but warned that much work remains to be done.
6. The counts of desirable and undesirable behaviour should be entered upon a simple graph (see Appendix 7 for a chart) to display the changes in patterns of behaviour for all to see.
7. Parents often ask whether their child should be allowed to see the records. I suggest being very relaxed about this. They probably will see them in any case and will ask what they are for. It seems best to say, in a noncommittal way, 'Oh, I am just recording how often you do what I ask you . . . or words to that effect. It is best not to make a big issue of the matter.

Managing the Implementation Stage

There are inevitable difficulties in the implementation stage. Table 5.2 shows some of the most common of these, together with approaches that at least some

Table 5.2 Problems and possible solutions at the implementation stage

Common problem	Possible solution
1 Keeping going: that is, persisting with the new way of managing the child.	Encouragement and support from the worker. Boosting self esteem. Help with assertiveness.
2 Conflicting advice from others	Emphasise research underpinning.
3 Extended family has different views upon how to manage the child	Try to get all the family together and explain that the child is confused.
4 Too many other demands on parents	Focus on just one area of difficulty to start with, and give much support.
5 Another crisis happens.	Put programme 'on hold', but fix restart date.
6 Neighbours complain	Talk to and explain plan to neighbours beforehand.
7 Pressure from school regarding the child	Meet the child's teachers and work collaboratively
8 Difficult to be consistent	Help parents to commend themselves for being consistent. 'I did it! I saw it through!'
9 'This way of managing him is weak. What he needs is a good thrashing!'	'It's a gentle approach, but it takes a lot of strength to put it into effect.'
10 Spouse/partner sabotages plan	Acknowledge disagreement, but ask spouse to 'opt out' for four weeks, while you work with main carer. Then re-evaluate.
11 Parents lose heart	Show file of success stories written by other parents. Highlight what these parents have already achieved.
12 Unable to manage time out.	Help negotiate 'family rules'. Involve children of four or older in planning rewards and sanctions.
13 Parents not complying with agreement	Say, 'I can help, but only if you keep to what we agreed. Please phone me if you need me'.

(With acknowledgements to the participants in many workshops that I have run.)

practitioners have found to offer solutions. The most important principle is that the families should keep going! We can assist this process by offering ongoing encouragement, troubleshooting particular difficulties and clarifying that what is happening for everyone is that old habits are being discarded and new skills learned. Just as it takes time to learn to swim, to ride a bicycle or to

Table 5.3 Rewards and penalties across the lifespan

Age	Rewards	Penalties or sanctions
0–4	Cuddles, hugs, kisses Approving attention Praise and admiration Simple outings: to a friend, to the park	Being disapproved of Being ignored Criticism and blame Being taken home from an outing Time out/calm down time
5–11	All the above, plus Stickers Staying up late Family outings: e.g. swimming	All the above, plus Loss of TV Loss of privileges Extra chores
12–18	All the above, plus Favourite meal Extend coming home time Friends invited for a meal Friend invited for a 'sleepover'	All the above, plus Ban on use of phone Make coming home time earlier. Friends not permitted to come for, e.g. three evenings Being collected from a party Being 'grounded' i.e. required to stay in, for e.g. two evenings
Parents	Choice of TV programme Chance to meet friends Uninterrrupted time to yourself Having ironing/cleaning done Having a meal cooked for you An appreciative note about child from school	Long arguments Loss of friends Constant interruptions Not being listened to/heard Being taken for granted A complaint about child from school

use a computer, so it takes time to learn to manage relationships differently, but practice helps to make perfect.

At this stage the parents may say that they, too, would welcome some reward for all their efforts to be consistent and to ignore difficult behaviour. To this end, one of the groups I have worked with has suggested the list of both rewards and penalties, not only for children but for their parents and carers too, which is given in Table 5.3.

REVIEWING AND EVALUATING THE PLAN

This stage takes place at a date agreed beforehand by all concerned. Discussion will take place informally about progress or the lack of it as the weeks pass but at a fixed point, usually six to eight weeks after the start, there needs to be a shared examination of the evidence – which should be available on a simple graph.

Reviewing and Evaluating: How Do They Differ?

The process of reviewing is essentially that of monitoring progress or the lack of it as the practitioner collaborates with the parents or family members. It is an ongoing process that takes place during the course of the implementation of the plan. By contrast, evaluation takes place once, right at the end of the intervention, but both use *evidence* as the basis for discussion.

Step 10 – Reviewing the Intervention

This requires the latter to review (literally, look at again) with those concerned how they are faring in respect of progress towards the desired goals for each of the child's difficulties written in the problem profile. Is there evidence to support one or more of the hypotheses? If the plans drawn up after the assessment have been followed then there should be information or reports from, say, other professionals such as speech therapists or audiologists to consider, as well as letters from a child's school or from counsellors. In addition there will be evidence arising from helping the parents interact with their child differently – typically in a more positive way.

In my own research many of the major difficulties were reported as much improved, and several of the lesser problems had disappeared completely – *and these would have been totally forgotten had they not been written down.* Both quantitative and qualitative evidence is likely to be available, together with views of grandparents, teachers and, of course, the parents and the practitioner.

It is crucial to *maintain* an approach based on cognitive-behavioural theory. Very often, when parents report that some behaviours continue to be a problem, they have unintentionally again begun to attend to a pattern of behaviour that they had formerly learned to ignore. This is one of the major areas of difficulty in implementing principles of cognitive-behavioural theory: having been involved in years of arguments over demands that they cannot grant or do not think it fit to grant, many parents find that with support from the practitioner they *can* manage to ignore them; *however, the parents' original pattern of responses to their child has been so deeply learned that it readily resurfaces in stressful circumstances* – and before they know it, they are back into the old, distressing but familiar routine of rows and arguments with their child. If they can be persuaded to continue to keep records, however, this lapse will show up on the record sheets and can be explored by the practitioner in reviewing progress.

Sometimes, reviewing progress throws up other factors that are impeding success and must be addressed. This requires the skill of 'troubleshooting'. I have experienced three particular areas of difficulty: the first is the impact of the behaviour of other people who influence the child's behaviour strongly; the second is lack of confidence on the part of one or both parents, leading to difficulties in making confident requests to the child; the third is difficulties experienced by parents in implementing the Time out strategy. Let us consider each in turn.

The impact of people in the wider environment

It is obvious that as a child grows older, his or her life is influenced by ever widening circles (systems) of people. Initially, it may be only the parents, childminders or nursery staff who have direct influence upon the child, but soon other children and other relatives have their impact – for good or ill. People typically want to be helpful but as they do not understand the principles of cognitive-behavioural theory they do not always make constructive suggestions. They say things like, 'we had to eat everything on our plates when I was a child', or 'boys will be boys; you don't want to make a cissy out of him!'

One major source of difficulty can be a family member who actively disagrees with what the practitioner is suggesting about how to respond to the child, saying 'Don't take any notice of what that health visitor/social worker is saying; what does she mean – to praise the child more? What he needs is a good thrashing!'

Other people, perhaps grandparents, again with the best of intentions, can sabotage new strategies of managing a child by actively undermining what the parents have requested – for example, that he should be ignored when he misbehaves. Grandpa may instead seek to divert the child by producing a present or a diversion whenever he becomes obstreperous – so teaching him that to behave in this way is the very thing most likely to prove rewarding. I found in my research that for a parent, particularly a mother, to lack someone who actively supported her or, more seriously, to have someone who deliberately undermined her, was a recipe for failure. Lone parents, by contrast, were often very successful: they could follow the guidance given without anyone undermining them.

A particular example of this from my research was one family's difficulty in managing three-year-old Danny. His uncle Bill, wanting to be constructive, taught him 'play-fighting' when the family visited each weekend. Danny loved this and took what he had learned into his nursery where he found it made him a very powerful fellow indeed; he could take whatever toys he wanted and the other children did whatever he told them. It took a good deal of insistence on the part of Danny's parents to stop Uncle Bill from teaching Danny to play-fight – because Danny had come to look forward to all this attention and wanted the 'games' to continue. When the play-fighting was eventually stopped, however, and with further calm management on the part of Danny's parents, his aggressive behaviour at nursery also gradually died away because it was no longer rewarded.

The effect of gentle, unassertive parents or caregivers

Practitioners should be alert to the possibility that very gentle, unassertive parents may find it extremely difficult or perhaps contrary to their values to impose their wishes on their child and indeed, may see this as the 'imposition of adult dominance upon impressionable children'. A typical scenario is a young, rather gentle mother who happens to have given birth to a tearaway; she may be a lone parent or she may have a partner who either dissociates himself from the job of bringing up children or, because he himself has not the slightest difficulty in getting the child to do as he is told, regards his wife or partner as ineffectual or stupid. He typically makes little effort to help her manage the child and, indeed, their different ways of handling him may itself lead to arguments between them. In these circumstances it is essential to be tactful both in acknowledging that the father has few difficulties with the child and in helping the mother to develop strategies that are both effective and acceptable to her.

It is important to insist that the child really does 'need a clear message' from her if he is, first, to attend to it and, second, to act upon it. I have spent much time, either in face-to-face situations or over the telephone, coaching these loving but unassertive parents, in delivering these 'clear messages' to their child – in a firm and confident voice. The parent plays himself/herself and I play the child. After a minute or so of role play, in which I'm asked to 'find my shoes as it's time to go out' or to 'come into the kitchen' I respond according to whether I felt my 'mother' really means business. If I receive a clear, firm and assertive request, I comply: if the request was unclear and unassertive, I ignore it. In these latter circumstances we have another go until I (as the child) can report that I feel 'She really does mean what she says this time: I'd better do as I'm told!' It is all very lighthearted and we laugh a lot. Sometimes I have to reassure parents that it is all right to be as firm as this; that is, this is not being domineering to the child – he needs to know that there are boundaries and that he is safe.

Difficulties in implementing the time out procedure

A third conclusion from my research, which links with the other findings, was that where parents could not implement the time out procedure (see Chapter 2) there was very little hope of their achieving a successful outcome. For their children had learned, sometimes over several years, to expect and to gain the limelight on every available opportunity and seriously to misbehave if this attention or their whims were denied.

Extensive research has repeatedly shown that the most successful strategy for dealing with these insatiable demands is a few minutes in Time out – that is, denying the child for very brief intervals the very thing that he demands – his own way – so that he can learn that positive attention is contingent upon his attending to other people, their needs and their guidance. It is no easy task, however, particularly for a lone mother, effectively to ignore a rude and aggressive child, especially if he is strong and has no respect at all for her or the rights of other people. However, ways *must* be found to ensure that the child is ignored – often by use of the Time out procedure.

One family with which I worked concerning the rudeness of their four year old daughter reported at the review stage, 'After all the progress we'd made, she started behaving really rudely again. We said to ourselves, What are we doing wrong? And then we realised: we'd stopped using Time out on the stairs! When we started using that again, and really ignored her while she was on the stairs, she soon began to behave well again. She just hated that Time out'.

Evaluating the Intervention

This takes place right at the end of a series of weekly meetings or conversations and is an opportunity for the family to offer a final judgement upon work undertaken together. The evidence of progess or otherwise will be to hand and it should be a fairly straightforward matter to compare the final situation with the starting point and to judge whether there is evidence of improvement or deterioration against each goal. As when reviewing, a number of different forms of evidence will be available.

Alternatively, this may be time for a fresh assessment: to consider what has been overlooked in the first assessment or what has happened to throw an initially good programme of intervention off course. In one situation in which I was involved, things had started well, and the mother reported excellent progress. In week five, however, she reported that 'Everything has fallen apart: he's worse than when we started'. I was at a loss but then remembered to ask whether anything out of the ordinary had happened since I had last spoken with her. 'Well', she said, 'We've had Easter and he did get seven Easter eggs . . . I thought I'd let him get them over with, so he ate them in two days . . . !' Here we had a completely different variable directly affecting the child's behaviour. When the effects of the chocolate wore off and the mother regained her confidence in how she was learning to manage the child, he resumed his pattern of improved behaviour.

It is important at this stage to ask the parents to complete once again the measures that they completed at the outset, using the Strengths and Difficulties Questionnaire (Goodman, 1997) or whatever measure the practitioner has employed. It is likely that the child will receive a lower score on this postintervention measure. If the work is being evaluated quantitatively, the data for the children's pre- and post-score can be analysed using a number of statistical tests. If only qualitative data are being gathered, statements about the child's behaviour before and after the intervention can be compared. Similarly, data concerning the depression level of the parents can be compared before and after intervention and a bank of data built up to show the impact of the 'Parenting Positively' programme.

II

HELPING FAMILIES WITH SPECIFIC DIFFICULTIES

6

HELPING FAMILIES WITH CHILDREN WHO ARE ANXIOUS OR DEPRESSED

DEFINITION OF EMOTIONAL DISORDERS

Rutter (1987) reported that emotional disorders were common among children. He defined them thus:

> Emotional disorders, as the name suggests, are those in which the main problem involves an abnormality of the emotions, such as anxiety, fear, depressions, obsessions, hypochondriasis and the like.

This chapter will focus upon anxiety and depression in preschool and primary school-age children.

PREVALENCE OF EMOTIONAL DIFFICULTIES IN CHILDREN

Some of the earliest studies of the incidence of emotional disturbance among children are those by Rutter, Cox, Tupling, Berger and Yule (1975a). They compared 1,689 10 year olds growing up in an inner London borough with 1,279 10 year-old children living in the Isle of Wight. The inner London children showed almost double the rate of disturbance of those in the Isle of Wight. This difference seems to be associated with the greater stresses of living in an urban environment, with greater density of housing and population and fewer places to play. Although these comparative data are not currently available, other data are. As we saw in the introduction, the most recent available figures show that among 5–10 year olds, 2.2 % of boys and 2.5 % of girls were seen as suffering from emotional disorders, fears, anxieties, phobias and depression, while among 11–16 year olds, 4.0 % of boys and 6.1 % of girls showed the same disorders (see Table I.1, p. 2).

Variables Protecting Children from Emotional Difficulties

Because not all children who appear to experience the same stressful circumstances do in fact display such symptoms of stress, research has been directed towards exploring which factors may give some protection against these symptoms and against mental disorders. Rutter et al. (1975a, b) noted the following protective circumstances:

- A low stress level within the home.
- Good circumstances compensating for stress at home, e.g. at school.
- Temperamental features of the child: easy, adaptable children are less vulnerable than awkward, negativistic ones.
- Heredity: some children may be genetically less likely to succumb to environmental stress than others. This conjecture has now been given empirical support by the studies of Caspi et al. (2002) who showed that a particular enzyme appears to confer protection against stress in those children fortunate enough to inherit it.
- Good relationships with at least one parent.

This work has been built on by Garmezy (1983), who reviewed studies of acutely disadvantaged children in an attempt to pinpoint what made them able to function well despite living amid poverty and prejudice. He found that black children, growing up in urban ghettos, benefited from:

- features of the child's disposition: the children were perceived as stable, competent and with a positive sense of self
- family cohesion and warmth: even where fathers were absent, mothers offered a well-structured environment and generous personal praise.
- support figures, e.g. in school, who served as positive models for the children.

These studies, together with others, e.g. Werner and Smith (1982), who studied the development of vulnerable children, converge on the following evidence as offering protection:

1. features of the child's temperament and disposition
2. family cohesion and warmth
3. supportive figures in the school or local environment.

Thus, in summary, it seems that psychosocial stress such as growing up in a family where there is low income, unemployment and overcrowding, together with marked discord between parents or caregivers, *particularly where these stresses are cumulative*, can place a child at risk of major difficulties.

Nevertheless, the protective factors noted above can substantially reduce this risk.

We shall now consider the research concerning children and anxiety and children and depression separately.

RESEARCH INTO CHILDREN AND ANXIETY

Forms of Anxiety

In a summary of research into anxiety disorders over the last two decades, Klein and Pine (2002) report that the most common anxiety disorders in children consist of phobic disorders, separation anxiety disorder, social phobia (serious shyness and fears of social situations), generalized anxiety disorder and panic disorder. We shall consider briefly each of these disorders.

Phobic disorder

This is defined as 'marked unreasonable fear of a specific object or situation, that is invariable (it occurs whenever the person encounters the feared object) The phobia must be of such severity that it impairs the person's well-being.' Children commonly experience a phobia of dogs. School phobia is an anxiety-related disorder (Rutter, 1987), but it is a complex response which may have many possible sources of origin (see Figure 6.1).

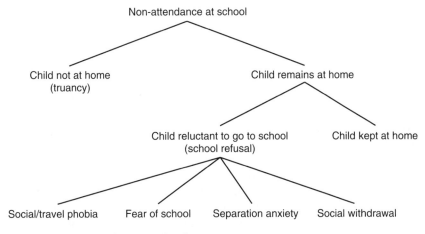

Figure 6.1   Nonattendance at school

Source: Reproduced with permission from Rutter (1987). *Helping Troubled Children*, 2nd edn. New York: Penguin.

Separation anxiety disorder

Herbert (1991) reports that 'Separation anxiety disorder is characterised by "excessive anxiety concerning separation from those to whom the child is attached". A child with separation anxiety disorder may be reluctant to go to school in order to stay near his/her mother or with some other important attachment figure. Headaches and stomach aches and other physical symptoms are also common.

Social phobia

Klein and Pine report that this condition is sometimes referred to as 'social anxiety disorder' because its key clinical feature is anxiety in social situations associated with fear of scrutiny, ridicule, humiliation or embarrassment. They clarify that for this condition to be identified the child must experience discomfort with peers, not only with adults. Such a child is likely to appear shy, socially withdrawn, embarrassed and timid.

Generalised anxiety disorder

Children with this condition are characterised by high levels of worry, often about many aspects of their lives. Such a child tends to worry excessively about school work and future events, and usually appears nervous or tense. The child may need much reassurance or comfort and may complain of a variety of physical ailments (e.g. nausea and dizziness) and shows frequent self-consciousness (Klein & Pine, 2002).

Panic disorder

This condition in adults is characterised by the repeated experience of unprovoked spontaneous panic attacks, marked by intense fear of impending danger. It is possible that children experience these disorders but it is more likely that they can identify the source or origin of their fears – so that the criterion of the panic being unprovoked and spontaneous is seldom met (Herbert, 1998).

Herbert clarifies that in addition to these primary types of disorder, some children also experience both phobic disorders and obsessive-compulsive disorders, in which certain rituals have to be frequently repeated to allay the child's anxiety. Such anxieties are often found among preschool and school-age children, especially shy and conscientious ones. The indications are that children coping with these difficulties often come from homes particularly concerned with cleanliness, etiquette and morality. Some children with these anxieties also lack social skills. This can lead to increasing isolation from normal group activities, leading to misery, which can intensify the obsessive symptoms.

Origins of Anxiety in Children: Natural Developmental Phenomena

It is entirely natural and normal for young children to be anxious and fearful. Ollendick and King (1991) suggest that:

> ... children experience a wide variety of 'normal' fears over their development and these fears appear to be related to their level of cognitive development [King, Hamilton & Ollendick, 1988]. Young infants are afraid of loss of support, loud noises and strangers, as well as sudden, unexpected, and looming objects. One and two year-olds show a range of fears, including separation from parents and fear of strangers. During the third and fourth years, fears of the dark, being left alone, small animals and insects emerge. Fears of wild animals, ghosts and monsters come to the foreground during the fifth and sixth years; and fears of school, supernatural events and physical danger emerge in the seventh and eighth years. During the ninth to eleventh years, social fears and fears of war, health, bodily injury and school performance become more pronounced (Herbert, 1991, page 309).

Most developmental fears, then, are transient. It appears that, under favourable circumstances, they fade away as a result of three main influences: first, children's naturally maturing cognitive processes, so that they come to understand that *monsters, such as dinosaurs, are no threat to them*; second, those who care for them *avoid reinforcing their fears* by giving simple cognitive explanations of upsetting noises like thunder; third, their caregivers *avoid showing fear* themselves.

However, there is increasing evidence that children of parents with anxiety disorders display more anxiety when compared with children born to non-anxious parents (Beidel & Turner, 1997). Some researchers suggest that genetic factors are responsible (Kendler, Karkowski & Prescott, 1999) whereas others suggest that modelling and imitation of the parent by the child provides the explanation. Probably both sets of factors are implicated.

Origins of Anxiety in Children: Specific Events

Hersov (1985) has highlighted the specific impact of certain events in a child's life, such as a car accident or being the object of abuse, physical or sexual. Some children observe things which happen to other people, child or adult, such as loss of a parent via separation or bereavement, which brings the realisation that this could happen to them. In yet other cases there is 'contagion of anxiety' from chronically anxious parents (Eisenberg, 1958).

There continues to be encouraging evidence (Kendall, 1991; Mendlowitz et al., 1999) of the impact of cognitive-behavioural therapy (CBT) strategies in helping anxious children and young people. These include, after due assessment, correcting inaccurate or faulty cognitive interpretations or misunderstandings, training in physical relaxation and developing coping strategies through self-encouragement or behavioural rehearsal. Some forms of CBT focus exclusively on the child and others engage family members (Barrett, 1998).

HELPING FAMILIES WITH ANXIOUS CHILDREN

Parents whose children are anxious or depressed are often deeply unhappy themselves: indeed, sometimes there is a vicious spiral of emotional distress in which each family member intensifies the difficulties experienced by the others. The sequences of the ASPIRE process (see Chapter 4) lend themselves to assessing, planning and intervening to reduce that distress.

Assessment

Anxious and depressed children are likely to find it very hard to communicate their difficulties – partly because they may feel that they will not receive a sympathetic hearing, partly because they are often shy and inarticulate and partly because adults, caught up in their own worries, do not notice that they are unhappy or isolated. It is all the more difficult, therefore, for us as practitioners to come close to them and to gain their confidence sufficiently for them to try to put their unhappiness into words. As with adults, a relationship-building approach showing concern and empathy is likely to be helpful.

Play and other activities as aids to assessment

It is, of course, essential to meet with the child and to gain his or her view of the situation as far as the age of the child permits. Children may be able to describe their fears or sadness and the situations which give rise to them – 'I'm afraid that now Mummy has left, Daddy may leave too' – but they may not. Sometimes there is an opportunity for them to convey something of their difficulties by drawing or painting and play materials should always be available to children. Oaklander (1988) describes some sensitive and imaginative activities in which it is possible to engage young children so that they may be able to express something of their troubles. There are many possible media: sand, clay, paint, papier mâché, as well as dressing up, drama and writing. There is danger, however, in adults' interpreting a child's play or creative activity: it is usually better to seek the child's account of the significance of a painting, a poem or story.

Box 6.1: Sentences for completion by troubled children
(Reproduced with permission from Herbert, 1991.)

I like to ....
What I most dislike ....
My best friend ....
I wish ....
My mum ....
My dad ....
If only ....
In my home the nicest thing is ....
The worst thing is ....
I wish I knew ....
I wonder ....
The thing I worry about most is ....

Children willing to meet with the practitioner alone can often be much helped by a calm talk in which the worker makes it clear that he or she wishes only to help, and how it may be possible to do so. Herbert (1991) has proposed a number of open-ended statements which can help a younger child to indicate in an indirect manner something of the troubles or worries (Box 6.1).

As part of the attempt to understand a child's anxiety or depression, the practitioner will usually ask how the parents have tried to deal with the situation. Often, understandably, they will say that they have talked to the child, told him or her that there is nothing to be afraid of or depressed about, asked him or her each morning how he or she is feeling and generally tried to reassure him or her. Something that they may not have thought of, which is only becoming apparent because of research within the framework of cognitive-behavioural theory, is that they may be unwittingly reinforcing anxious or depressed behaviour in their child by unduly attending to it. This is, of course, likely to be only part of the story but it is a significant part and the removal of this attention can, of itself, reduce the child's level of distress.

In all these situations of assessment, the constructive nature of the relationship between worker and parent(s) is paramount – based upon fundamental principles of counselling: empathy, warmth, genuineness and unconditional positive regard. The parents or caregivers will need time to unburden themselves of their own distress associated with the child's difficulties. Sometimes, talking to the practitioner in a nonjudgmental and confidential setting will be the first opportunity parents or caregivers have had to speak freely of a situation without feeling that they are being implicitly criticised. This active listening, as has been emphasised, is essentially a component of counselling and can markedly reduce tension for all concerned. It is *step 1*.

Step 2 – Information Gathering

The Common Assessment Framework offers a helpful holistic process for a comprehensive survey of the child in his or her setting. (see Figure 4.2, p. 87).

Child's developmental needs

This dimension includes all aspects of the child's physical and psychological wellbeing, and notably his or her emotional and behavioural development. The child's educational progress and his or her social presentation and sense of identity are also located on this dimension. We shall seek information from parents about when they first noticed that their child appeared tense or worried – indeed, what they noticed about him as a baby and toddler. Was he tense as an infant or did this develop later? What seemed to distress the child in early life? When does the anxiety seem worse and when better? In respect of life events, parents can sometimes pinpoint a date or an event that they think contributed significantly to the child's difficulties: an accident, an admission to hospital, the move to a new school, or a separation of the child's parents. How has the child responded when they asked what was the matter?

Organic factors will include variables that interact with physiological systems and which make it intrinsically more likely that the child will experience anxiety: for example, a tendency to be self-conscious and self-preoccupied leading to a tendency to blush, to wet himself or to develop a rash in stressful situations. Some children experience deeply painful shyness so that they literally cannot look at another child or adult and are forever glancing past them or looking away. This social anxiety may be genetically underpinned or it may have been learned, either as a result of little contact with the hurly burly of young children's play or of a very upsetting rejection.

It will be important to ask how the parents understand or make sense of their child's anxiety or depression – but remember that parents or family members are unlikely to be familiar with the concept of 'anxiety' and its connotations although they *are* likely to have encountered the idea of 'stress'. The child may be described as tense or worried but it is unlikely that parents will have an understanding of the physiological underpinnings of anxiety or depression or of how, for example, there can be generalisation of anxiety from one situation to other apparently very different situations.

Family and environmental factors

This second dimension takes into account the circumstances of the wider family. Here we shall note information which concerns events or experiences which family members or the child himself may have had which seem to contribute directly or indirectly to the child's anxieties. For example, bereavement of a beloved family member is typically a very distressing experience and one that may wound a child profoundly. Similarly, family separation or divorce can prove devastating to young children who cannot begin to understand such a complex development with so many interruptions to their lives: changes of house, school and sometimes friends and relatives.

Parenting capacity

This third dimension concerns the ability of the child's parents to give the necessary care to the child in line with his or her age, emotional needs and individual development. When making an assessment of an anxious child, practitioners will notice how the parents interact with him or her. Do they describe the child in negative ways, likely to reinforce the child's sense of failure or difficulty? Do they speak optimistically of the future? Do they cheer and encourage him, or do they see him as a 'problem'? All these subtle messages to the child are unintentionally reinforcing the child's inhibition and probable low self-esteem.

Additional information to inform the assessment

There is evidence that children often do not understand what they are being asked to do (that is, the instruction is too vague or too general: 'will you behave!') I have included a space where the practitioner can attend quite specifically to that issue. In the summary of assessment document (Table 4.1, p. 95) I have incorporated also a space where the *strengths* of the family, and indeed of the child, can be deliberately identified and highlighted for both the family members and the practitioner to recognise. With so much attention being given to misbehaviour or at least in the case of a very shy child, to his or her difficulties, it is urgent that everyone should notice and record some positive features of the family and of its most vulnerable member(s).

I also incorporate space for an analysis of the detail of what we may call 'immediate variables', that is, an analysis of events in the child's daily life in terms of antecedents, behaviour and consequences (A–B–C). Such an analysis often throws a great deal of light upon the behaviours of an anxious child, and sometimes also upon that of a depressed child.

The Case of Ellie: a Very Anxious Little Girl

Consider Ellie, whose mother, Julie, is asking her health visitor for help with her little girl's behaviour. Ellie is just four, an only child, who will not let Julie out of her sight. The little girl follows her mother *everywhere* – all round the house, into the garden, even to the toilet. Her mother feels increasingly

---

Box 6.2: Initial information concerning Ellie to inform the assessment

1. *Child's developmental needs*
   (a) Ellie seems a very fearful little girl indeed. Her life experiences are much curtailed by her fears.
   (b) She has always been 'shy'.
   (c) She had a number of allergies when a toddler but these seem to have improved.
2. *Family and environmental factors*
   (a) Ellie's father was killed in a car accident when she was three; she still asks for him.
   (b) Her mother is still deeply depressed.
   (c) Ellie's grandparents try to be helpful, but she will not stay with them.
   (d) Ellie has had little contact with other children, apart from a dancing class once a week. She will not stay at a playgroup or nursery.
3. *Parenting capacity: interactions within the family (A–B–C):*[*]
   (a) Ellie receives a great deal of attention when she behaves fearfully.
   (b) There are few opportunities for her fearfulness to diminish as she meets few adults and fewer children.

[*]Julie may not understand this concept, but it is useful to introduce it at this stage.

---

annoyed with the little girl. If Julie visits a friend, Ellie stands by her throughout the visit, rejecting all encouragement to play with other children. She insists on sleeping in her mother's bed and gets panicky if this is refused.

Further information may come to light as the asssessment proceeds. It can be entered on the summary sheet as shown in Table 4.1.

Step 3 – Identifying Problem Behaviours

It is likely that Julie will need help in beginning to think of her little girl's difficulties in terms of her *behaviours* but let us assume that she is able, with support, to identify the following:

1. Ellie cries a great deal.
2. She does not play with other children.
3. She screams when left with a neighbour or at playgroup.
4. She follows her mother round all the time.

When asked to list these behaviours in order of the distress they cause her, Julie acknowledges that although she feels upset by her little girl's unhappiness, it is being followed about that irritates her most. So the list emerges:

1. Ellie follows her mother round all the time.
2. She cries a great deal.
3. She does not play with other children.
4. She screams when taken to a playgroup.

Step 4 – Identifying Positive Features of a Child's Behaviour

This request may also surprise Julie, but she is able to distinguish her little girl's strengths and qualities, although she probably needs help in stating them in terms of *observable behaviours*:

1. Ellie paints and draws readily: she is very imaginative.
2. She can pick out tunes on the piano: she seems very musical.
3. She goes readily to a small ballet class for five little girls; Julie has to stay too. Here she smiles and occasionally laughs. She has one friend, Clare.

Step 5 – Discovering Desired Outcomes

To the question of what target behaviours would Julie like her little girl to show more frequently, she works out, with help, the following:

1. To allow Julie to leave the living room for the kitchen or bathroom without Ellie following her.
2. To go to a nearby playgroup three mornings a week; Julie to stay if necessary.
3. To let her Granny look after her for a day without screaming.

Step 6 – Arriving at a Formulation of/Rationale for the Difficulties

When the practitioner has gathered as much relevant information as possible, or as much as she has time for, then it should be possible, drawing upon material offered by Julie, to formulate some provisional rationale for Ellie's difficulties. For example, the following analysis might be helpful:

1 *Developmental factors concerning Ellie*
   (a) Ellie seems temperamentally to be a very sensitive child.
   (b) The allergies she had as a baby, although less troublesome now, still cause difficulties.

Table 6.1 Preliminary assessment of/rationale for aspects of Ellie's difficulties

Activator	Behaviour	Consequences
1 Julie is talking on the phone with her friend	Ellie begins to cry piercingly	Julie interrupts her phone call and reads Ellie a story to calm her down
2 Julie takes Ellie to the playgroup	Ellie screams and says she wants to go home	Julie takes her home

2 *Family factors*
   (a) Ellie was deeply upset at her father's disappearance and is still very upset.
   (b) She has seldom been cared for by anyone else.
   (c) Her mother is also still deeply sad and depressed.
   (d) Once, when her mother was very ill and was admitted to hospital, Ellie's Granny came from Scotland to care for her. Ellie was very upset and took many weeks to settle once her mother returned home.
3 *Parenting capacity. Interactions within the family (A–B–C)*
   In discussion with Julie, some of these could be tactfully considered in the way shown in Table 6.1.

This formulation of the difficulties might need much discussion, for while the precipitating factors may 'make sense' to Julie – indeed, they are obvious precipitants of anxiety in a young child – the examination of Ellie's behaviour when her mother is on the telephone or when she is taken to the playgroup, in terms of activators–behaviour–consequences, may seem irrelevant and even irritating. The practitioner needs to help Julie to understand that, with the best of intentions, she may be playing into her little girl's difficulties. Together they can try out different strategies.

Julie may not understand that by interrupting her telephone call and by taking Ellie home from the playgroup she is rewarding Ellie for her inappropriate behaviour. She is teaching her that screaming will be rewarded by Julie's full attention and that showing fear at playgroup will be reinforced by Julie's taking her home – so confirming for Ellie that a playgroup is not a safe place. At this point we are simply sowing the seeds of Julie's looking at Ellie's difficult behaviours both from her understanding of her little girl's distress but also from the slightly different viewpoint of what patterns of behaviour she is herself unwittingly reinforcing. There is no need to insist on one perspective. We can go on to suggest testing a number of hypotheses or 'possibilities'; the number is likely to vary according to the age of the child. In respect of Ellie, they might be:

Table 6.2 A scale for parents to estimate levels of anxiety in their young children

0	5	10
Generally clam, relaxed behaviour	Generally calm, some episodes of tension or clinging	Generally tense, panicky behaviour

(a) Ellie's overall anxiety will diminish in frequency and intensity as she learns from repeated experience that her mother does not abandon her.

(b) Ellie's anxiety will reduce if it is possible for her to talk about her Daddy.

(c) Ellie's episodes of crying will diminish as Julie manages to avoid attending to them – for example, when she is on the telephone.

(d) Ellie's anxiety will slowly diminish as, by very gradual steps, she becomes less sensitive to formerly stressful circumstances, such as the playgroup.

(e) Ellie will gain confidence if she is able to spend more time with her friend, Clare.

In order to test these hypotheses, probably one at a time, it is desirable to have some measure of her present level of distress – a yardstick or benchmark against which to assess progress or deterioration. One can ask parents to estimate their child's average anxiety level over the past week, using a 10-point scale such as the one in Table 6.2. Parents can then estimate any changes in their child's average daily anxiety level as the plan takes effect. These can be charted simply and any changes monitored and discussed.

Step 7 – Seeking One Week's Counts of a Positive and a Negative Behaviour

Julie can then be asked to identify a pair of behaviours, one negative and one positive, whose frequency she can record over the next week. She can be helped to identify one positive feature of Ellie's behaviour and one negative feature. She may choose as follows:

Negative behaviour: Ellie cries for a spell of three minutes.
Positive behaviour: Ellie draws or paints for three minutes.

When the information identified above is available, say within one week, it might look as shown in Table 6.3.

Table 6.3 Number of instances of Ellie's positive and negative behaviours over one week

CHARTING BEHAVIOURS		Name: Ellie				Week beginning: 16 May (Week 1)		
Behaviour	*Sunday*	*Monday*	*Tuesday*	*Wednesday*	*Thursday*	*Friday*	*Saturday*	*Total*
Behaviours to encourage and praise – Amusing self (e.g. by painting)								
Morning								
Afternoon				✓				
Evening						✓		2
Behaviours to discourage – Following mother								
Morning		✓✓	✓✓✓	✓✓	✓	✓✓	✓	
Afternoon		✓	✓	✓✓	✓✓	✓	✓✓✓	
Evening	✓			✓			✓	24

Step 8 Planning – with the Parent(s)

The practitioner and parent(s) are partners in a shared endeavour to help Ellie. Some of the ideas that have to be discussed may be very difficult for them: for example, Julie may find it very painful to talk to Ellie about her Daddy. She may need support in doing so, not in an intense way but in a supportive way in which she herself may weep and show her distress. Despite her own pain, she will probably understand that to show her own natural emotion is, in the long run, in her little girl's best interests.

Ellie, too, can be involved as fully as her understanding permits – so that it can be explained to her that Mummy and the health visitor/social worker know she gets very upset that her Daddy is no longer able to be with her. There are organisations to support children and parents with bereavement and it seems that talking about the lost person, and asking any questions as and when they arise is most helpful to a bereaved child. Parents will want to give explanations in line with their own views or beliefs; the important thing seems to be that the child should be dealt with openly and truthfully as far as is possible. Ellie will also need reassurance that it is understandable that she is frightened when she thinks her mummy is going to leave her, but her mummy is *not* going to leave her; she will continue to look after Ellie. Once this has been confirmed, the topic should not be returned to again and again. This might easily increase Ellie's anxiety.

In respect of the immediate variables, A–B–C, it is crucial that we explain to parents what is known about desensitisation from the standpoint of cognitive-behavioural theory. Most people are familiar with the idea of taking very small steps when gaining confidence in a new skill; it can be clarified that just as we advise adults to 'avoid running before they can walk', and just as we teach children to swim not by throwing them in at the deep end but by gradually helping them to trust themselves to the water, so anxious children gain confidence by taking *very* small steps.

I sometimes tell parents and children of our dentist's way of introducing children to dental treatment (Box 6.3). To the children, the whole thing was intriguing. The dentist told me to tell our children that sometimes drilling did hurt a bit, but it soon wore off. Going to the dentist became a matter of great interest and even enjoyment!

Helping the parent explain the plan to the child

There will probably be at least two important things to explain to Ellie and these must obviously be pitched to her level of understanding. First, her mummy knows that Ellie is afraid that her mummy will leave her. She will not leave her but she is not going to say this over and over again. Second, it is really important that Ellie lets her mummy go to the loo without interrupting her. So, in future, when she wants to go to the lavatory, she will get out the

Box 6.3: Gradual steps for introducing a child to the dentist

Step 1 They accompanied me when I was having a checkup. They were each allowed to sit in the chair for a moment or two.

Step 2 They accompanied me when I was having my teeth polished. They were allowed to have a very brief inspection.

Step 3 They accompanied me when I was having a small filling. They were allowed to have a brief polish.

Step 4 I took them when I made an ordinary visit; each had a brief check.

Step 5 I took each one separately for a proper check. No treatment was necessary.

crayons and paper or a jigsaw for Ellie and say once, in a matter-of-fact way, that she will be in the bathroom for a short time.

Plan of action

The details can be worked out with Julie and Ellie and their suggestions taken into account, for example:

1. Ellie can use her crayons while her mummy, Julie, goes to the bathroom.
2. If Ellie amuses herself and does not cry, Julie will read her a short story as soon as she comes out of the bathroom.
3. If she does cry, however, there will be no story and no cuddles at that time.

This explanation will help the little girl understand why her mother has changed her pattern of reactions to her; she is likely to respond positively within a day or two. Julie, too, is likely to begin to understand the logic of the approach. She is to explain to Ellie, in effect, that *she intends to reward Ellie for desirable behaviour and avoid rewarding her for undesirable behaviour*. Reassurance will come as the little girl learns to trust that her mother will do as she said and as she gains no additional attention for her anxious behaviour. One can confidently predict that so long as the assessment has been sound and so long as the mother remains calm and avoids reinforcing her little daughter's anxieties when looking after her, Ellie's fearfulness will gradually fade away or 'extinguish'.

In other situations, for example at other people's houses, if Ellie cries she should be ignored – so as not to reward her screaming with attention. However, when Ellie amuses herself with her paints or drawing for a spell of three minutes, she should be told gently (not overenthusiastically) how well she has done.

Step 9 – Implementation of the Plan

Ellie's mother is likely to be ready to try the suggestions offered but there may well be problems in implementing the plan. Ellie has learned to control her mother so effectively over so long a period, as a means of managing her fears, that she is likely to put up heavy initial resistance to her mother's changed way of managing her. Her fearful behaviour may become worse rather than better for a few weeks and her mother may find it necessary to seek support from the practitioner, either face to face or by telephone. In my own research (Sutton, 1992, 1995) I was able to show that contact by telephone for many children's difficulties was as effective as face-to-face contact and brought about equally good results. A two-minute telephone call can be extremely economical, in terms of both time and money. This plan can be adopted for the next month, with contact between practitioner and parent at least twice weekly initially and then once a week as those becomes less anxious. Data such as those shown in Figure 6.2 are very commonly obtained. Ellie and Julie will both need much commendation and encouragement.

As the new strategies begin to take effect and as Julie sees their impact so systematic work upon a new pair of behaviours is called for – in Ellie's case, increasing the amount of time she spends amusing herself and avoiding attending to her crying in *any* setting. If, however, no progress is made and Ellie's distress has not diminished by the end of the agreed time, in this case a month, then another plan must be considered. Sometimes one finds that

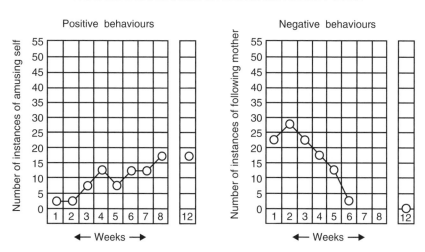

Figure 6.2 Ellie's positive and negative behaviours over eight weeks and at three months' followup

although the parent has intended to be consistent, in a moment of irritation she has said to the child, 'I can't stand much more of this: I'm going to send you to Scotland again and get a bit of time to myself'. The next moment she regrets her words, but the damage has been done and Ellie's fearful behaviours may reintensify. Sometimes, we hear about such unintended lapses; at other times we do not; we just hear that the plan for helping Ellie didn't work!

Step 10 – Review and Evaluation

Ordinarily, one can anticipate that, so long as Ellie's mother is patient and does not attempt to rush things her little girl's anxiety will decrease. As she gains confidence, the plan can be extended to making short outings from the house, taking plenty of time over each step. Soon they can plan their outings – perhaps next to a shop, where a small treat may be purchased for Ellie *and* for Julie. Over the course of time, Ellie may go with her mother to a park and then gradually to the local playgroup where the staff are aware of the need to introduce this little girl very gradually to the buzz of a playgroup.

In my own years as a playgroup leader and before I had ever heard of cognitive-behavioural theory I spent many hours carrying small tots around the room while their anxious mothers first walked round the hall in which the group was held, then a week later went to the lavatory alone – sometimes the first occasion in which they had done so in years – and then, gradually, extended the period when the mother was out of her child's sight until the child could manage alone for a whole morning. It was wonderful to see the changes in both parent and child as the confidence of both gradually rose. At another level, of course, the practitioner is likely to support Ellie's mother in ensuring that her own needs are met, perhaps by seeking counselling in respect of her bereavement and of her needs to develop aspects of her own life.

RESEARCH INTO CHILDREN AND DEPRESSION

Prevalence of Depression

Rutter (1986) reported that in the early Isle of Wight study of 10–11 year old children:

> ... 13% showed a depressed mood at interview, 9% appeared preoccu-
> pied with depressive topics, 17% failed to smile, and 15% showed poor
> emotional responsiveness.

The data from the Department of Health (1995a) report that major depression in children spans a range of 0.5%–2.5%, depending on the location of the study. More recent data (see Table I.1, p. 2) do not distinguish depression in children from other affective disorders such as anxiety so the earlier figures can still serve as a general guide as to prevalence. Hersov (1977) has suggested that there is probably an interaction effect between genetic factors and life circumstances and that this contributes towards whether a given child will respond to a difficult life event such as parental separation, with depression or not. However, other studies, for example Wilde, Keinhorst, Dickstra and Walters (1992) found that many children's depressions were associated with chronic and longstanding difficulties as much as with specific life events. So a 10 year old may say, 'Mummy is always saying she can't afford things: I'm afraid that there soon won't be enough food for us'; or she may say, 'I can help with looking after Danny [a brother with Down's syndrome] now, but what will I do if Mummy gets ill?' Many of these worries have their origins in reality and all our energies and resources are needed to help the children concerned.

Indicators of Depression

Depression is a condition characterised by disturbance of at least three systems:

- *affect* or emotions of sadness or misery
- *behaviour* marked by slowness or lethargy
- *cognitions* or thoughts of hopelessness or sometimes suicide.

Herbert (1991) offers a checklist (Box 6.4) of the main signs of depression in children and young people.

There is evidence (Bernstein & Garfinkel, 1986) that depression may also be accompanied by severe symptoms of anxiety, so Herbert emphasises that the assessment must be comprehensive enough to allow for the identification of both disorders.

Origins of Depression in Children

Harrington (1994) reports three major types of research into the factors contributing to depression in children and young people. First, there are those which study the impact of parental depression upon children: in this area several works, notably the review by Rutter (1988), have shown the association between the mental disorder of parents and children's emotional and cognitive development. Thus depression in mothers is likely to lead to reduced mother-child interactions and may indeed contribute to depression in the children. (In my own research, 11 of the 23 mothers studied scored 15

Box 6.4: Main signs of depression in children and young people

(Reproduced with permission from Herbert, 1991.)

- A demeanour of unhappiness or misery (more persistent and intense than 'the blues' from which we all suffer now and then).
- A marked change in eating and/or sleeping patterns.
- A feeling of helplessness, hopelessness and self-dislike.
- An inability to concentrate and apply oneself to anything.
- Everything (even talking and dressing) is seen as an effort.
- Irritating or aggressive behaviour.
- A sudden change in school work.
- A constant search for distractions and new activities.
- Dangerous risk taking (e.g. with drugs/alcohol; dangerous driving; delinquent actions).
- Friends being dropped or ignored.

---

or above on the Beck Depression Inventory at the preintervention stage; at postintervention only 4 of 22 mothers reached this score, while at 12 months' followup only 2 of 18 mothers did so.)

The second set of studies are those in which three kinds of risk factors have been isolated:

1. *Acute life events,* such as loss of a parent. Rutter and Sandberg (1992) have shown that it is not only the loss *per se* but also the associated reduction in parental care which renders children vulnerable. The impact of such events, however, will clearly be influenced by the circumstances and meaning of the loss for the children concerned.
2. *Chronic adversities.* Wilde et al. (1992) showed that depression was often as much associated with long-standing problems as with a sudden life event.
3. *Vulnerability factors.* Brown and Harris (1978) showed that early experience of loss of mother before the age of 11 years rendered children vulnerable to subsequent depressive disorders.

The third type of approach is to study children who have experienced a specific 'life event'. Harrington (1994) reports that:

> Depressive symptoms have been found in association with many types of adverse life experience, including divorce (Wallerstein & Kelly, 1980; Aro & Palosaari, 1992) and disasters (Yule, Udwin & Murdoch, 1990). Bereaved preschoolers often have depressive symptoms and Weller et al. (1991) reported that around one-third of bereaved prepubertal children met criteria for depressive disorder.

Depressive symptoms have also been found in association with both physical abuse (Allen & Tarnowski, 1989) and sexual abuse (Goldston et al., 1989). Depressive disorders occur in about 20 % of maltreated children.

In seeking to explain the mechanisms by which these life events lead to the internal mood state of depression, Harrington (1994) suggests that the concept of 'learned helplessness' provides the best explanatory framework. According to this model, the child (or adult) experiences *powerlessness* in the face of uncontrollable life circumstances and therefore comes to adopt a negative cognitive set (Beck, 1976). He or she develops a negative view of himself or herself, of the world and of the future.

Harrington also reports the evidence of low social competence as being implicated in the development of depression in children and young people and cites Patterson and Stoolmiller (1991), who found that rejection by peers was often associated with depression in young people and this too can lead to antisocial behaviour.

What Children Get Depressed About

The events or beliefs listed in Box 6.5 appear frequently to lead to depression.

HELPING FAMILIES WITH DEPRESSED CHILDREN

You will recall that in the Isle of Wight studies 13 % of 10–11 year old children were found to be depressed and, although the issue is beyond the scope of this book, it is distressing that at followup at age 14–15 *over 40 %* of the same young people 'reported substantial feelings of misery and depression'. These are deeply disturbing figures.

This book focuses upon children of primary school age so cannot address the issues of adolescence but the same basic approach is adopted for all

---

Box 6.5: Life events that may predispose a child or young person to depression

1. Loss by bereavement of or separation from a person emotionally important to them: mother, father, brother, sister or other close relationship.
2. Anticipated loss: for example family separation.
3. Beliefs that they carry responsibility for a major life event within their family: for example a family member leaving the household.
4. Social unacceptibility: leading to loneliness and isolation.
5. Lack of friends.
6. Disability, both its direct impact and also its indirect effects such as associated isolation from the peer group.

children. First, as always, a comprehensive assessment, using the Common Assessment Framework, is essential but this will be made more effective if, as *step 1*, a supportive relationship with the parent is developed.

Assessment – the Example of Amrit

It will be necessary to interview parents and caregivers of depressed children in an effort to understand their view and knowledge of the child's life experience. This is likely to start from the standpoint of

1. *The child's developmental needs*, including caregivers' perception of the child as a toddler, characteristic patterns of shyness or of outgoingness, sensitivity or other temperamental features, as well as friendships and their disruption by changes of school or other factors. It will be necessary to gain the parents' view of the onset of the depression, whether gradual or sudden, and what they believe precipitated it.
2. *Family and environmental factors.* These may include bereavement or other major losses of family or friends, accidents which have left them with major physical or other difficulties, family break-up or experiences at school or elsewhere which have left the youngster feeling vulnerable.
3. *Parenting capacity.* Here the practitioner will be noting in a provisional and constructive way how the parents speak of the child, their level of understanding of and concern for him, and whether or not they may be unwittingly reinforcing the child's depression. Most parents are distressed to see their child's depression, but do not understand how their own actions, however well meant, may be intensifying their child's unhappiness. We shall discuss this further below.

It will, of course, be necessary to talk with the child separately, to see whether his views accord with those of the parent(s). Few children will be so articulate as to be able to identify the direct cause of their unhappiness but again responses to open-ended questions may offer clues as to the contributory factors.

The following example of Amrit, a little Asian boy of nine, sets out the various illustrative steps.

Step 1 – Build Supportive and Empathic Relationships

Amrit has been noticed by the school nurse as a lonely and apparently unhappy child. She has gained his confidence and has had one meeting with his mother, Smita, who says she is effectively a lone parent, is on Income Support, is depressed herself, and can't cope with Amrit's moods. However, she agrees to meet with the school nurse again. On this occasion, Smita explains that she

---

Box 6.6: Initial information concerning Amrit to inform the assessment

1. *Child's developmental needs*
   (a) Amrit is a child of dual heritage.
   (b) He is beginning to put on a lot of weight.
   (c) He seems to be lonely and to have low self esteem.
2. *Family and environmental factors*
   (a) Amrit's father has had several spells in prison.
   (b) Amrit sees his dad only rarely — every three or four months.
   (c) Roy, Smita's new partner, and Amrit do not get on well.
3. *Parenting capacity*
   (a) Smita admits she 'nags' Amrit when he eats a lot; then he eats more!
   (b) Smita would like Amrit to go to football training, but if he does not go she often says, 'Let's go to the cinema then . . .'
   (c) Amrit often spends all weekend in his bedroom, playing on his computer. Smita lets him; she gives him his meals there on a tray.

---

is a lone parent; she was knocked about by Amrit's dad, who is white, and she doesn't want to talk about him. She realises Amrit is very unhappy, but can't see that telling Amrit about what his dad did to her and why she left him will help Amrit at all. She used to be very cross with Amrit if ever he got noisy or at all aggressive as she was afraid that it was his Dad coming out in him, but now she wonders if she curbed him too much.

Step 2 – Gather Information

In the course of gathering information (Box 6.6), the nurse learns that Amrit's Dad is in prison and that his mum doesn't want him back. She is making something of a new life for herself with a new partner, Roy.

Step 3 – Identify the Problem Behaviours

Smita understands well that Amrit may be missing his father, and says she will do what she can to help him. When asked to identify the particular patterns of behaviour causing concern, she can state several:

1. Amrit keeps saying he's 'no good'.
2. He is overweight for his age.
3. He spends much of his time alone.
4. He has few friends.
5. He has started to avoid going to school.

Play and other aids to assessment. As with anxiety, a variety of aids can be helpful in enabling a child to reveal something of his unhappiness, but here too interpretations by the worker are to be avoided. Amrit, as a nine year old, may choose to draw or paint rather than play with sand, or he may feel able to answer some of the questions developed by Herbert (1991); see p. 137 above.

Step 4 – Identify a Positive Profile

With careful enquiry, a depressed child's strengths and positive qualities can usually be brought to light. A perceptive teacher has noticed that Amrit has written a story of great sensitivity; another is aware that he is particularly responsive to the natural world and a third remembers how he 'came alive' when talking about animals. So soon Amrit's positive profile can be set out:

1. He always responds to his teacher's greeting.
2. He takes great care of the family pet, brushing it and preparing its food.
3. Since he learned to make a cup of tea, Amrit brings his mother a cup every morning without fail.

Step 5 – Identify Target Behaviours

Smita says that there are several patterns of behaviour that she would like Amrit to develop:

1. To attend football and sport sessions each once a week as before.
2. To speak to her friends when they visit the house and not to hide away.
3. To spend at least two hours weekly out of the house with a friend or group.

Amrit seems frightened when asked what patterns of behaviour he would like to change in his own life but with help is able to say that he wants to eat fewer snacks and he would like to play football again.

Step 6 – Arrive at a Formulation

This formulation of the difficulties shown in Table 6.4 might need discussion, for although the developmental factors together with family stressors may be clear to Smita and Amrit, it will probably be difficult for them to understand that by offering attractive alternatives to activities with children of his own age, Smita may be making it *more* likely in the long term that Amrit will become depressed.

Table 6.4 Preliminary assessment of aspects of Amrit's difficulties

Child's developmental needs	Environment/family factors	Parenting capacity
(a) Amrit is a child of dual heritage. Both his Asian and White heritage need appreciation (b) He is rather overweight. (c) He seems depressed.	(a) Amrit's father has had several imprisonments. (b) Amrit seldom sees him. (c) Amrit and Roy, Smita's new partner do not get on.	(a) Smita is a loving mother, who cares for Amrit dearly. (b) She will do anything she can to help Amrit.

What are this family's strengths?
1. The mother loves the child dearly. She has sought help for Amrit and will do all she can to help him.
2. She actively asks for help and for guidance on how to cope with his depression.

Communication. Are clear messages being given? i.e. does the child understand what he is being asked to do?
Not really. Amrit is nagged for being overweight but then fed rich foods in his room.

Activator	Behaviour	Consequences
1. Amrit says he feels unhappy and doesn't want to go to football.	He dawdles in getting ready – until it is certain that he will be late.	Smita shouts at him, but then says 'oh well, we'll go out to the cinema . . .'
2. Smita calls Amrit for dinner from his bedroom.	He delays and shouts 'in a minute' but does not go.	Eventually Smita brings him a meal on a tray.

Priorities for action agreed with parents

1. School nurse will meet Amrit and spend more time winning his confidence.

2. Mum will keep a food diary of everything that her child eats.

3. Mum will record one negative behaviour and one positive behaviour for Amrit for one week. (See page 287.)

Step 7 – Collect Details of Behaviour

Smita and Amrit agree to collect a record of how Amrit spends his time for one week.

Step 8 – Planning

It is likely to be possible to help Amrit and Smita by a plan with a number of steps:

1. To help Smita herself by listening empathically to her story.
2. To ask what she thinks would help Amrit: for example:
   (a) talking with Amrit about his dad
   (b) enabling Amrit to meet his dad regularly – even though this is hard for her
   (c) going to places with Amrit: the library, museum, but not as an alternative to activities with his school
   (d) helping him take up his interest in sport again: swimming, football
   (e) inviting a child whom Amrit suggests home to play after school
   (f) helping Amrit lose weight – keeping a chart.

Involve the child in the planning

Amrit must be involved in clarifying the ideas about how his depression has developed and in exploring plans for the future; in each case, his wishes are incorporated where possible. Amrit may well reveal that while he knows his mother has ceased visiting his dad in prison and seems to want to break all contact with him, he, Amrit, does not want to break contact; in fact, he very much wants to strengthen it but fears to tell his mother. He may also say that he is afraid of Roy, who shouts at him.

Three further components of the plan to help Amrit may then emerge:

   (g) the practitioner will talk with Smita about Amrit's wish to see his father
   (h) the practitioner will discuss with Smita how to improve Roy's and Amrit's relationship
   (i) the worker will talk with Smita about how to enable Amrit to learn more of both aspects of his heritage.

Step 9 – Implement the Plan

This takes place over the next few weeks, with records to show first the initial states of affairs and then the impact of agreed changes: these might relate to:

- The number of times Amrit has visited his father and how much time they have spent together.
- Diary of Amrit's developing interest in his Indian *and* his British heritage.
- Amount of time spent by Amrit taking part in activities, as distinct from in his bedroom.
- Time spent by Amrit in swimming, football and other sport.
- Weight change as Amrit begins to reduce his intake of food and to take exercise.
- Measuring Amrit's depression pre- and post-intervention using the Strengths and Difficulties Questionnaire (Goodman, 1997).
- The impact of the worker's gentle questioning of Amrit's assertion, 'I am no good'. What is the evidence for this statement? This is a cognitive therapeutic approach. The aim is to help children and adults recognise that they are themselves diminishing their sense of worth by rehearsing such statements. Instead they are helped to work out positive, self-encouraging statements. This approach is known to reduce depression in young people (Kendall, 1991).

This is the stage at which to return to the original goals set out in Step 5 and to highlight any progress that has been made towards them. They may need amending but there is likely to be some progress. There will be setbacks but it is the areas of improvement that should be highlighted and reinforced.

Step 10 – Review and Evaluate

These are based upon the evidence of the impact of the plan – reviewed at agreed intervals and adapted as necessary. The practitioner acts as facilitator and troubleshooter and gives encouragement to all concerned. The intervention would be finally evaluated at the end of an agreed period of intervention and booster meetings would be arranged.

7

HELPING FAMILIES WITH CHILDREN'S SLEEPING PROBLEMS

Since the publication of the first edition of this book, a number of studies have been published that approach the various strategies for managing young children's crying and sleeping problems from a fresh vantagepoint: that of their cost. In addition there has been the development of a research focus upon the sleeping patterns of very young infants and indeed of the costs of irregular sleeping in these tiny babies. These new fields will be considered below.

Disturbed sleep causes great stress for families. As anyone who has paced the floor with a screaming baby in the small hours knows, one can feel desperate for something, *anything*, that will stop the crying. So sleeping difficulties are included within this book because, although they are of a rather different order from others, there is much help that can be given by appropriately trained staff. Improving sleeping patterns often contributes to the wellbeing of all concerned and to the reduction of other difficulties attributable to fatigue and stress.

However, sleeping problems are *not* an area to be tackled by inexperienced staff, and above all not by staff working without supervision. Things can go wrong and even though it is difficult to delay intervention when parents are begging for help it is better to wait for skilled supervision than to embark on a plan to resolve sleeping difficulties and to fail. Such a failure reinforces the enthusiasm for the toddler for midnight play and reduces the confidence of parents in the practitioner.

DEFINITION OF SLEEPING DISORDER

To say that a child has a 'sleeping problem' requires clarification. This term is used to distinguish children who depart from statistical norms, in that they display sleeping patterns that are markedly different from those of most of their contemporaries, which affects the child's wellbeing as well as that of family members. Let us examine the research on sleeping difficulties in the light of these concepts.

Skuse (1994) identifies three main areas for the study of sleep disorder:

1. Children who fail to settle at night – bedtime difficulties.
2. Children who wake in the night and do not readily return to sleep.
3. Disorders of sleep: sleepwalking, nightmares and night terrors.

To this may be added the field of the crying and sleeping patterns of very young babies. Each will be considered below.

THE PREVALENCE OF SLEEPING/WAKING DIFFICULTIES

Epidemiological Studies

Many practitioners regard a 'sleeping problem' as a culturally invented 'disorder', pointing out that to place very young children to sleep alone is a Western practice considered by many other cultures as little short of barbarism. Yet the fact remains that many families do expect their infants to sleep alone, although Scragg et al. (1996) have recommended, on the basis of their research in New Zealand, that to reduce the risk of sudden infant death infants should sleep in the same bedroom as their parents until they are at least six months old, preferably in their own cots. There is also now general concensus among researchers that babies should be placed on their backs to sleep (Wigfield, Fleming, Berry, Rudd & Golding, 1992; Hunt, 1994).

The sleeping patterns of infants

The study by Sadler (1994), undertaken as part of the Avon Longitudinal Study of Pregnancy and Childhood (ALSPAC) surveyed the parents of 640 babies when they were 6 months old. Researchers found that among babies:

- only 16% slept through the night
- 84% were not sleeping through the night
- 17% woke more than once per night, ranging from twice to 8 times
- 5% woke once every night
- 9% woke most nights
- 50% woke occasionally
- 16% had no regular sleeping pattern.

In respect of waking difficulties, there is an unfortunate assumption that unless a baby settles readily and 'sleeps through the night' from a very early stage, there is something wrong. This is inaccurate. Reporting a major study, Skuse (1994, p. 476) writes:

> Whether or not night waking is regarded as a problem by parents will depend on what they believe to be normal. Few think that infants less than three to four months of age can be expected to sleep through the night without interruption. Even after four months there is considerable variation in their expectation. Scott & Richards (1990) recently conducted a survey on this matter. They found that about one in four infants, at one year of age, were waking five or more nights a week. Ten per cent of their mothers did not regard that as a problem. However, 37 % of those whose babies woke less often did regard their sleep pattern as a problem. These findings have implications for studies that rely solely on parental reports for their identification of children with sleep disorders.

Bedtime problems and waking difficulties

It may be difficult to distinguish between these two fields in very young children so they will be considered together. Richman, Stevenson and Graham (1982) found that 11 %–14 % of 2- and 3-year-old children were waking frequently at night and 8 % were continuing to do so when they were aged 4, while Butler and Golding (1986) found that no less than 46 % of children who had sleep problems as infants continued to have them at age 5. Douglas (1989) suggested that the more serious the sleeping problem in young children is, the more likely it is to persist.

There is thus great variability in the age at which infants and young children 'sleep through the night'. It seems that the first year of life is one in which immature infants have to make huge adjustments from living in the womb to living in the world, to sensations of hunger and satiety, to changing sequences of light and dark and that, as with all other areas, each infant with his or her own genetic endowment will adjust to its environment in different ways.

Disorders of sleep

Vela-Bueno et al. (1985) who examined 900 children aged from 6 to 12 years, found that 20 % reported nightmares. Skuse (1994) indicates that these, which are dreams occurring during the REM stage of sleep (see below), are best understood as a form of post-traumatic stress response, as the child or adult attempts by reprocessing the frightening events to assimilate them into consciousness. Night terrors are much less frequently reported, occurring in only 3 % of children (Klackenberg, 1987); they appear to take place during the non-REM sleep cycle and are not fully understood. For some children both nightmares and night terrors seem to be responses to very stressful experiences such as viewing horror films on television. Sleepwalking seems to occur very occasionally in about 30 % of children, but is common in only 2.5 % (Klackenberg, 1987); the peak age for this disorder is between 5 and 7 years and its frequency diminishes after 9 years. There appears to be some genetic underpinning to the difficulty as monozygotic twins are much more likely to be concordant for sleepwalking than dizygotic twins.

Costs of Sleeping Difficulties in Infants

Morris, St. James-Roberts, Sleep and Gillham (2001) undertook a study involving 610 mothers and their young infants, which estimated the financial cost to the National Health Service of the infants' crying and sleeping in the first 12 weeks of life. When all the detailed costs of services were calculated, Morris et al. concluded:

> the mean cost to the NHS of infant crying and sleeping problems in the first 12 weeks was £90.64 ... per baby. In 1997 there were 725,800 live births in the UK. Therefore the annual total cost to the NHS was £65,786,512 ...

These researchers point out that the costs of over-the-counter remedies are not included in the £65 million: only the costs to the NHS. Morris et al. went on to report that the behavioural intervention (see details below) incurred a small additional cost and produced a small but statistically significant additional benefit. The educational intervention, however, apparently had no significant effect in comparison with controls.

RESEARCH INTO THE ORIGINS OF BEDTIME AND WAKING PROBLEMS

Studies of Affected Children

Extensive research has taken place concerning possible associations between sleeping difficulties and specific variables. Richman (1985) concluded that first- or second-born children were more likely than later children to have sleeping difficulties, but Skuse (1994) suggests that an alternative interpretation is that later children experience less parental anxiety about whether they will sleep or not as their parents become more experienced. There is no greater tendency for one gender to be more prone to sleeping problems than the other (Thoman & Whitney, 1989).

Several studies, such as Quillin and Glenn (2004), have shown that breastfed babies tend to wake more frequently during the night than bottlefed infants but Skuse (1994) cautions that infants who wake at night are not necessarily hungry: it may fall to the health visitor to advise anxious parents as to whether nutrition is likely to be a factor for a given age of child.

Nikolopoulou and St James-Roberts (2003) undertook a groundbreaking study concerning infants at risk of developing sleeping problems. They enrolled a community sample of 316 parents and their newborn infants in an effort to identify the risk factors at 1 week of age, which increased the likelihood of the babies' failing to sleep through the night at 12 weeks of age. The most notable finding was that infants who had a high number of feeds (more than 11) in 24 hours at 1 week old were 2.7 times more likely than control group infants to fail to sleep through the night at 12 weeks of age. How these researchers instituted a plan to assist longer sleeping will be considered below (p. 166).

An association not commonly known is that between maternal depression and children's sleeping problems. Richman (1985), for example, showed that the mothers of toddlers with these difficulties were far more likely to be depressed, to be coping with family stress and to lack a confiding relationship than were those of toddlers in a control group. It is hard to distinguish which comes first, maternal depression or toddler behaviour difficulties. In my own work (Sutton, 1995), the level of maternal depression fell significantly when the sleep and behaviour problems of their young children improved, so it seems likely that maternal depression and sleeplessness in young children interact, forming a vicious circle that is hard to break.

Underpinning Physiological Processes

The human body experiences rhythmic changes that prepare it for cycles of activity, interspersed with cycles of quiescence, which prepare it for sleep and restorative rest. These physiological processes are powerful, so sleep does eventually take over but can still be disrupted or thrown out of phase with the cycles of the rest of the world. Nurses do adjust to night duty but often with discomfort and physiological distress; similarly, infants do eventually develop a sleeping pattern but it may not be the conventional, rhythmic one for which their caregivers long. There are, however, steps we can take to encourage the usual 'day for activity: night for sleep' routine.

The pineal gland, deep within the brain, responds to light and dark and the changes associated with this gland trigger the sleep process. Armstrong, Quinn and Dadds (1994), in a study of the sleep patterns of normal children in Australia, found that the circadian rhythm is typically established by about four months of age and it is therefore helpful if, right from birth, babies come to associate darkness with sleeping. Babies *can* sleep in bright and noisy rooms but it is often helpful if they learn the same patterns as the rest of the world as they grow older. It is also helpful if they can learn to sleep through the sounds of most households, doorbells or telephones ringing or television in a neighbouring room, rather than waking at the slightest sound. The young child's body responds to a calm and soothing environment by reducing physiological

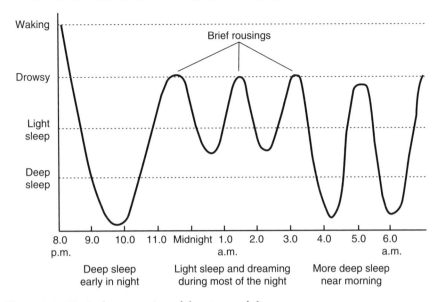

Figure 7.1 Typical progression of the stages of sleep

> *Source*: Adapted from Ferber (1986). *Solve Your Child's Sleep Problems*. London: Dorling Kindersley.

arousal and by lowering blood flow and muscle tone in preparation for sleep; so parents can take advantage of this naturally occurring cycle by ensuring that the hour or so before they wish the child to go to sleep is one of relative calm, without stimulating interactions and involving quiet activity only.

As is commonly known, patterns of sleep are of two main kinds, rapid eye movement (REM) sleep, accompanied by dreaming and increasingly known as *active sleep* (Ferber, 1986), and non-rapid eye movement (non-REM) sleep, known as *quiet* sleep. The function of REM sleep seems to be linked with the processing of emotional material, while that of non-REM sleep seems to be largely restorative. These two types of sleep follow each other cyclically through the night, as shown in Figure 7.1 (Ferber, 1986).

Bedtime Problems

These are addressed first because they happen earlier in the night than typical waking problems but the two are, of course, intimately linked. Some problems may have arisen because a child has been ill and has needed much attention at bedtime or in the night, but often bedtime difficulties arise from not establishing a routine at the time of evening when the family wishes the child to sleep. Often parents appear not to take advantage of the child's readiness to fall into quieter activities as night approaches and the physiological level of arousal begins to fall. In some families early evening is accompanied by the return of a parent from work and understandably he or she wishes to spend enjoyable and sometimes very stimulating time with the child. Thus, at the time when the children would, given a little encouragement, cooperate in preparing for sleep, demands are being made upon them to wake up and play lively games. I recall one father who used to tuck his two-year-old son under his arm and rush around with him as though he were a rugby football, to the delight of the little one but to the despair of his mother, who then had to try to get a wildly excited child ready for sleep.

In other families a child has been put to bed at a reasonable time for his or her age but has objected loudly; new parents, lacking strong role models and the confidence that comes from experience, allow the toddler to rejoin their more stimulating interactions and to eat their snacks. In no time at all, the toddler stays up until the parents go to bed, while they feel power-less to do anything about it. I recall one family with a delightful little daughter, aged two-and-a-half, who charmed her loving mother and her gi-ant of a father for several hours first one evening and then every evening – only for them to find themselves quite unable ever to insist that she stay in bed and allow them some time alone. She regularly stayed up until mid-night, sitting on her Daddy's lap, demanding and receiving stories, television and snacks until *they* fell asleep, exhausted. The little one was still ready for more!

Other children repeatedly come downstairs, pathetically claiming that they are afraid or cannot sleep but with broad smiles upon their faces. In my experience, they are often allowed to sit in a corrner of the sofa and told that they can stay as long as they are quiet. It then becomes increasingly difficult for families to invite friends in for the evening or to go out themselves; visiting adults are likely to be less tolerant of a toddler at 9.30 p.m. if their own children have already been asleep for two hours.

I am aware, of course, that children's bedtime and sleeping routines are culturally influenced and that each family will have its own expectations about both. I am not trying to be prescriptive; rather, I am drawing upon research findings to support those families who ask for help with what *they* *perceive* to be a bedtime or sleeping difficulty in their child. They set the goals, not me.

Waking Problems

Newborn infants

Morris et al. (2001) worked with 610 mothers and their babies to explore the impact of three different means of facilitating sleep in the infants when they were 8–14 days of age:

- 205 were randomly assigned to a behavioural programme
- 202 were assigned to 'an educational booklet and telephone helpline' group
- 203 were assigned to a 'routine services' group.

It was found that at the age of 12 weeks, 82% of the babies in the behavioural programme group slept through the night, compared with 61% in the combined educational booklet/helpline and 'routine services' control group. The components of the behavioural programme will be clarified below (see p. 166).

Toddlers and young children

We see from Figure 7.1 and Table 7.1 that it is natural for children to experience both *active* and *quiet* sleep, to rouse frequently and briefly and to go back to sleep again. As Ferber (1986) puts it:

> What most parents don't realize is that what they view as abnormal wakings in the night are actually quite normal. And what they do to try to treat the 'abnormal' wakings – namely going in to help their child go back to sleep – is actually *causing* the disturbance (p. 55).

What seems to happen is that when children rouse briefly, as they pass through the cycles of the sleeping sequence, they momentarily check their environment for familiarity and security. If they have become accustomed to a specific set of 'sleep cues' or 'sleep accessories', a blanket, a Teddy, a bottle and even a Mummy, all to hand for security, when they rouse they check that these accessories are all more or less in place. If they are, they readily self-soothe and fall back to sleep: but if they are not – and the more accessories the more long drawn-out the checking may have to be – instead of falling back to sleep they become more wakeful and distressed. Sometimes this sequence can occur five or six times a night as the sleep patterns cycle through. Thus, the waking is not abnormal: what is problematic is the difficulty the child is having in going back to sleep.

Table 7.1 Summary of the stages of sleep in children

Part of night	Approximate times	Type of sleep	Pattern of sleep
Early	8.00–11.00 p.m.	Deep non-REM	Several brief wakings
Middle	11.00–5.00 a.m	REM	Several brief wakings
Late	5.00–6.00 a.m	Deep non-REM	Brief wakings

RESEARCH INTO THE MANAGEMENT OF BEDTIME AND SLEEP PROBLEMS

Many studies show how a range of professionals can help families with sleeping difficulties. What used to be regarded as a specialist field of skill, the province of paediatricians and psychologists now rightly features in the repertoire of skills of many health visitors, social workers, school nurses and community psychiatric nurses. As this is work requiring high levels of skill and responsibility, however, I reiterate the need for experienced supervision for practitioners.

Helping Families to Assist New Babies to Sleep Through the Night

In the study by Nikolopoulou et al. (2003) mentioned above, (p. 162), reference was made to a 'behavioural programme' to assist with enabling longer periods of sleep in the babies. This asked parents to take several main steps:

1. To introduce a regular 'focal feed' between 10 p.m. and midnight.
2. To settle baby into the cot to sleep and not to rock, hold or feed him just before sleeping.
3. To maximise day/light differences in the environment, i.e. arrange for the baby to associate darkness with sleep by placing him to sleep in a darkened room.
4. To 'stretch' the intervals between night-time feeds once infants were growing satisfactorily beyond three weeks of age. This was to avoid linking night waking with being fed.

The authors report that this approach led to the babies concerned being able to sleep through from midnight to 5.00 a.m. on at least two of three nights by eight weeks of age. They also report, however, that many parents found achieving this pattern of sleeping by their babies stressful in itself!

Helping Toddlers Get Off to a Good Start: the Usefulness of Routines

There is increasing evidence of the usefulness of helping babies and young children develop flexible routines (Ferber, 1986; Kerr, Jowett & Smith, 1997). As the young infant grows, cycles of waking, feeding and sleeping become established and Ferber has shown how these mesh with and become part of

> **Box 7.1:** One possible bedtime routine (Sutton, 1996)
>
> 1. Quiet activities for an hour before bed – or as quiet as possible!
> 2. Child is told 10 minutes before bedtime 'bedtime's in 10 minutes/very soon, so start to put your toys away'.
> 3. Help a young child to put toys away.
> 4. Carry or lead a young child to the bathroom.
> 5. Child uses toilet.
> 6. Bath or wash and brush teeth.
> 7. Into bed (we suggest the child should not come downstairs again).
> 8. Short, calm story or look at picture book together (5 minutes).
> 9. Tuck child up, give a kiss and say something like 'sleep well; see you in the morning'.

the child's developing circadian rhythms. Reasonable regularity is thus beneficial; indeed, Ferber claims that in households where there is little structure children do not receive these regular cues and it may therefore be more difficult for them to develop patterns of sound sleep. A routine can be valuable in preparing the child for sleep. Box 7.1 shows one possible routine, which I have published elsewhere (Sutton, 1996).

Using Principles of Cognitive-behavioural Theory

This body of theory has been found to be central in dealing with children's sleeping difficulties. It is being taught to health visitors and other practitioners all over the country and they in turn are now running successful sleep clinics (Roberts, 1993).However, despite the availability of excellent books such as *Solving Children's Sleep Problems*, by Lyn Quine (1996) and *The Good Sleep Guide* by Angela Henderson (2000) these difficulties continue to pose difficulties for many families. We shall consider below two of the main approaches in managing toddlers' bedtime and waking problems.

Graded desensitisation: the gradual approach

Desensitisation, which we encountered in Chapter 6, is a procedure whereby a child or adult is helped to overcome a fear or anxiety by being exposed very gradually to small increments of the feared situation. At each step, the practitioner ascertains that the person is entirely relaxed and comfortable before slowly introducing the next. This is the procedure that helps many children who have acquired a fear of being alone at bedtime. The steps of

Box 7.2: The steps of a desensitising process for an anxious child: the 'gradual' approach

1. The child should be naturally tired at bedtime.
2. The parent should explain to the child that there has been a lot of upset for everyone at bedtime, so in future Mummy/Daddy/Grandma/Carer will be doing things a bit differently. The aim will be that eventually the child can go to sleep happily by himself.
3. The child is put to bed in a calm, matter-of-fact way. If the parent is upset, the child will pick this up and behave anxiously in response.
4. If the parent has previously had to lie on the bed she should say she won't do this but she will sit by the bed. She should insist that the child stays in bed making it a condition of having a story. She should stay until the child falls asleep if absolutely necessary.
5. After three or four nights, she should move a few feet nearer the door, but again she must be prepared to wait until the child falls asleep. Over the next week or so, again, she should move the chair a little nearer to the door, leaving toys or books for the child if he is not sleepy but insisting on looking at her own book rather than watching him. She shouldn't speak to him or even glance at him but instead concentrate on her own book.
6. Over time, her chair should be moved towards and in due course out of the door. She should keep completely calm but be ready to return the child to his bed if he comes searching for her. Parents should not be afraid to be very firm, but calm, in requiring the child to stay in bed.
7. If this approach is used, it must not be rushed. School holidays, or at least a weekend, is a good time to make a start.
8. If another caregiver can be encouraged to take part in the bedtime or waking routine, this enables the child to become less dependent upon the mother.

the 'gradual approach', which have been found to be very helpful to fearful children in many situations, are shown in Box 7.2.

Avoiding rewarding waking: the direct approach

The above procedure is obviously time-consuming and some parents, after trying it, say they can't be doing with such a long drawn-out approach! They want a speedy solution and, for them, assuming the practitioner has undertaken a careful assessment and has screened out other possible explanations for the difficulty, a direct approach may be more fitting. This may be so particularly if it appears that the child is 'trying it on'. It must be the parents' choice. The steps of the 'direct' approach are shown in Box 7.3.

Box 7.3: The steps of managing bedtime or waking: the 'direct' approach

This approach should not be used with children below the age of 12–15 months. Other authors or researchers may suggest an earlier age but I cannot myself recommend this.

1. The child should be naturally tired at bedtime.
2. The parent should explain calmly but firmly to the child that there has been a lot of upset for everyone at bedtime so in future Mummy will be managing things differently. She will check that the child is all right but she will not bring him downstairs again however much he calls out. He can have story books if he wants them. Soon he will be able to go to sleep happily by himself.
3. As in the other example, the child is put to bed in a calm, matter-of-fact way. If the parent is upset, the child will pick this up and exploit her distress.
4. The parent says 'goodnight' and then leaves the room, leaving the door open or closed as usual.
5. If the child does scream, the parent waits one minute and then does as she said she would. She stands at the door, out of sight, and says in a very firm voice, 'It's sleep time, Johnny. I'm here, but I have my work to do. Goodnight'. Then she leaves but may potter round upstairs tidying up so that the child can hear that she is still around.
6. If the child goes on screaming, she waits three minutes then goes in and says the same. If the child goes on screaming, she waits five minutes, then goes in and says the same. If the child goes on screaming she waits seven minutes, then goes in and says the same and so on. She increases the interval by two minutes each time and sounds very firm but calm each time she has to go in.
7. If the child gets out of bed, she makes sure he cannot leave the room; she fixes the door, perhaps with a stair-gate but *never* locks the door. If the child goes to sleep on the floor, she lets him; he can be lifted into bed later on.
8. If the child wants the door left open, she makes this a condition of staying in bed. He can choose: either he stays in bed and the door can be open or he keeps getting out of bed and the door must be closed.
9. If the child makes himself sick, he will have to be cleaned up but this should be done without comment and he should be put straight back to bed. The same routine can also be used in the middle of the night. *There should be no speech and no eye contact.* The parent should remain as calm as is humanly possible!
10. The point of dealing with the child in this way is that it reassures him but does not reward him with attention for the waking behaviour.
11. It is essential to keep records when dealing with a bedtime or waking problem. They will show if things are getting better or worse (see Appendix 10).

HELPING FAMILIES WHOSE CHILDREN HAVE BEDTIME/WAKING PROBLEMS

Parents whose children settle or sleep poorly are often very stressed as the shortage of sleep affects the functioning not only of the child but of the whole family throughout the day. The steps of the ASPIRE process (see Chapter 4) lend themselves to assessing and reducing this stress. The first contact is crucial; it is an opportunity to allow people to release pent-up tension and frustration, to show empathy and understanding to them and, by means of patient and careful listening, to gather crucial information that will assist in relieving or resolving the sleeping difficulty. The mnemonic REST is useful here. It is particularly relevant to the needs of the parent who has a child who is not sleeping. The letters stand for Reassurance, Empathy, Support and Time out (Keefe et al., 1997). This is Step 1 of the process.

Assessment

Step 2 – Gather Information

Holistic assessment of the child's sleeping difficulty within the overall family is essential. Completing the assessment framework (see Figure 4.2, p. 87) with the service user will provide crucial information, while using Appendix 1 may elicit further relevant detail. This will include information concerning the child, his or her development, health, education and other predisposing variables such as hospital admissions, separations or other distressing events that may be, or may have come to be, associated with bedtime; it will include relevant developmental or organic factors such as a tendency to asthma on the part of the child. It will also include details concerning family and environmental factors, such as bereavements which affected the child as well as information on the parenting capacity of those caring for the child.

The example of Sebastian, aged four

Let us consider Sebastian, a 'precious child' in that he was longed for for many years before he was conceived. He is an only child of older parents and one who has learned, because of inexperience on the part of his parents, that if he keeps demanding long enough and often enough they give way. His mother, Felicity, is deeply unhappy; she gave up her work as a financial consultant in her delight at conceiving and told her friends of her intention to become 'a perfect mother with a perfect child'. Her husband, Hamish, is as disappointed as his wife and the two parents alternate between issuing harsh threats, never carried through, and indulging the child's whims. If Sebastian does not get his way he resorts to screaming, tantrums and hitting and kicking his mother.

In line with the dimensions of the assessment framework, we can identify whether there are factors relating to Sebastian's developmental needs, to family and environmental factors and to the parenting capacity of Felicity and Hamish. Key features of these three sets of factors are set out in Box 7.4 as part of the rationale for or formulation of the difficulties that these parents are experiencing with their little boy. It is crucial that this discussion should be seen as provisional and tentative because fresh information relevant to the assessment may come to light at any time.

Step 3 – Identify Problem Behaviours

Unless it is already apparent that many of the child's difficulties are exclusively attributable to an organic difficulty or to an event in the child's life,

---

Box 7.4: Preliminary assessment of/rationale for Sebastian's difficulties

1. *Child's developmental needs e.g. organic factors, disability*
   Sebastian has always been a very lively little boy, apparently needing less sleep than many children of his age.
2. *Family and environmental factors*
   (a) Sebastian is a 'precious child'; his parents waited many years before he was conceived.
   (b) His mother gave up a satisfying professional life to give him full-time care. She now regrets this deeply.
   (c) His parents had had little to do with babies or children before Sebastian was born; when the extent of the baby's impact on their lives was apparent, they lost confidence.
   (d) Sebastian's mother is understandably depressed: she feels totally powerless over bedtimes.
3. *Parenting capacity interactions within the family, including A–B–C**
   (a) Sebastian's parents love him dearly and give him excellent physical care. However they have great difficulty in setting firm boundaries, especially at bedtime.
   (b) Unwittingly, by sometimes insisting that Sebastian stay in bed and then sometimes allowing him to come downstairs, they have been rewarding the very behaviour they want to stop – while at the same time complaining about this behaviour.
*Parents may not understand this concept, but it is useful to introduce it at this stage.

such as abuse, it is appropriate to ask the parents to identify their difficulty in terms of exactly what the child *does* that constitutes the bedtime or sleeping problem. So, in the case of Sebastian:

1. Sebastian keeps coming downstairs after he has been put to bed; he does not eventually settle in bed until his parents go to bed at 11.00 p.m.
2. Once downstairs he gets out all his toys and spreads them all over the floor.
3. If reprimanded he calls his mother horrible names and kicks her.

Here it will be apparent that Sebastian is being rewarded, unintentionally but systematically, by the consequences of his behaviour. This makes it highly likely that the behaviour will happen again – and again and again.

Step 4 – Identify Positive Behaviours

When requested to identify the positive features of their child's behaviour, both parents are delighted to identify distinctive and pleasing characteristics. For Sebastian:

1. Once asleep he stays asleep; he sleeps soundly until roused next morning.
2. When asked to help lay the table or wash up, he complies readily.
3. He helps his Daddy in the garden, sweeping leaves and digging weeds.

Step 5 – Clarify Realistic Goals

So far we have identified the main 'problems' and 'positives' in Sebastian's behaviour. Now, briefly, we need to establish what the parents really want. We need to help them cast their minds forward to identify the key areas of their child's behaviour where they long for improvement. Here we have to help them strike a balance between requiring perfection ('he must go to bed and fall asleep right away') and not setting standards in accordance with what is known from social learning theory. ('Well, he could stay downstairs with us once a week ... ' This arrangement would be giving Sebastian 'intermittent reinforcement/reward' for his coming downstairs, the very contingency most likely to keep him behaving in this way.) Here our judgement will help us to negotiate three specific goals that our experience tells us are likely to be attainable – and to rank these in order of their attainability. For we, too, need success; we need the encouragement that comes from people saying 'we've had the best night's sleep in years!' So we should use the same theoretical ideas to structure success for families and for ourselves. For Sebastian, the three goals might be:

1. That Sebastian will stay in his room once put to bed.
2. That he will speak calmly and quietly to his mother.
3. That when told 'no' he cannot have something he will accept this calmly and quietly.

Step 6 – Problem Formulation Shared with Parents

When the practitioner has gathered as much relevant information as possible, then, drawing upon material offered by the parent(s) and, as appropriate, by the child himself or herself, it should be possible to *explore with the family* some preliminary rationale for/formulation of the child's difficulties. If the child is old enough to contribute to this formulation then, of course, this information must be incorporated. The overall formulation might be as shown in Box 7.4. Exact information concerning the timing and extent of the difficulty is necessary. Appendix 10 can be photocopied to permit accurate data concerning either bedtime or sleeping problems to be gathered (see Table 7.2). Often the information that becomes available is of no less interest to the parent(s) than to the practitioner. Sometimes the child comes downstairs or wakes less often than is thought; sometimes other patterns, such as the way the children respond differently to their mothers and to their fathers, become apparent – thus opening the way to a discussion of how parents are responding differently to the child.

Step 7 Gather Baseline Data as an Aid to Assessment

Accurate information is needed now concerning the extent of Sebastian's negative behaviour – his 'coming downstairs' after bedtime – and one of his positive behaviours, say, his 'helping in the house', such as laying the table. This information could be collected on the chart shown as Appendix 7.

Let us assume that the records for the first (baseline) week show that Sebastian came downstairs 25 times (see Table 7.2) and was helpful only 3 times.

Step 8 – Planning with the Parents

The practitioner and parent are partners in a shared endeavour to help the whole family. It is vital that we convey both support for the individuals

Table 7.2: Baseline information for the number of times Sebastian comes downstairs during 1 week (see Appendix 10)

SLEEP CHART   Name: Sebastian (4)   Date: 14 March

Shade in the times of sleep, and mark with small crosses any periods of prolonged crying. Mark instances of coming downstairs with a D.

	7 a.m.	8	9	10	11	noon	1 p.m.	2	3	4	5	6	7	8	9	10	11	12	1 a.m.	2	3	4	5	6	Total for day
Sunday													D	DDD	DD	D	D	▓	▓	▓	▓	▓	▓	▓	8
Monday														DD	D	DD		▓	▓	▓	▓	▓	▓	▓	5
Tuesday														D	D			▓	▓	▓	▓	▓	▓	▓	2
Wednesday														D	D	D	D	▓	▓	▓	▓	▓	▓	▓	4
Thursday														D	D	D	D	▓	▓	▓	▓	▓	▓	▓	3
Friday														D	D			▓	▓	▓	▓	▓	▓	▓	2
Saturday														D				▓	▓	▓	▓	▓	▓	▓	1

Example:

	7 a.m.	8	9	10	11	noon	1 p.m.	2	3	4	5	6	7	8	9	10	11	12	1 a.m.	2	3	4	5	6	Total for week
Sunday		▓				▓							▓	▓	▓	xxxxx									
Monday	▓					▓							▓	▓	▓	▓									

Box 7.5: Plan developed by:

Felicity Anderson, 12 Copse Road, Blastow, Kent
Hamish Anderson, 12 Copse Road, Blastow, Kent
Rosemary Brown, Health Centre, Canterbury
Our overall aim is to improve Sebastian's sleeping patterns

1. Mrs Anderson will explore with her former employer the possibility of doing some part-time work.
2. Rosemary Brown will telephone three times weekly to offer support.
3. Sebastian's mummy and daddy will explain to him that, come what may, he will not be allowed to come downstairs once he has been put to bed. Each time he comes down, he will be taken *straight* back to bed.
4. Each evening Sebastian stays in bed quietly he will win an animal sticker to put on a chart. His daddy will help him make the chart. Any week when he achieves five or more stickers out of seven, his daddy will take him swimming on Saturday morning.
5. If he does come downstairs there will be no snacks and no toys will be allowed. Mummy and Daddy will not talk to him or even look at him. He will be taken straight back to bed.
6. Normally Daddy will be at home at bedtime on Friday, Saturday and Sunday evenings so that both Mummy and Daddy can follow the plan in the same way.
7. Mummy and Daddy are very pleased with Sebastian's helpfulness, his laying the table and working with Dad in the garden. He will have a chart to record these good behaviours and Mummy will tell Gran how well Sebastian has behaved when she comes each Sunday.

---

concerned as well as confidence that we have a strategy for helping them. Again REST is a valuable mnemonic to bear in mind – see p. 170. At this stage the practitioner discusses with the parent(s) how they may test out the ideas above. The plan written above may be developed concerning Sebastian:

Step 9 – Implementation of the Plan

At all stages the safety of the child is paramount so the practitioner should familiarise herself with the layout of the house and sleeping area and check the environment for safety. Then, on the agreed day, the plan is put into action.

Ordinarily, practitioners would expect to make no more than once weekly visits or contacts but in serious situations where parents are desperate for support a brief visit or telephone call after two nights or even after one night

SHOWING THE INCREASE OR DECREASE WEEK BY WEEK

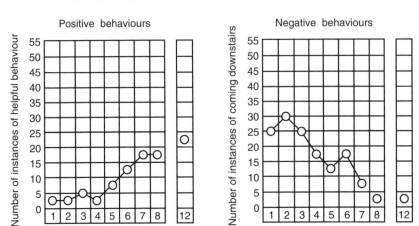

Figure 7.2 Sebastian's positive and negative behaviours over eight weeks and at three months' followup

is usually very welcome. One would not expect any change at this stage: on the contrary, things are likely to be worse at this point as the child realises that limits are being set to his behaviour. The role of the practitioner is to 'troubleshoot' – to be sufficiently familiar with and confident in the use of the theoretical framework to encourage parents not to give up once their child becomes more difficult. Deteriorating behaviour at this stage is a very good sign! It is evidence that the child has noticed the change in routine and, in line with theory, is increasing his misbehaviour. If the parents can stand firm at this point, this is likely to be a prelude to his adapting to the new arrangements. We must recognise the demands this places on parents, however, and give *much encouragement* for their efforts to follow the plan.

Over the next six weeks at least, the parents are asked to keep careful records of Sebastian's patterns of bedtime behaviour. This will not be easy for them but information arises from this about whether things are getting better or worse, when difficulties happen and the relationship between events in the child's life and their impact upon behaviour. Typically, things are likely to be much improved after a month but sometimes it takes longer for the child to respond to the new methods of management. Figure 7.2 shows a very typical course of events as the child receives fewer and fewer rewards for coming downstairs and more and more attention and praise for his prosocial behaviour.

As there is improvement towards one goal, so a further pair of behaviours, one negative and one positive, can be identified and targets set. The newly learned strategies for managing the first pair need to be consolidated but the links between aspects of improvement in the child's behaviour and the new ways in which the parents are handling him/her are probably by now becoming apparent. Unless there is absolutely no change in the child's behaviour parents should be asked to persist in their efforts. If there is absolutely no such evidence then different explanations may need to be considered and tested in a similar way.

Step 10 – Review and Evaluation

Through all the weeks of attempting to put the theoretical principles into practice it is essential to learn from the parents' experience. For example, I have recently been in touch with the family of a five-year-old boy who repeatedly hit and punched his mother when she tried to send him back upstairs when he came down after being put to bed. She tells me that she learned that she had to sit on the stairs outside his bedroom and the instant that the child showed his nose outside, she stood, gave him a hard stare, and ordered him back to bed. It gave her great satisfaction to give her child an 'order' and see it obeyed after realising that for many months she had been carrying out *his* orders! She found the approach extremely effective and it was necessary to sit at the top of the stairs for only a few evenings before her son learned that Mum was now in charge!

Another Example: Rajita, Aged 15 Months

Assessment

The use of the assessment framework does not reveal anything untoward about the situation. During Steps 1–2 the practitioner builds supportive relationships with Rajita's parents and gathers relevant information. Rajita is the daughter of Poonam (her mother) and Vickram (her father). She is a delightful little girl but her parents are desperate because of shortage of sleep. Rajita had always been put to bed by Poonam, but as Poonam has had to take an evening job, Vickram now has to put Rajita to bed.

Step 3 – Identify problem behaviours

1. Rajita wakes up five or six times during each night.
2. She insists that her mother lie beside her to get her to go to sleep.
3. Each time she screams until she is given a bottle of milk.

Here it seems probable that Rajita, who is having to adjust to a new routine, has learned to expect both being settled to sleep during the night by her mother and having a bottle feed as well. Thus, she is being reinforced for waking up by two very gratifying rewards. It is most unlikely that she will change this routine of her own accord!

Step 4 – Identifying positive profile

1. She goes to bed readily: there is never any problem at that time.
2. She is a very loving little girl: she comes to kiss her mummy and daddy.
3. She 'helps' her mummy prepare meals in the kitchen.

Step 5 – Identifying desired outcomes

The parents know that there will be broken nights. They understand that Rajita is still a tiny child who is taking time to move to a consistent pattern of sleeping. They hope, however, that within two months they will experience only two broken nights each week.

Step 6 – Formulation of Rajita's poor sleeping patterns

The overall formulation might be as shown in Box 7.6.

Box 7.6: Preliminary assessment of/rationale for Rajita's difficulties

1. *Child's developmental needs*
   (a) Rajita is eating well during the day; night feeds are not necessary.
   (b) She is warmly dressed; she does not seem to be waking because of heat or cold.
2. *Family and environmental factors*
   (a) Rajita, aged 15 months, is not used to sleeping alone.
   (b) Poonam has had to take up evening employment; Vickram now puts the toddler to bed.
3. *Parenting capacity: interactions within the family (A–B–C)*[*]
   (a) Both parents are devoted to Rajita. They will do anything to, as they think, show her that they really love her. They believe she wakes because she is insecure.
   (b) Rajita wakes repeatedly during the night from 10.00 p.m. Each time her mother goes and gives her a bottle. Each one takes about 15 minutes.
   (c) The number of wakings is increasing – from about three to about five nightly.
   (d) Unintentionally, Poonam may be 'teaching' Rajita to wake, by giving her a bottle and cuddling her each time she does so.

[*]Parents may not understand this concept, but it is useful to introduce it at this stage.

> **Box 7.7**: A plan for Rajita and her family
>
> 1. Rajita is too young to be involved in the plan but her parents agree to work together.
> 2. The existing routine should be maintained, but in future Rajita's mother will make a point of spending at least 20 minutes playing with the little girl each afternoon.
> 3. At night, she will put first water and milk and then water only in the bottle, when initially she continues to go to her.
> 4. She will choose which of the two strategies described above (p. 168 and 169), the gradual or the direct approach, is more acceptable to her.
> 5. Both parents will continue to keep records and to encourage each other to be consistent.
> 6. The worker will telephone three times a week to offer support.

Step 7 – Gather data

Data are collected just as for Sebastian but as this is a tiny child, with the approval of the general practitioner, records must be kept to see how frequently Rajita is waking for unnecessary attention during the night.

Steps 8 and 9 – Planning and implementing the plan

When the baseline information is available, the plan in Box 7.7 is likely to help Rajita's parents in discussion with the family health visitor:

It is very likely that, given a consistent response night by night to Rajita's waking, she will gradually relinquish her pattern of waking and sleep for longer and longer periods. If Poonam has to go to her, she will avoid talking to her or looking at her. With the worker's support the family's goal of only two nights' broken sleep each week is likely to be achieved by the end of two months.

Step 10 – Review and Evaluation

It will be essential to offer 'booster' contacts to both these sets of parents after the main intervention has finished. This is to reinforce the very newly learned child-management practices, which, as we should expect from our understanding of cognitive-behavioural principles, may all too swiftly extinguish or fade away. Both Sebastian's and Rajita's parents need repeated reinforcement and encouragement for their efforts to change their ways of managing their child. *We should use the theory to maintain the effectiveness of every intervention.*

8

HELPING FAMILIES WITH CHILDREN WITH EATING PROBLEMS

It is difficult to understand that such intense and primary needs as those for food and drink can become so subverted that young children not only take insufficient nourishment to meet their growth needs but actively turn away from food so frequently that they lose weight. This often causes acute anxiety to parents, who may believe that their child will starve to death and, in their distress, may get into frequent confrontations with the child – who becomes ever more reluctant to eat. How common are these difficulties and how can we help families who experience them?

PROBLEMS OF DEFINITION

It is not easy to establish a clear definition of what constitutes an eating problem because of differing terminology and different criteria used by different researchers. For example, the expression 'failure to thrive' carries unhelpful connotations and the alternative expression 'faltering growth' is gaining currency. As to criteria, in some research studies it has been sufficient for the mother to report that there is a problem for her view to be accepted into a research study; for others, the problem must have been of a particular duration, and for yet others (Dahl & Kristiansson, 1987) certain strict criteria must be met such as:

1. The mother and health visiting nurse must agree that a problem is present.
2. It must have persisted without interruption for at least one month.
3. Simple advice on management provided by the nurse must have been insufficient to resolve the problem.

As infants develop, a clearer means of delineating a feeding difficulty becomes available: the measured loss of weight according to centile charts. Children typically gain weight according to 'centiles', which represent norms; for a child to 'fall off' his or her typical centile gives grounds for concern, while falling through two or more centile spaces over time gives major grounds for concern.

PREVALENCE OF EATING/FEEDING PROBLEMS

Birth to 12 Months

With such variability, it is not surprising that there is little agreement over the prevalence of feeding difficulties. The Swedish study, referred to above, by Dahl & Kristiansson (1987), who screened babies between 4 and 7 months, found that only 1.4 % of the infants met their tight criteria for an established feeding difficulty. Another Swedish study by Lindberg, Bohlin and Hagekull (1991), however, of infants between 6 and 12 months, found that about 25 % had feeding problems, while an American study by Forsyth (1989) of babies between birth and 4 months reported that about 33 % of mothers indicated that they had a moderate or severe feeding problem. Criteria for what constituted a 'problem' clearly differed greatly, nevertheless it is of great interest that the mothers' conclusion that they had a problem was so very much stronger than the views of the independent researchers who set stringent but impersonal criteria. In view of the movement to empower parents and to view situations empathically rather than clinically, services are required to meet the perceived needs of the *parents*, rather than those of researchers.

Pre-school Children

There are more studies of the prevalence of eating problems in pre-school children, and the major report by Minde and Minde (1986) concluded that 12 %–34 % of children were affected. Other studies suggest an even higher figure. Workers in the Child Support Project in Swindon, United Kingdom, found that parents reported that many difficulties began at the time of moving to mixed feeding or weaning but that some stemmed from the period of about 15 months, when babies are typically beginning to develop a sense of independence. Skuse (1994) suggests that, while for a proportion of these children there may be a genuine persistence of difficulties from the earlier months of life, for many the difficulty has arisen through a conditioning process (see Chapter 2 and below).

RESEARCH INTO THE ORIGINS OF
FEEDING/EATING PROBLEMS

There are several major fields of research in this area: we have space only to consider three:

1. Circumstances which seem to be linked with feeding or eating difficulties.
2. Some features of so-called 'failure to thrive'.
3. The relevance of principles of cognitive-behavioural theory in helping families.

Circumstances Linked with Feeding Problems

Several sets of circumstances may combine so that feeding gets off to a poor start. The first is the rare circumstance of inadequate milk on the part of mothers who are breastfeeding their babies, which may contribute to the infants' restlessness and fretfulness. This circumstance is more likely to be imaginary than real and more temporary than permanent but many mothers, hearing their babies crying, assume that they are hungry and, swiftly losing confidence in their ability to breastfeed, cease trying to do so. With encouragement and information from supportive and experienced midwives, health visitors or other professionals, however, many mothers can produce a sufficient supply of milk for their babies.

The second set of circumstances that may pose difficulties is the introduction of weaning – the supplementation of breast milk by solid foods. Skuse (1994) makes a strong case for abandoning the term 'weaning' and using instead the expression 'mixed feeding' – a practice I shall adopt in this book. He reports that 'the present-day recommendation in the UK is that solid food shall be introduced into an infant's diet between the ages of about four and six months' (Department of Health and Social Security, 1988).

This seems to accord with the possibility that there may be a 'sensitive period' when solid foods are more readily acceptable than at other times. Skuse (1994) comments:

> If children are not exposed to solids that require chewing by about 6–7 months of age, they tend to be resistant to accepting these textures in later childhood (Illingworth & Lister, 1964). Feeding problems can then result, with refusal to accept lumpy foods and even vomiting.

A third contributory factor, according to Skuse, is colic, which is associated with the baby experiencing acute abdominal discomfort, often in the evening.

This leads to crying, which persists despite every effort on the part of the caregivers to offer comfort. This seems to affect between 10 % and 30 % of infants and to persist for about 3 months. Spasms of pain may interrupt feeding and produce tension in all concerned. As Skuse says, the persistence of difficulties of this kind can seriously undermine parents' confidence, particularly if they are new. Other problems may arise either through reflux vomiting or through lack of coordination between the many systems necessary for sucking and swallowing – such as may occur, for instance, in children born with cerebral palsy.

A fourth contributory cause may be the way that parents respond to the first signs of reluctance to eat on the part of the child. Parents are usually anxious that their child will eat, not only in order to gain weight appropriately but because eating well is a socially approved behaviour in young children, so they often overencourage eating, regardless of the size of the child's appetite or of what has been eaten since the last meal. Mealtime all too readily becomes an aversive, rather than an enjoyable, experience for the child and a vicious spiral may be established in which the parents become ever more anxious and the child ever more determined to eat only minimal amounts.

Many readers will be familiar with scenarios in which children are required to eat certain types of food or certain amounts of food at mealtimes – sometimes, in the worst situation, with the same food brought to them again and again. It is extraordinarily difficult to make a child eat who has set his will against doing so – but the anxiety levels of the parents in such circumstances are intense; it is no simple matter to reduce them. The child ultimately always has the upper hand.

Overlap with the Field of Failure to Thrive/Faltering Growth

The research field of eating problems overlaps substantially with that of failure to thrive. I emphasise immediately that this book focuses upon general eating difficulties, and practitioners seeking information and guidance on failure to thrive are referred to the excellent practice guide, *Children who Fail to Thrive*, by Iwaniec (2004).

Several researchers, for example Iwaniec, Herbert and McNeish (1985a), highlight studies which attempted to distinguish particular antecedents in the history of children who fail to thrive by comparison with children with non-problematic histories. They quote, for example, Pollitt, Eichler and Chan (1975), who studied the economic, social, family, nutritional and medical circumstances of 38 families in which a child was failing to thrive by comparison with controls. The researchers anticipated that the target group would show higher levels of mental ill health and more stressful marital histories but in fact this was not found to be the case. Iwaniec, Herbert and McNeish (1985a) report:

> The largest between-group statistical differences were found in the scores drawn from the mother–child interaction check-list. The mothers in the experimental group showed less frequent verbal and physical contacts, were less positively reinforcing and warm. These differences in verbal interactions were noted on various socialization tasks. Substantial differences were also noted in maternal affection, described as 'inoperant' in many of the index mothers.

Researchers such as Lachenmeyer and Davidovicz (1987) also pinpointed feeding difficulties as key variables leading to the onset of failure to thrive and factor analytic studies, such as that of Bithoney and Newberger (1987), confirmed that disturbed feeding situations were deeply implicated in the aetiology of the disorder. Another factor that has been highlighted as possibly contributing to a disturbed feeding situation is the increasing preoccupation many women have with body shape and slimming. For example, a Scandinavian study by Brinch, Isager and Tolstrup (1988) found that 17% of the children of women with a history of anorexia nervosa failed to thrive in the first year of life and a controlled study using actual observation of the 1-year-old children of mothers with eating disorders found that the index mothers interrupted their children more at mealtimes and were more critical of them than the mothers in the control group (Stein, Woolley & McPherson, 1999).

Treatment models have not, until fairly recently, been well developed. Iwaniec, Herbert and McNeish published two seminal papers in 1985. The first examined numerous features, demographic, social and individual, of a group of parents whose children failed to thrive and distinguished several sets of specific circumstances that characterised them:

- Most of the mothers demonstrated ambivalent feelings and behaviour to their children.
- Some of the mothers felt indifference and hostility towards their children (but Iwaniec and colleagues note that almost two-thirds felt that their children had first rejected them in that they had refused 'that very basic symbol of mother care – food').
- The child's poor physical appearance and apathetic behaviour brought much criticism from health visitors and neighbours – which in turn led to tension and further anxiety in the feeding situation.
- A history of feeding problems (inability or reluctance to suck) while the infants were on liquids.
- The majority of mothers dated the onset of really *acute* feeding difficulties from the time when solids were introduced.

Iwaniec et al. (1985a) identified a theoretical formulation that seems central to both understanding the development of the feeding problems and suggesting how to relieve them. They reported:

> All parents in the non-organic index group reported specific feeding difficulties with their children ... the majority dated the onset of really acute feeding difficulties from the time when solids were introduced ... *the possibility that the child has learned to fear broad aspects of the feeding process is overlooked* [present author's italics].

The second seminal paper published by Iwaniec et al. (1985b) concerned the successful testing of a model of intervention based upon principles of social learning/cognitive-behavioural theory applied within a 'systems' framework. It is to this that we now turn.

RESEARCH INTO THE MANAGEMENT OF EATING DIFFICULTIES

The Relevance of Cognitive-Behavioural Theory

Iwaniec et al. (1985b) worked with the parents of 17 children who were failing to thrive using an innovative model of intervention and comparing the progress of these children with children in two control groups. The parents of the children in the first (focus) group were offered help based upon principles of cognitive-behavioural theory within a 'systems' framework and they were able to demonstrate that the children gained weight to an extent that brought them within the normal ranges which characterised the controls. This seminal work is being widely disseminated as a model of *preventive intervention* (Hampton, 1996).

There were two main stages in the approach. First, help was made available via the many systems of which the family were a part: this involved the researchers in arranging for parents to be offered occasional places at community resources such as a day nursery; approaching welfare agencies to ensure that parents were receiving all the financial support to which they were entitled; enabling parents to attend a self-help group; and enlisting community volunteers. Second, individually tailored help was given within the framework of cognitive-behavoural theory to do two main things:

1. To desensitise (where necessary) the mother's tension, anger and anxiety when in the child's company.
2. To provide her with a set of strategies for learning new responses to the child.

The essential point is that the tension was seen as a *learned* response to the child's difficult feeding behaviour – and thus as one that the parent can, with help, replace with other, more constructive responses, provided she is offered support and encouragement.

The Application of Cognitive-Behavioural Principles

The principles are systematically applied as set out in Box 8.1. Iwaniec, Herbert and McNeish (1985b) reported:

> There were several 'rejecting' mothers in our sample and they usually found this [nurturing] very difficult and at times distasteful. This aversion gradually lessened when the child began to smile back, seek her presence and in other ways respond to her overtures. This period of therapy requires a lot of support for the mother and the whole family ... It could take three months of hard work to bring a mother and child closer together and to the point of beginning to enjoy each other.

The evidence from this study was very positive: of the 17 children whose families took part in the study, 11 showed 'satisfactory' improvement (i.e. they improved to the extent that the children resumed growth to the point where height and weight were within normal limits); 5 achieved 'moderate' improvement with weight gain renewed; for only one was there no improvement.

Building on this work, and in an attempt to avoid admission to hospital and the cycle of weight loss and gain so often noted, interdisciplinary teams in Swindon and Trowbridge, Wiltshire developed a resource for offering families a service in their own homes. The main bodies of theory employed were humanistic psychology, child development theory within a multiracial and multicultural community and cognitive-behavioural theory. The first, associated with the names of Rogers and Maslow, is invoked in that the infants and young children concerned are in danger of not having their most fundamental needs met – the needs for food and drink, together with individual nurturing and care. The second underpins the monitoring of each child's development and takes into account each one's progress according to recognised developmental charts; knowledge of norms for child development is central to the effective work of the project. The progress of children from ethnic minority groups is considered carefully in order that norms that apply to white children should not be used inappropriately. The third main body of theory employs cognitive-behavioural principles. Figure 8.1 is a flow chart showing the sequence of events which follows referral to the project. My own evaluation of the Infant Support Project (Hampton, 1996) reported that 73 of the 108 children showed satisfactory gain as measured by either weight or height gain, or both.

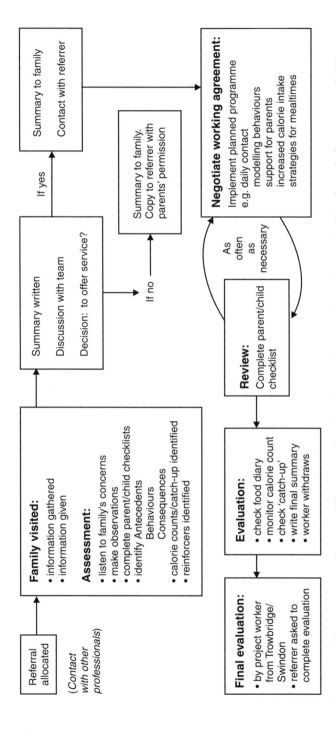

Figure 8.1 The sequence of events following referral to the Feeding to Thrive Project (with acknowledgements to Di Hampton, Feeding to Thrive, Chippenham, Wilts)

Box 8.1: Programme for increasing mother-infant nurturing, Stages 1–3 (after Iwaniec et al., 1985b)

Stage 1 – to reduce tension and anxiety at mealtimes

- A very structured approach is followed.
- Parents are asked never to feed the child when feeling very tense or angry.
- They are asked to avoid screaming, shouting and threatening the child.
- They are helped to develop a quiet and calm atmosphere at mealtimes.
- The parents are coached in talking reassuringly and pleasantly to the child.
- If the child refuses food, the parents are guided to leave him or her for a while and to avoid getting into a confrontation with him or her. If the child persists in refusing the food, they are advised not to exert pressure.
- The food is arranged attractively and the child is given very small portions.
- When he or she does take food, the mother is guided to show her pleasure and to encourage the child.

Stage 2 – to promote and encourage attachment and bonding

- The objective of developing closer relationships with the child is explained to the parents (the authors report that sometimes a contract to support the approach is devised). The mother is asked:
  - Each day in the first week, to play for 10–15 minutes with her child.
  - Each day in the second and third week, to play for 15–20 minutes with her child.
  - Each day in the fourth and later weeks, to play for 25–30 minutes with her child.
- The parents, who sometimes need help in learning how to play with their child, are supported in this activity by the practitioner.
- Parents are shown how to interact gently with their child, to smile at him or her, to give him or her encouragement and praise and to touch and stroke him/her (for some parents who have never received this nurturing behaviour themselves this is very difficult. They too need much encouragement and clear examples by the worker which they can copy.)
- Fathers are encouraged, wherever possible, to take part in the child's care.
- The earlier feeding strategies are continued and weight is monitored regularly.

Stage 3 – to consolidate gains and to promote independence

- The plan for this stage is explained to the parents and their involvement sought.
- The mother is asked to take her child with her almost everywhere she goes, for two weeks of increased mother-child interaction.
- She is asked to smile at the child a lot, to talk to him or her and to cuddle and hug him or her often.

- She tries to engage the child in play with any other children of the family.
- The earlier feeding strategies are continued and weight monitored.
- If improvements are noted and are maintaining, the practitioner gradually withdraws.

HELPING FAMILIES WITH CHILDREN WITH EATING DIFFICULTIES

Here I am not considering children who have reached the stage of displaying faltering growth but those who may be displaying the patterns of eating difficulty that *might* lead to that condition. For example, the innovative work by Hampton and colleagues required videoing mealtimes of children who were eating poorly and, although that is undoubtedly often revealing, I seek here to avoid it.

Assessment

Step 1 – Introduce Yourself

In tense situations, the practitioner may have to work hard to overcome resentment and hostility. Parents understandably tend to locate the problem in the child and are likely to be bewildered and unable to grasp any other explanation. In such circumstances the quality of the relationship developed between the family and the practitioner is crucial; it must be seen by the family members as supportive, friendly and noncritical otherwise one will join the ranks of the many other people dismissed as having nothing to offer.

Step 2 – Gather Information

The assessment framework offers a valuable structure for organising information. The three dimensions of this framework are used here.

1 Child's developmental needs

Many children will already have been seen by health visitors, paediatricians or other professionals and will have been screened for conditions predisposing to eating problems such as allergies, difficulties in absorbing certain nutrients, or other organic difficulties. Great tact will be necessary to help families accept situations where no such factors have been found because the probable implication is that there are difficulties intrinsic to the feeding situation which are contributing to the child's problems. However, if an appropriate health professional has not yet been involved then the information we are able to gather may well contribute useful pointers to the aetiology of the difficulties.

2 Family and environmental factors

The practitioner will use discretion about how much detail is required. Have there always been difficulties or did things become markedly worse at a certain stage of development, such as at the introduction of mixed feeding? Do all family members experience difficulty in getting the child to eat, or, deepest humiliation of all for the mother, is it only her food that is rejected whereas husband and grandmother experience no problems? The practitioner is likely to be drawing upon counselling skills of empathic listening, showing positive regard and demonstrating personal warmth if this kind of story unfolds. Appendix 1 is an instrument with a section about feeding, which can help practitioners gather detailed information relevant to the development of the feeding difficulty.

3 Parenting capacity

Here whether the parents and caregivers still have confidence in their ability to give the child basic care is of the greatest importance. Once they have lost confidence, their attempts to encourage the child to eat may well become disorganised, confused and even threatening. Although they actively want the child to eat, the nonverbal messages of frustration or the mixed messages of encouragement and criticism are likely to bring about a vicious spiral of anxiety in both parent and child. Here again, responsiveness on the part of the practitioner conveying elements of REST (Reassurance, Empathy, Structure and Time out for the parents) are likely to bring the best results.

The Example of Lisa

Let us consider the situation of Clare and Keith, parents of Lisa, a little girl of just over three years born with a cleft palate. She has had extensive surgery, which has repaired the palate leaving only a slight scar on her upper lip, but this has contributed to much tension around feeding. Clare, in particular, is becoming increasingly anxious and there is some concern that Lisa has already fallen through one centile space.

Step 3 – Identify the Problem Behaviours

It will probably be beneficial for some person who is emotionally uninvolved to be present during at least one meal to observe in a supportive way the interactions of Lisa and her mother or father. This might be the practitioner or some 'friend of the family' who wishes to be supportive to them all and who will be empathic with the parents in their distress. It may then be possible to identify eating or mealtime circumstances that are causing difficulties. For example:

1. Lisa screams if her mother, Clare, tries to get her to eat. She turns away from her.
2. If they are placed in front of her, she will eat a very limited range of foods: bananas, ice cream and baked beans, and nothing else.
3. She will eat a little more if her Daddy (Keith) or her granny sits with her.

Step 4 – Identifying Positive Profile

It is next necessary to identify features of the child's behaviour that the parents already enjoy and would like to see happening more frequently. These positive behaviours can be in areas quite removed from the eating situation. This serves to reassure parents who are losing confidence that there are features of their parenting that are entirely successful. For example, family members will be reassured to hear the worker's appreciation of some aspect of their parenting: the child's friendliness, her ability to find things or her smile. Such parents are usually *very* demoralised; they have had difficulties in a field of great significance: that of nurturing their child. They need *much* empathic support. We are trying to foster positive, warm, nurturing interactions between parent and child as these serve to reduce anxiety and tension – so reducing angry, rejecting interactions and also, indirectly, to demonstrate positive ways of interacting with the child. Thus, Clare and Keith might identify:

1. Lisa's outgoingness; she is friendly to people who come to the house.
2. Lisa's kindness to other toddlers; if one cries, she tries to give comfort.

Step 5 – Discover Desired Outcomes

Most parents whose children have eating difficulties have few unreasonable expectations. They generally want their children to eat a reasonably balanced diet and to maintain their weight and growth. In precise terms, this might be stated as follows:

- Goal 1: that within eight weeks, Lisa will be eating a diet comprising protein, carbohydrates, fats, etc. during each week (precise figures to be devised by a dietician).
- Goal 2: that Lisa will maintain this diet over the subsequent 12 weeks.

Step 6 – Summarise Key Information and Offer a Rationale

A matter-of-fact approach, which emphasises that feeding problems are common and that the practitioner is particularly interested in them, often serves to reassure parents. Enabling them to talk to other parents who have had a successful outcome to their child's difficulty may be an effective strategy. If this is not possible then another good approach is to show letters from 'satisfied customers' – a number of brief notes kept in a loose-leaf file, in which parents who have had successful outcomes have written about their child's eating problems and how they felt about them, both *before* and *after* they received help.

The overall formulation of the difficulty, offered supportively to the parents, might be as shown in Box 8.2. This situation is potentially serious, as an analysis in respect of the Antecedents/Activators–Behaviours–Consequences might reveal the following:

Steps 7 and 8 – Planning

Support from a cognitive perspective for Clare and Keith

In accordance with the cognitive component of 'cognitive-behavioural theory', the practitioner (let us call her Miranda) realises that to support these parents, help is needed that is specifically directed towards addressing their negative assumptions about Lisa's difficulties and Clare's part in them. Such help in this case is likely to have components both of (a) education/information giving and (b) reassurance by explaining the theoretical approach taken by the practitioner.

(a) Education/information giving

The practitioner and parents are now partners in a joint endeavour to help Lisa. It is crucial to explain to the parents that she seems to have a *fear of eating* in her mother's presence: she is not just being naughty. No-one is to blame for this but everyone can work together to improve matters.

(b) Reassurance through an explanation in terms of theory

Once their anxiety has been reduced via the empathy and support of the practitioner, the parents may be ready to attend to a cognitive explanation of what is known about *generalisation* – the way in which Lisa's initial painful experiences at the time of her operation have made her acutely sensitive to the activities and sensations of eating, so that she feared eating in case it brought pain. (The parents will probably already understand this very well at one level but will be unable to give the circumstance its due weight because of their anxiety.)

Box 8.2: Preliminary assessment of/rationale for the difficulties of Lisa, aged 39 months

1. *Child's developmental needs or those intrinsic to the child: e.g. developmental stage, disability*
   (a) Lisa's cleft palate has required substantial surgery, upsetting to all concerned.
   (b) Feeding has been difficult from the start, sometimes initially associated with pain.
   (c) Lisa is losing weight; she is on the point of falling through a second centile space.
2. *Family and environmental factors*
   (a) Lisa, aged 3 years, is the first child of Clare and Keith.
   (b) Clare feels helpless and inadequate because of the feeding difficulties. Lisa is her first child, and her medical needs cause Clare much anxiety.
   (c) Clare's mother-in-law, Lisa's grandmother, tries to help but Clare feels criticised by her.
   (d) Clare worries about whether she might have harmed Lisa during her pregnancy.
   (e) Keith is self-employed. He has tried to adjust his work so that he can come home to help feed Lisa, but this is straining his relationship with Clare.
3. *Parenting capacity: interactions within the family, including A–B–C**
   (a) Lisa had never had the care of young children before Lisa was born. She wants to do her very best for her little girl, but her best does not seem good enough.
   (b) When Lisa refuses food Clare has provided, Clare feels *very* tense and angry.
   (c) Clare acknowledges that she has tried to forcefeed Lisa, who screamed and screamed.

*Parents may not understand this concept, but it is useful to introduce it at this stage.

Family strengths

Everyone agreed that the family needed help.
Everyone has agreed to work together in the situation. They just want clear guidance.

Moreover, Lisa's fear, linked with the feeding situation, has now *generalised* to the person who provides the food: her own mother. To know that Lisa's screaming at the sight of Clare makes sense and that Lisa's learned fear can be unlearned are both ideas likely to prove very reassuring to Clare. The

Table 8.1   Analysis of immediate context and long-term consequences of Lisa's refusal of food.

Activator	Behaviours	Consequences	Distant (long-term) consequences
1 Clare approaches Lisa with a bowl of cereal.	1 Lisa screams and tries to throw the bowl on the floor . . .	1 Clare gets very upset and tries to force Lisa's mouth open.	1 Clare and Lisa become increasingly fearful of each other.
2 Another meal time arrives . . . Clare says 'I just can't go through this again . . .'	2 Lisa becomes rigid whenever she sees her mother. (Her fear has generalised from the mealtime situation to the mere sight of Clare.)	2 Clare refuses to try to care for Lisa. (She cannot bear Lisa's rejecting first, the food she provides and then, Clare herself.)	2 Father and grandmother have to take over the care of Lisa . . .

Source: Adapted from Iwaniec (2004). *Children Who Fail to Thrive: A Practice Guide.* Chichester: Wiley.

practitioner can help Clare learn to interact with Lisa calmly so that Lisa's fears can fade away. This is called a process of *desensitisation,* employed for example when people have acquired fear of dogs or feathers. Miranda is deliberately normalising this fraught situation.

Support from a behavioural perspective for Clare and Keith

The practitioner can make a number of predictions based on her theoretical knowledge and her experience (which will vary according to the age and circumstances of the child). In respect of Lisa, these might be:

1. Lisa's fear of her mother going into the kitchen will diminish if Clare keeps going in and coming out again without any food in her hands and without looking at Lisa.
2. Lisa's tensions about food, arising from the necessary medical treatment, will subside if mealtimes can become relaxed and casual occasions.
3. Lisa will be less fearful of eating if Clare explains to her that, although she had tried to force her to eat in the past, she will never do so again.
4. Lisa will gradually become used to having her mother present at mealtimes if her mother and her Daddy together sit to eat with her whenever possible behaving in a very relaxed and casual way about what Lisa eats.
5. Lisa will gradually become used to eating if, when her Daddy provides her with food, her mother also, casually, puts some of Lisa's favourite finger

foods, such as yoghurt-covered sultanas, near her plate – but takes no interest initially in whether she eats them or not.
6. Lisa will gradually respond to eating a wider variety of food if she is told, in a calm and casual way, 'well done, Lisa' at the end of a meal.

Keith and Clare have already begun to realise that they must reward Lisa's occasional willingness to extend the range of her foods, and an explanation of the A–B–C formulation is likely to make sense to them. It will be helpful to give them a simple chart showing the days of the week and the times of day when Lisa eats or drinks anything. (Appendix 10 can be adapted.) Guidance should be given about, for example, the type of milk or cheese she should be offered so that, although her diet is small, it is nutritious. Clare will need much help in accepting, at least temporarily, Lisa's rejection of her but may be reassured by the worker's confidence that her little girl is likely to regain her love for her. Clare will certainly need the practitioner to practise how to remain calm in her interactions with Lisa, particularly when the food she has prepared is rejected. Because of her anxieties that she may have harmed Lisa in some way during her pregnancy, she may agree to referral to a counsellor if the current practitioner has not received appropriate training in counselling. Clare will probably know who or what would help her most: perhaps a medical explanation from a specialist health visitor or perhaps a talk with the paediatrician who first helped care for Lisa. She may need several forms of support.

The strategies in Box 8.3 are put forward as a range of ways of, first, making the eating situation far more relaxed and, second, desensitising Lisa and her mother to the learned fears associated with eating. The fears have been learned over many months; it is likely that for Lisa and Clare to regain confidence about eating will also take many months. The plan must not be hurried.

Involving the child in the plan

Lisa, too, can be involved as fully as her understanding permits – so that it can be explained to her that Mummy understands that she seems frightened to eat. Mummy did once try to make her eat but she will not do that again. Everyone hopes she will come to enjoy eating like most people do but for the time being they're not going to pay much attention to it.

Step 9 – Implementation of the Plan

The next step will be for Clare, Keith and Lisa's Granny to attempt to put the plan into effect. There are bound to be disappointments and set-backs as Lisa tests out the new 'management' and as her mother has further experiences of rejection. However, if the plan is followed carefully, and as the practitioner gains experience in the use of cognitive-behavioural principles, he or she is likely to be able to 'troubleshoot' the difficulties that will inevitably arise.

Box 8.3: A possible plan to help Lisa eat more

Parents: Clare and Keith Davis, 27 High Street, Hightown. Tel. 985309
Child: Lisa, aged three
Practitioner: Susan Jenkins, Health Centre, High Street, Anytown.
                    Tel. 875097

Agreement between Clare and Keith Davis and Miranda Jenkins concerning Lisa Davis

Overall aim: To enable Lisa to gain weight
Specific goals are: 1. To increase Lisa's calorie intake
                        2. To enable Clare to feel more confident in caring for
                           Lisa. (To be measured on a self-report scale of
                           0–10.)

Clare and Keith agree

1. For the first week. there will be no change in the plan of caring for Lisa.
2. Gradually, Clare will resume caring for Lisa in all other respects except feeding. She will play briefly with her, read her short stories, bath her, help her dress and so on.
3. Keith will continue to give Lisa her meals as far as his work permits; Clare will eat her own meals in Lisa's sight but offer her nothing.
4. As Clare feels calmer and more relaxed, she will place some finger food near Lisa, saying nothing to her and not even looking at her.
5. If ever Lisa does eat the finger food, Clare should say nothing – although if this pattern becomes established, she should say casually, 'that's nice; well done'.
6. The parents will keep a record of Lisa's intake of food on a daily basis.
7. If Lisa gets messy or sticky, Clare will clean her up without comment.
8. Clare will make her interactions with Lisa as relaxed and calm as she can during the rest of the day.

Miranda Jenkins agrees

1. To visit the family weekly and to phone each Wednesday morning to offer support.
2. Provide a chart on which Clare can record everything that Lisa eats.
3. Liaise with the paediatrician who referred the case to Miranda and keep her informed.

It will be important for Keith to cooperate with the plan and for Miranda to enlist the support of Lisa's Granny, who may be tempted, because of her own anxiety and impatience with her daughter-in-law, to try to hurry the plan forward. On some occasions it may be necessary to ask the various family members actively to support the plan so that they do not try to take matters into their own hands and sabotage it.

Step 10 – Review and Evaluate

The main measure of the effectiveness of the plan will, of course, be Lisa's weight gain. She should be weighed at regular intervals; this will be a reliable indicator of whether there is or is not evidence to support the various hypotheses. If, for example, it seems that the hypothesis that Lisa has learned to fear the feeding situation is not supported, then another must be systematically tried. Cognitive-behavioural approaches offer a wide range of theoretical principles to help families deal with feeding and eating difficulties. The principles can be discerned at any meal, whether they be the satisfaction and rewards that people typically gain from eating or the difficulties which arise when eating ceases to be enjoyable.

9

HELPING FAMILIES WITH CHILDREN WITH SERIOUS BEHAVIOUR PROBLEMS

DIFFICULTIES OF ARRIVING AT DEFINITIONS

There have been many attempts to distinguish differences between types of misbehaviour in young children in the hope of clarifying, for example, whether any have an organic basis, whether patterns of early onset give more grounds for concern than do those of later onset, and whether there are innate predispositions towards aggressiveness. There is still much disagreement between researchers but some progress has been made.

For example, there is increasing consensus that a pattern of behaviour marked by extreme restlessness and impulsiveness, named attention deficit hyperactivity disorder (ADHD), is sufficiently different from, say, a general tendency to aggressive behaviour for it to be accepted as a distinct syndrome; further, among child psychiatrists, a pattern of behaviour called oppositional defiant disorder (ODD), distinguished from other conditions by the degree of interpersonal verbal aggressiveness displayed, has also been identified. Ways of managing these difficult behaviours are very similar, however, so no effort will be made here to distinguish between conduct difficulties and oppositional defiant disorder, although attention deficit hyperactivity disorder will be considered separately in Chapter 10.

Children with severe behaviour problems are described as 'conduct-disordered' according to the two major systems of classification: the *Diagnostic and Statistical Manual*, 4th edn (DSM-IV) (American Psychiatric Association, 1994) and the *International Classification of Disorders*, 10th edition (ICD-10) (World Health Organization, 1992). Both systems of classification require the presence of at least three of the features shown in Box 9.1 and, although this has been devised with older children in mind, it is included to indicate the types of behaviour that may give grounds for concern. It has also

> **Box 9.1:** Features of children's behaviour which may lead to an assessment of conduct disorder (data from American Psychiatric Association, 1994)
>
> | | | |
> |---|---|---|
> | Lies | Initiates fights | Uses weapons |
> | Is destructive | Is cruel to animals | Is cruel to people |
> | Stays out late | Sets fires | Steals |
> | Runs away | Engages in robbery/mugging | Forces sex |
> | Bullies | Burgles | |

become evident that ADHD is characterised by 'comorbidity', in other words, that the condition sometimes occurs together with other disorders, such as marked anxiety.

As we saw in the frontispiece and in Chapter 1, serious behaviour problems in early childhood are grounds for great concern, especially if they are exhibited in more than one setting, for example at home as well as at playgroup or nursery. The precursors in young children of the terms in Box 9.1 are destructiveness, disruptiveness, defiance and physical and verbal aggressiveness.

As noted, the patterns of behaviour shown in Box 9.1 are descriptive of the conduct of children over the age of 10 or so; however, recent research is suggesting that the terms 'oppositional defiant' and 'conduct disorder' may be validly applied to preschoolers. For example, Keenan and Wakschlag (2004) assessed the rates of indicators of oppositional defiant and conduct disorders in children aged two-and-a-half to five-and-a-half who were referred to a clininc for treatment and a comparison group of nonreferred children. They found that the referred children had significantly higher rates of indicators of conduct disorder than nonreferred childen. Such research, although telling us nothing about the aetiology of the children's behaviour, alerts us to the need to offer help and support to the parents of children as young as two-and-a-half, or even earlier.

PREVALENCE OF AND CONTINUITIES IN CONDUCT DISORDERS

Serious misbehaviour has been the focus of extensive research both in the United Kingdom and the United States because of the increasing evidence of the link between early antisocial behaviour and subsequent aggressive and offending behaviour (Robins, 1966, 1981; Caspi et al., 1996). A broad consensus is emerging upon a number of issues.

Prevalence

Studies undertaken in different countries and in different parts of those countries all indicate a much higher rate of serious misbehaviour for boys than for girls (Offord, Boyle & Racine, 1991; Earls & Jung, 1987) and all show a higher rate in urban environments than in rural ones (Rutter et al., 1975a, 1975b). In the United Kingdom, as we saw in Table I. 1, (p. 2) prevalence rates are reported as 6.9 % of boys and 2.8 % of girls in the 5–10 year old age range, and as 8.1 % of boys and 5.1 % of girls in the 11–16 age range. These are separate from those who may be diagnosed as displaying ADHD.

Longitudinal studies confirm this very worrying picture. The British National Child Development Study (Davie, Butler & Goldstein, 1972) followed the development of some 15,000 children born in one week in 1958. Assessments by teachers when the children were 7 indicated that 14 % were considered to present serious problems and a further 8 % were showing some signs of disturbed behaviour; again, boys were more highly represented than girls. A study by the Thomas Coram research Unit (Tizard, Blatchford, Borke, Farquhar & Plewis, 1988) of children aged 4 to 7 in inner London infant schools reported 16 % as having definite behaviour problems in the eyes of their teachers and a further 17 % as having mild behaviour problems. The teachers' views were confirmed by independent observers in the classroom.

Continuities from Early Childhood into Adolescence and Adulthood

There have been many attempts to follow up children seen as having behaviour disorders in childhood into later life. The seminal study by Robins (1966) found that nearly half the children with this diagnosis in her large sample of children in a US town went on to develop antisocial personality disorder as adults. Some of the children who did not become antisocial showed other forms of disturbance, including alcoholism or schizophrenia. Olweus (1979) reviewed a number of studies on this topic, some of which followed up subjects for long periods, in some instances as long as 20 years. He concluded that the degree of stability in the area of aggression was substantial; moreover, he found that 'marked individual differences in habitual aggression level manifest themselves early in life, certainly by the age of 3'. Further, Zoccolillo, Pickles, Quinton and Rutter (1992) in a major longitudinal study of adults who had spent much of their childhood in foster care, showed that the great majority experienced a variety of social problems in adult life.

Other studies give further grounds for concern. Robins and Price (1991), in their longitudinal study of young people with conduct disorders, found, as reported by Earls (1994), that, 'Conduct disorder may predict adult substance abuse about as efficiently as it predicts antisocial behaviour . . . ' There was a difference, however, between young men and young women. Earls reports: 'For females, conduct disorder predicted depression and anxiety disorders more strongly than it did antisocial behaviour and substance abuse'.

Many researchers, such as Loeber (1990), have found a relationship between early age of onset and more serious forms of disturbance. It is increasingly accepted that the more serious and the earlier the onset of behaviour disturbance, the greater the probability of its continuing into adolescence and beyond. Indeed, Henry, Caspi, Moffitt and Silva (1996) reported research about predictors of violent and nonviolent criminal convictions, age 3 to age 18, as follows:

> Previous criminological research has consistently found that a small subgroup (approximately 5%) of offenders accounts for a disproportionate percentage (50–60%) of all crimes committed (Wolfgang, 1972). This subgroup is typified by early onset of antisocial behavior, high rates of offending and disproportionately violent offending (Elliott, Huizinga & Morse, 1986; Moffitt, Mednick & Gabrielli, 1989) The remaining 95% of offenders appear to represent a group whose criminal behavior begins later and is less frequent and less violent . . . The primary difference between the two offender groups is to be found in the complex interplay between environmental and individual difference characteristics that originate in early childhood . . . The theories differ in detail but . . . all theories agree that the child at greatest risk for later serious offending exhibits an early emerging pattern of undercontrolled behavior. These early emerging behavioral difficulties, interacting with environmental characteristics (such as disorganized family environments), can have a profound impact on social development.

In analysing these same issues, Webster-Stratton and Herbert (1994) concluded that certain risk factors contribute to the continuation of disorders:

- Early age of onset (preschool years) of oppositional-defiant disorder (ODD) and conduct disorder (CD). Those children with conduct symptoms prior to age six are at greater risk for developing antisocial behaviour as adults than those whose problems start during adolescence.
- Breadth of deviance (across multiple settings, such as home and school). Those children most at risk of continuing antisocial behaviour as adults had conduct problems which occurred not only in the home but also at school and in other settings.
- Frequency and intensity of antisocial behaviour. The likelihood of becoming an antisocial adult increases in direct proportion to the number of different behaviour problems evidenced as a child.
- Diversity of antisocial behaviours (several versus few) and covert behaviours (stealing, lying, firesetting) at early ages. The greater the variety of both covert and overt behaviour problems, the greater is the likelihood

of becoming an antisocial adult, although aggressive behaviour is probably the most stable over time.

- Family and parent characteristics (Kazdin, 1987). Children whose biological parent has an antisocial personality are at greater risk.

RESEARCH INTO THE ORIGINS OF CONDUCT DISORDERS

The evidence suggests that a multifactorial model encompassing many contributory factors is necessary to understand conduct disorders. The frontispiece shows the major contributory variables that, research suggests, contribute to the development of problem behaviours. Earls (1994) suggested five main contributory sets of variables that pose a risk for the development of such behaviour: community factors, family environment, poor mental health of the parents, psychosocial factors in the child and factors intrinsic to the child. Each will be considered briefly below.

Community Variables: Socioeconomic and Structural Factors

Many studies have shown the association between children's behaviour problems and parental poverty, poor quality of housing in inner city areas, unemployment and general disadvantage (Rutter et al., 1975a, 1975b; Rutter, 1978). Many explanations for these close associations have been put forward. We saw in Chapter 1, p. 16, how there was an impact of the environment even among children as young as two years, over and above any genetic liability. It may not be that the environment impacts directly upon infants: rather, it may be that disorganised and deprived environments affect parents, whose capacity to care for their children is, in turn, placed under stress. In such neighbourhoods, particularly if there is a high level of crime, it is harder to get local people to form friendships and supportive neighbourhood networks (Sampson et al., 1997). It is also more difficult for parents, schools and faith communities to reinforce positive, prosocial attitudes. However, the work of many Sure Start initiatives gives grounds for hope that substantial improvements can be made in children's lives by improving the family circumstances and living conditions of their parents.

Family and Parenting Variables

Extensive research is available in this area. Bandura and Walters (1959), in an early comparative study, compared 26 aggressive youths aged 14–17 with 26 nonaggressive youths matched for age, IQ, socioeconomic status and social background, focusing particularly upon the parenting practices of each group. They noted that the parents of the aggressive young people were more likely to:

- use physical punishment
- disagree with each other
- be cold and rejecting to their sons.

Bandura further reported:

> Parents of non-aggressive adolescents rarely reinforced their sons for resorting to physical aggression in response to provocation. Parents of aggressive delinquents, on the other hand, tolerated no aggressive displays whatsoever in the home, but condoned, actively encouraged and reinforced provocative and aggressive actions towards others in the community.

We saw in Chapter 1 (p. 17) how various parenting styles affect the young people concerned, and how authoritarian parents tend to be very demanding of their children, but not very nurturing. If the authoritarian style escalates into harshness it is not surprising that the young people concerned react with hostility and develop a relationship with the parent concerned which is marked by conflict. Research has thrown light on the impact of harsh parenting in the very earliest years of life. Raine, Brennan and Mednick (1994) studied 1-year-old infants and their mothers and found that, in line with the studies of the impact of low birth weight, there is evidence that birth complications, combined with harshness and rejection by the mother at 1 year old, are associated with an increased risk that the child will be involved in violent crime by age 18.

Herbert (1978) has focused upon the stresses experienced by parents and, writing from the standpoint of cognitive-behavioural theory, has highlighted the difficulties that parents, often isolated and distressed, encounter in providing firm and consistent management for active and challenging children. In an early comparative study of Asian and English children, all aged between 9 and 12, Kallarackal and Herbert (1976) found the Asian children more stable and less unruly than their English counterparts, and they attributed this in part to the way in which the Asian parents managed their children. They wrote: 'We do think that the quality of Indian family life may positively help to reduce the risk of developing deviant behaviour in Indian children... Indian parents were found to be insistent on close supervision of children and firm discipline at home.'

There has been much interest in the impact of abuse in childhood upon those children's subsequent lives. Studies by Lane and Davis (1987) and Widom (1989) showed that about a quarter of children who had been physically abused or neglected in childhood became offenders. Research continues upon the specific variables that lead to some children following a route into offending but by far the greater number avoiding it.

The impact of violence on television has been much under scrutiny. The evidence in this field is becoming much clearer. For example, Browne and Hamilton-Giachristis (2005) concluded from their scrutiny of five meta-analyses that

> There is consistent evidence that violent imagery in television, film and video, and computer games has substantial short term effect on arousal, thoughts, and emotions, increasing the likelihood of aggressive or fearful behaviour in younger children especially in boys.

A number of other researchers, such as Huesmann, Moise-Titus, Podolski and Eron (2003) have found a close relationship between children's exposure to TV violence and their aggressive and violent behaviour in young adulthood.

Parental Mental Ill-health

It is known that there is an association between parental mental ill health and children who are the subject of child protection conferences: parental mental illness was identified in a quarter of cases reviewed by Farmer and Owen (1995). A number of studies have investigated the impact of the mental health of parents upon their children's behaviour. Lahey, Russo, Walke and Piacentini (1989) examined aspects of mental health in mothers and found that maternal antisocial personality has a direct effect on child conduct disorders. Earls (1994) comments:

> How to interpret this relationship in causal terms is open to question. Is it through the production of a disorganized rearing environment, as suggested by the Kolvin et al. (1988) study, or are both the mother's and the child's deviant personality genetically mediated?

It is my own view that the 'disorganized rearing environment' contributes more to the total variance than the genetic factors although inherited temperamental factors, such as a tendency to hyperactivity, may well contribute in some children. I have arrived at this conclusion because, as already indicated, in one of my own studies (Sutton, 1995) I found that the preintervention mean score of the mothers on the Beck Depression Inventory bordered on 15, the cutoff score indicating clinical depression, but that this fell dramatically over the course of 8 weeks to within normal limits as the mothers learned skills of managing their aggressive and disruptive children. If these tendencies to behave very aggressively had been innate in the children, it would have been unlikely that they could have been so easily overridden by a short parenting programme.

The work of Cooper and Murray (1998) is very important in this field. As already reported (p. 16) these researchers worked with a community sample of mothers who were experiencing postnatal depression and compared outcomes for children born to depressed mothers with those born to mothers who were not depressed. There were clear distinctions between the two groups: Cooper and Murray reported of the comparison between children born to depressed mothers and those born to well mothers:

- Cognitive development in the context of postnatal depression is adversely affected, especially among male children and socioeconomically disadvantaged groups.
- The children of postnatally depressed mothers tend to have insecure attachments at 18 months, and the boys show a high level of frank behavioural disturbance at 5 years.
- The adverse child outcome in the context of postnatal depression is related to disturbances in the mother-infant interactions.

Behavioural and Cognitive Variables

Important contributions have been made by many researchers, for example Hollin (1991) and Kendall (1991), in drawing attention to factors arising from a cognitive-behavioural analysis of serious misbehaviour. They stress how inconsistency on the part of parents may lead to the very patterns of behaviour of which the parents frequently complain, namely aggressiveness and disruptiveness. Parents do not typically understand that this misbehaviour is often unwittingly reinforced by their attention in the form of repeated reprimands to their children, which are, however, often not followed through, and by their neglect of their children's positive and desirable behaviours. This analysis has already been discussed in some detail in Chapter 2.

Within a primarily cognitive framework, Dodge and Frame (1982) have shown how aggressive children perceive people and events differently from non-aggressive children. Lochman, White and Wayland (1991) summarised this growing body of research as follows:

> aggressive children have been found to encode and retrieve significantly more cues that convey hostile connotations than do non-aggressive children...aggressive children are hypervigilant in scanning their social environment, attending to more immediate cues, especially hostile cues, than do non-aggressive children...
>
> In the milliseconds after cues are perceived, aggressive children form inferences about others' intentions, and these efforts to decipher the meaning of others' behaviour have been found to be significantly influenced by their higher rate of detection of hostile cues and by their prior expectations that others would be hostile towards them ... As a result, aggressive boys have been found

to be 50 % more likely than non-aggressive boys to infer that antagonists in hypothetical provocations acted with hostile rather than neutral or benign intent.

Dodge, 1980

RESEARCH INTO INTERVENTION IN CONDUCT DISORDERS

Since the publication of the first edition of this book, when I deplored that shortage of rigorous studies into ways of intervening in conduct disorders, I am glad to report that this situation has been at least partially remedied. In his review of groups of interventions showing evidence of effectiveness Kazdin (1995) identified two groups of interventions which he described as 'highly promising', cognitive problem-solving skills training and parent management training. Cognitive problem-solving approaches tend to be most helpful for older children and teenagers. In the United Kingdom, Lane, Gardner, Hutchings and Jacobs (2004) surveyed a range of these and reported a number of effective family and school-based programmes being used in Britain. They included:

The Incredible Years (Webster-Stratton, 1992)
Triple P Positive Parenting Programme (Sanders, 1999)
Multi systemic therapy (Henggeler, 1999)
Functional family therapy (Gordon, 2003)

As this book is focusing upon preventive work with very young children these approaches will not be discussed further here.

Parent Management Training

Kazdin summarises the steps of this as follows:

1. The parents meet with a therapist/trainer who teaches them specific procedures to use in managing their child.
2. Parents are trained to identify, define and observe problem behaviours carefully. This is the A–B–C analysis.
3. The sessions cover principles of social learning theory: positive reinforcement, mild punishment (e.g. loss of privileges) and contingency contracting.
4. The sessions provide opportunities for parents to discuss how their attempts to practise the techniques are or are not proving effective and for the trainer to offer guidance and encouragement to continue.

Box 9.2: Parenting 'packages' shown by rigorous evaluation to be effective (when employed by an empathic and skilled facilitator)

- *Living with Children* (Patterson 1976). The earliest of the approaches based on social learning theory, which showed how parents could, with support, gain knowledge and skills to manage their troubled and troublesome children calmly and positively. It was from this approach that my own materials, *Parenting Positively*, Sutton (1995) have been developed. These have also been shown by independent evaluators to be effective.
- *The Incredible Years* (Webster-Stratton, 1992; Webster-Stratton et al., 2001). A package of materials accompanied by a large array of manuals and videos now widely used in the United States and the United Kingdom. An additional package of materials is available for teachers.
- *Triple P* (Sanders, 1999). An Australian package of materials for work with parents, incorporating resources for differing levels of family problem and child misbehaviour.
- *Parenting Partnership* (Davis, Day & Bidmead, 2002). A resource for working with families with multiple and varied difficulties, of which work with children with behaviour problems is one strand.

NB A number of other packages, such as *The Solihull Approach* (Douglas, 2001) and *Strengthening families, Strengthening Communities* (Steele, Marigna, Tello & Johnson, 1999) have been developed but these cannot be placed in the first rank of materials as they have not yet been evaluated according to the most stringent criteria, namely using randomised controlled trials (RCTs).

There is now much evidence of the effectiveness of parent management training using cognitive-behavioural principles, particularly with serious behaviour problems (Herbert, 1981 Sutton, 1992, 1995; Barlow, 1997; Richardson & Joughin, 2002; Scott, 2002). Some of the conclusions which may be drawn from the evidence include those shown in Box 9.2.

In Box 9.3 we see the typical outcomes of these rigorously evaluated parenting programmes.

Key strategies typically taught in parent management training

1. Developing rewarding relationships between parent(s) and child – e.g. play, taking part in enjoyable activities or outings together, cooking, swimming.
2. Targeting specific behaviours: negative and positive.
3. Tracking and recording these behaviours.

Box 9.3: Outcomes of cognitive-behavioural procedures for serious behaviour problems

1. Children's behaviour improves in ways that can be measured both quantitatively and qualitatively (Scott, Knapp, Henderson & Maughan, 2001a; Scott, Spender, Doolan, Jacobs & Aspland, 2001b).
2. Mothers' levels of depression fall to within normal limits (Sutton, 1995).
3. Siblings of referred children also improve, as parents practise the strategies with them as well.
4. In preschool children, the capacity for attachment behaviours, cuddling, kissing, saying affectionate things, re-emerges (Sutton, 2001).
5. There is maintenance of improved behaviour for one–three years after training (Kazdin, 1995; Sutton, 1992). One study reported maintenance of gains 10–14 years later (Long, Forehand, Wierson & Morgan, 1994).

---

4. Giving warm praise and encouragement.
5. Identifying antecedents to and consequences of the behaviours.
6. Giving clear messages to children. See Box 9.4.
7. Giving clear sanctions and penalties: time out as a last resort.
8. Using the principles for a range of behaviours: aggressiveness and disruptiveness, but also wetting, eating difficulties and shyness. See Box 9.5.

Coaching parents in the use of Time out/calm down

I found in my research that, whereas many parents found it difficult to praise their children, some found it even more difficult to use time out. Indeed, I

Box 9.4: Giving a child a clear instruction

1. If possible, give a few minutes' warning of a change in activity; a meal, going out.
2. Keep very calm, even if the child ignores you or shouts at you.
3. Go to the child and say his name.
4. Put your hands on his shoulders.
5. Look him or her in the eye.
6. Say firmly, 'John, we have to go out. Please find your shoes'.
7. As he begins to comply, say something like, 'Well done; thank you'.
8. If he does not begin to comply within, say, one minute, repeat the above.
9. If he still does not comply, explain that a penalty will come into effect; for example no television that day. Try to keep as calm and 'matter of fact' as is humanly possible.

> **Box 9.5:** Parenting positively. Some general guidelines for parents
>
> 1. Work out some house or family guidelines: for example 'all toys must be put away before bedtime'. Everyone helps each other to carry out the guidelines. See Box 9.6.
> 2. Find three behaviours each day-for which you can praise a child. Catch them being good!
> 3. Reward behaviour you want to encourage, by attending to it and showing how pleased you are with it.
> 4. Ignore small misbehaviours: whining, pestering, tantrums. Turn your back on the child.
> 5. Try to be consistent. If you promise or threaten something, you must carry out the promise or threat.
> 6. Speak directly and firmly to your child when giving instructions.
> 7. Ask others who care for the child to use these same guidelines.
> 8. Take a day at a time.
> 9. You'll have some bad days. Try to commend yourself for what you have already achieved.
> 10. Try to find someone you can confide in when it all seems to be falling apart. Don't give up.

found that those parents who either did not use time out when it was appropriate or used it inconsistently were unlikely to be successful in learning to manage their children effectively. Box 9.6 therefore shows the principles for using time out.

HELPING PARENTS WITH CHILDREN WITH SERIOUS BEHAVIOUR PROBLEMS

This book focuses upon prevention and the evidence has accumulated extremely fast over the last decade, so the intervention that will be emphasised here is that of parent management training – the second of the groups of approaches that Kazdin considers to be 'highly promising'. Humanistic principles (associated with respect for and empathic listening to the families concerned) underpin all the approaches (programmes) shown to be effective, all of which also incorporate cognitive-behavioural principles.

We turn now to exploring how we can introduce the essential core of these approaches but without identifying with any specific commercial package. We can start by using the steps of the ASPIRE process.

Box 9.6: Sample family rules: to apply to parents/carers as well as children

(With thanks and acknowledgments to a group of Family Support Workers in Luton)

Up to 2 years

- Hold hands when we're out and about
- We sit at the table to eat and drink
- Say Please, Thank you and Sorry
- We kiss, or blow a kiss, Goodnight
- No hitting or smacking in our family
- No shouting or swearing in our house
- Toys are put away when we've finished playing

Age 3–6 (approximately)

- We say nice things to each other
- We help each other
- We listen to each other at meal times
- TV off during meal times
- Evening meal together – at the table if possible
- Up and dressed in time for breakfast
- School clothes and school bag prepared the night before
- When accidents happen, tell a grown up truthfully
- No secrets from parents (surprises are all right)

Age 7–11 (approximately)

* Get homework done before play
* Change out of school clothes and put them away
* If we want to go out, we check with a grown up first
* TV/computer games for only * amount of time per day
* Dirty washing in the wash basket – or it's not washed
* Bed time is at . . . . . . o'clock, and we stay in our rooms until morning (Visits to toilets excepted)
* We ask before we 'borrow' other people's belongings

Age 12 plus

* No smoking in the house
* No illegal drugs in the house
* Alcohol is used under supervision
* When we want to go out, we always let parent(s) know where we are going and confirm when we will be back
* If we have a mobile, we have it on when out of the house
* We get permission from friend's parents or carers before going to their house
* Fridays/Saturdays/Sundays are family days; other arrangements to be made after discussion

* If we want to ask friends home, we check with parents/carers first
* We respect each other's privacy: we knock before going into each other's room
* We have a family meeting every ... weeks to agree/clarify family rules

Step 1 – Build Supportive and Empathic Relationships

As already discussed, families whose children have serious misbehaviour problems are often very agitated about their circumstances. They have often tried everything that they can think of in an attempt to manage their children, following advice from grandparents, neighbours and friends for a few days at a time, only to abandon each strategy when the child's behaviour fails to improve. Thus, in order for the practitioner really to help, *it is for the parents to say which are the priorities in helping them.* These may have little to do with managing their children. There may be pressing debts, mental health issues, unacceptable housing and a range of other concerns to be coped with before the parent(s) have time to consider their managment of their children. Such wide-ranging therapy for mothers is obviously desirable but, because there are so many thousands of children whose parents are asking for help with their difficult behaviour, this is unlikely to be available. In these circumstances, we have to refer families to other appropriate agencies: we cannot take on the whole world.

In what follows, I am taking it for granted that practitioners consistently offer parents the warmth, genuineness and unconditional positive regard that Rogers (1951) insisted upon as central to his 'client-centred' therapy, and which Truax and Carkhuff (1967) showed to be essential components of effective counselling and psychotherapy; These are the humanistic principles referred to above. I also take it for granted that, where resources are available, parents are offered supportive counselling. This relationship-building is Step 1 of the process.

Assessment – in line with the Framework for Assessment

Step 2 – Gather Information

Child's developmental needs

Within this domain we shall need to gather brief information about the child's health, educational progress, his overall development and, according to age, his sense of identity and his relationships with other members of his family (see p. 87). This information is not likely all to be forthcoming at once, as parents of children with serious misbehaviours are likely, perhaps more than some other groups of parents such as those whose children are anxious or withdrawn, to need time to unburden themselves of their embarrassment and distress, as their children's conduct can be publicly humiliating. They are also more likely to see the problems as located in the child.

However, with a child with serious behaviour difficulties, we also need additional information or more detailed information to supplement the headings shown on the framework. For example, how did the mother experience her pregnancy? We know from the work of O'Connor et al. (2002) (see p. 14) that the experience of high stress in the third trimester can predispose a child to hyperactivity. What is a typical diet of the child in question? We know from the work of Bateman et al. (2004) that a diet high in colourings or E factors can contribute substantially towards a child's difficult behaviour. Did anything intensify the child's difficult behaviour? If so, these circumstances should be written down in chronological order. Sometimes parents can pinpoint a date or a period that they think contributed significantly to the child's difficulties: an episode of postnatal depression, an accident, an admission to hospital, or a separation of the child's parents.

Completing Appendix 1 with the parents may provide invaluable additional information concerning the aetiology of the child's difficulties. Completing the Strengths and Difficulties Questionnaire (Goodman, 1997) which can be found on the internet will help parents specify the nature of their child's behaviour difficulty, provide a score on a standardised tool of assessment and also highlight the child's strengths; this is likely to be a helpful counterbalance to focusing upon his or her shortcomings. This questionnaire can also be completed by the child's teachers, so giving a more rounded picture of the child. Older children could complete it themselves.

Family and environmental factors

Here we shall be gathering information concerning the family's general circumstances in terms of employment, housing, and what support, if any, that its members receive from the wider community. It may be that the family is extremely isolated, perhaps linked with the child's difficult behaviour and perhaps independently of that. Social isolation is an extremely unpleasant experience for families to deal with, so this factor may be making a major contribution to the difficulties with which the parents are coping.

Parenting capacity

As already discussed, parents with challenging children may find the sheer hard work of managing their children beyond them. Amid so many demands, and sometimes with many other children to care for, parents or caregivers may have just given up, existing in a miserable atmosphere full of shouting and hostility, which may escalate into violence. For example, consider the giving of instructions: to come for tea, to clear up an activity or to get ready for bed. Parents with challenging children often do not give clear instructions. Like us all, they tend to shout from one room to another, to call up the stairs or to give no warning that it is necessary, say, to put the TV off because it is time to go out.

An Example: Simon, Aged Six Years

Simon's developmental needs

Let us consider Simon, who has never been an easy child but whose behaviour is reported as 'difficult and getting worse'. He has terrible tantrums and appears as a wilful and rude child. Donna, Simon's mother, had a difficult pregnancy and found the demands of motherhood exhausting. Simon's relationship with his mother is tense and marked by rude and hurtful remarks. His behaviour deteriorated when his father left the household. His dad has 'access' but does not always keep to the agreement that Simon will spend Saturdays with him. Simon is told to expect him only to find that he does not turn up. Simon then, understandably, becomes impossible to manage for the whole weekend.

Family and environmental factors

Because his mother, Donna, has come to dislike her son so much, and because she now has a new partner, Clancy, Simon's mother sends him to every club and activity that she can find. Simon does like some of these clubs, particularly those with opportunities for physical activities, but he is beginning to be unpopular with the club leaders because of his rudeness and bad relationships with the other club members. Simon's grandmother used to have him for occasional Saturdays but even she is refusing to have him because of his rudeness and aggressiveness.

Parenting capacity

Simon behaves reasonably well when he is alone with Donna and is getting her full attention (and his own way) but the situation becomes difficult when she has to ask him to do things or stop doing things. Donna has a long, long list of criticisms of her son, which she has written down in preparation for her meeting with the worker. She has no positive characteristics of Simon written on her list. Further, Clancy and Simon do not get on, with Clancy frequently on the point of hitting Simon when Simon cheeks him and tells him 'you can't tell me what to do; you're not my dad'.

Step 3 – Identify problem behaviours

Having gathered preliminary relevant background information and identified major developmental or family factors we can move to ask Donna to identify specific problems in Simon's behaviour. These might be:

1. Simon is aggressive: he often kicks and hits his mother.
2. He is deliberately disruptive: he overturns furniture and throws it about.
3. He damages things deliberately books, crockery, household tools, electrical equipment, but not his own belongings.

The arrival of Clancy, Donna's new partner, is making things worse. Simon's behaviour is deteriorating. It is also apparent that Simon is being repeatedly rewarded for his disruptiveness and rudeness by Donna's and Clancy's attention to his misbehaviour in the form of reprimands, rows and complaints.

Step 4 – Identify a positive profile

When asked if Simon shows any positive forms of behaviour, Donna winces and says that he used to be very loving but this seldom shows itself now. However, she is able to think of three behaviours that Simon still occasionally displays and which she would like to increase.

1. He sometimes brings Donna the newspaper to read before she gets up.
2. However awful his behaviour, he still says 'sorry, Mum' when he goes to bed.
3. He looks after Toffee, the family dog, very well.

It will of course be essential to meet with Simon and to gain his view of the situation. There may well be early events or other factors that are contributing to his disruptive and aggressive behaviour, of which Donna and Clancy are unaware. It may be that Simon is being bullied and has not told Donna about it. If this is so and if, with Simon's permission, the practitioner can tell Donna about this, she is likely to be very concerned for her child.

Step 5 – Clarify what Donna really wants

As Donna is Simon's mother and Clancy's future in the household is uncertain, it will be Donna who says what she really wants in respect of Simon's behaviour but it will probably be necessary to try to involve Clancy in the plan. It emerged in the assessment that Simon is missing his own dad badly and she knows already that it is his dad's failure to turn up to collect Simon that acts as the antecedent or trigger to Simon's worst behaviour, Donna is likely to have some sympathy for Simon over this matter. In respect of Simon's day-to-day behaviour, she may well be able to specify the following goals:

1. That when she has to say 'no' to something that Simon demands, he will accept this.

2. That he will speak calmly and quietly to Clancy even if he is feeling angry.
3. That he will do what she asks him more often than not.

Step 6 – Develop a formulation: share key ideas with parents/carers

At this stage there are likely to be two tasks confronting the worker:

1. To help the family make sense of why the problems developed in the first place, taking into account the life events of the parents, the extended family and the child. This can be seen as a 'formulation' of the problem.
2. To teach the parents some basic strategies for managing Simon when his behaviour becomes troublesome. These are based on common sense but it will be necessary for all those who care for the child to work together. We can assure them confidently that there is excellent research evidence for the effectiveness of the strategies, which we will work together with them to put into practice.

I have found it useful to describe problems, both those stemming from the child and from all the family circumstance, in terms of 'stresses' with which the various family members are coping. This term is usually acceptable; everyone experiences stress and it is a nonstigmatising word. So we can reframe what we have heard of their circumstances in terms of the stresses they have caused. In this case we can convey our empathy for Donna and Clancy in their difficult position, but then we can show our concern for Simon; he is likely to be deeply distressed by the changed relationship with his dad and to idealise him in his absence. At the same time he also has to adjust to the arrival of Clancy as his mother's new companion, and Simon is only six years old!

The overall formulation might be as shown in Box 9.7.

Step 7 – Gather data as an aid to assessment

Donna has identified three positive and three negative behaviours whose frequency can be recorded. It will be wise to start with the least complex of the three behaviours because the practitioner herself needs to experience success in her efforts to help parents before tackling deeply entrenched or longstanding difficulties. Thus, starting with damaging toys or tools would probably be the wisest course, or another not-too-deeply-entrenched behaviour. The positive behaviour that she would like to increase is Simon's carrying out an instruction when asked.

It is a mistake to embark upon a plan of intervention without gaining a 'baseline' against which to measure improvement or deterioration. In this first week Donna should continue to handle Simon just as she has before, not attempting to do anything differently. She should, however, gather the

---

Box 9.7: Preliminary assessment of/rationale for the difficulties of Simon, aged six years

1. *Simon's developmental needs*
   (a) Simon is still quite small for his age; this embarrasses him.
   (b) Simon seems to be a lonely child; he has no friends.
2. *Family and environmental factors*
   (a) Simon's Dad left when Simon was four. He seems to be missing him very deeply.
   (b) Simon may be being bullied or otherwise unhappy at school.
   (c) Clancy joined the family eight months ago. Simon resents him.
3. *Parenting capacity: interactions within the family (A–B–C)**
   (a) The activator (cue) to the worst misbehaviour is Simon's dad's failure to collect him on a Saturday morning.
   (b) Unintentionally, Donna and Clancy have been rewarding the very behaviour they complain of in Simon by their inconsistent reactions to it.

*Donna and Clancy may not understand this concept but it is useful to introduce it at this stage.

'baseline' counts of both the negative, the destructive behaviour and the positive, the helpful behaviour. The chart (see Appendix 6) used to collect the data is likely to look something like Table 9.1.

Parents often ask whether they should hide the record sheets while they are gathering the baseline and other data. My view is that they should be matter-of-fact about them: they should have them available to record information, make no attempt to hide them and if questioned about them by their son or daughter, give a truthful but non-committal answer – something along the lines of 'oh, I'm just keeping a count of how many times you kick me – or swear at me – and how many times you do something I ask you to do'.

Step 8 – Planning

Donna, the practitioner and Clancy, if this seems fitting, are now participants in a shared effort to help Simon. As a six year old, he too can be involved in the plan. As indicated, one way forward is the method of testing hypotheses. We may or may not use this terminology with the parents but we ourselves should be clear about which hypotheses we are testing. In respect of Simon, they might be:

1. Simon's aggressive behaviours will decrease if it is possible to explain to Paul, his Dad, how much his little boy is missing him. Simon needs

Table 9.1 Number of instances of Simon's positive and negative behaviours over one week

CHARTING BEHAVIOURS					Name: Simon		Week beginning: 14 May	
Behaviour	Sunday	Monday	Tuesday	Wednesday	Thursday	Friday	Saturday	Total
Behaviours to encourage and praise								
Morning	√	√	√	√	√	√	√	
Afternoon	√						√	
Evening	√				√		√	12
Behaviours to discourage								
Morning	√√						√√	
Afternoon	√√						√√	
Evening	√√	√	√√	√√√	√	√√	√√	24

his reliable support and encouragement (an agreement might be one way forward). See Chapter 12.

2. Simon's destructive behaviours will decrease:
   (a) as he experiences more attention for his positive behaviours
   (b) if there are clear sanctions for his damaging things.
3. Simon's non compliance (disobedience) will reduce as he experiences more consistent responses to his demands.

In order to test out these ideas, it will be necessary to use the baseline measures of Simon's positive and negative behaviours as benchmarks against which to assess progress or deterioration (see Table 9.1). This baseline information is likely to offer Donna some surprises. Typical reactions on the parts of parents are:

● The positive/negative behaviour is much more frequent than had been expected.
● The positive/negative behaviour is much less frequent than had been expected.
● The positive/negative behaviour occurs at specific times of day/days of the week.
● The positive/negative behaviour occurs in association with certain people, etc.

When the new information arising from these records has been discussed and its implications explored, we can work with Donna in a systematic attempt to improve Simon's behaviour.

Features of the plan for Donna and Simon

It would be desirable to develop a formal plan as shown in Box 5.4, page 120, but for economy the essential features are shown in list form.

1. *Reward/reinforce positive features of Simon's behaviour.* Donna should pay clear, direct attention to the positive aspects of Simon's behaviour – for example, his bringing her a morning cup of tea or his saying 'sorry' but in particular his carrying out an instruction. We should ask Donna to tell Simon clearly and directly after each instance of the positive behaviour that when he behaves in this way she is very pleased with him. This praise may open the way to some renewed communication between Donna and Simon. At this stage, when mother and son are trying to rebuild their relationship, Donna should have Simon's needs to the fore and she should avoid talk of Clancy.

2. *Penalise instances of negative behaviour*. There are three main strategies for dealing with these, as we saw in Chapter 2:
   (a) *Ignore petty, demanding behaviours* so that they fade away because they are not reinforced with attention. Whining, pestering, grumbling and fault finding can all usually be successfully dealt with in this way.
   (b) *Give and carry through on a firm punishment*, e.g. the loss of television time or a pocket money fine.
   (c) *Time out/calm down time* (Webster-Stratton & Herbert, 1994). This involves removing the child from the reward of being in the centre-stage to a place where he can be totally ignored. For details of using time out/calm down, see Box 2.11, p. 62.
3. *Helping Donna explain the plan to Simon*. If a child is to be dealt with in a different way, with his positive behaviours attended to and commended and the negative behaviours ignored or mildly punished, then it is only sensible to explain the intended changes to him; otherwise there will be an unnecessary confusion for the child while he is trying to 'work out the new rules'. We should therefore advise Donna to set time aside to explain the new way in which she will respond to Simon and if this will be difficult the practitioner can go through the necessary steps by means of a simple role-play.

Some families find it helpful if the worker writes down the precise steps to take in some specific circumstances – for example, turn your back on petty, irritating behaviours and attend to the ones you would like to see happen again. I myself have a notebook with a carbon page, so that both the parents and I have an identical copy. The plan to help Donna and Simon might look something like that in Box 9.8.

Step 9 – Implement the plan

Over the next few days, it will be important for the worker to be in touch with Donna as she attempts to put the plan into effect. Sometimes a weekly contact is sufficient but in line with cognitive-behavioural theory it may well be appropriate to offer more immediate contact – say within two or three days of her embarking on the new regime. This is to reinforce Donna's efforts to alter her patterns of responding to Simon. She should be encouraged to follow the agreed plan and to continue to keep records (Figure 9.1) to see if the problem behaviour becomes worse or better.

Step 10 – Review and evaluate the intervention

To review the intervention is to monitor it on a regular basis – usually weekly or twice weekly to see how far it is being successful. It will require the

Box 9.8: Sample plan devised by Donna, Simon and Melanie (family aide)

Name of child: Simon   *Date of birth*: 10 October

The following factors seem to be important in the child's difficulties:

1. Simon is missing his Dad badly and wants regular contact with him.
2. He is being called horrible names at school and is sometimes being bullied.
3. He is finding it hard to get used to Clancy being about and taking Donna's attention.

Target behaviours for this week:

Positive: (deliberately placed first) Simon's bringing Donna a cup of tea or newspaper.
Negative: Simon's damaging toys or household items.

Action plan agreed by Donna

In order to try to help Simon, Donna has agreed to the following:

1. To contact Simon's dad and agree to cooperating fully over access arrangements.
2. Go to Simon's school and report that Simon is being bullied.
3. To find three things for which to praise Simon each day: e.g., bringing her a cup of tea, taking his dishes to the washing up machine and giving Toffee his dinner every day.
4. To tell Simon that she knows it is hard for him to say 'sorry' after one of his outbursts, and although she would rather not have the breakages, she is glad he says 'sorry'.
5. Each school day, Donna will spend 10 minutes listening to anything Simon would like to tell her about school. She will show interest and not tell him off about anything.
6. If Simon damages toys or household items she will give him one warning. If he continues, she will send him to spend four minutes calm down time in the hallway, where he will be completely ignored. If he does damage there he will stay a further four minutes. Damaged items will not be replaced.

Action plan agreed by Melanie

1. Will meet with Donna and Clancy within the week to explain the plan to Clancy.
2. She will contact the family in one week to see how the plan is working.

This will be reviewed on . . . . Signed . . . . Signed . . . .

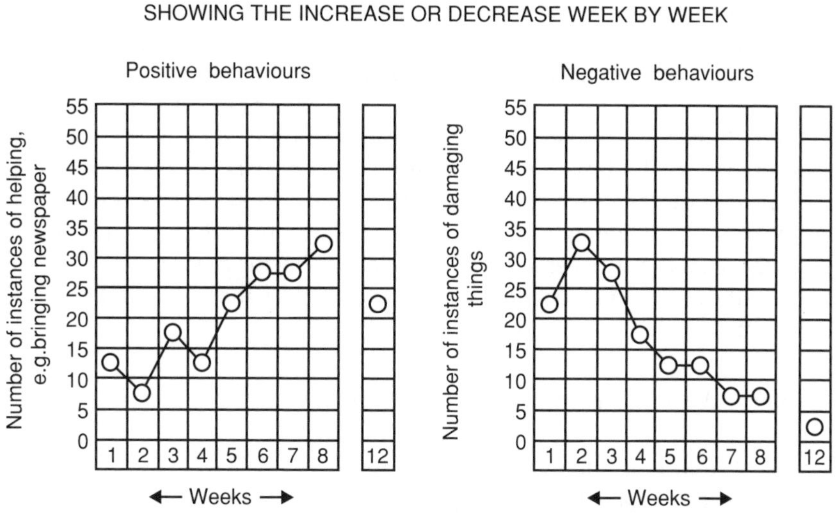

SHOWING THE INCREASE OR DECREASE WEEK BY WEEK

Figure 9.1 Simon's positive and negative behaviour over 8 weeks and at 3 months' followup

practitioner to be in touch with Donna frequently, particularly at the beginning of the intervention, for three purposes:

1. To commend and reinforce Donna's efforts to manage Simon by positive methods.
2. To consider the quantitative data – that is, the counts of positive and negative behaviour that Donna is recording on the charts and to encourage Donna to persist in her efforts to attend to Simon's positive behaviour rather than the negative.
3. To consider the qualitative information – that is, Donna's accounts of her experiences in trying to respond differently to Simon's troublesome behaviour.

Donna has some questions to ask:

Question 1. What should she do if Simon misbehaves at someone else's house, if, for example, they are visiting friends or relatives?

Answer: Donna should express confidence in Simon before they leave home and say that she is looking forward to going visiting with him. She should say this as if she means it, even if she has her worries.

Question 2: What should she do if Simon nevertheless misbehaves at her friend's house?

Answer: Donna should say to her friend that Simon does sometimes misbehave. Is there a safe, dull and boring place where, as at home, Simon could be required to spend four minutes alone? In other words, Simon should be dealt with as far as possible in exactly the same way as if they were all at home. If she uses other sanctions at home, such as loss of pocket money or of TV time then these should be imposed when at the friend's house so that Simon has to cope with hearing the sanctions being spoken of in public. He may increase the misbehaviour but Donna must stand firm, drawing if necessary on her friend's backing. If absolutely necessary they should go home at once and still the sanctions will be put into effect.

Question 3: What should Donna do if Simon behaves badly when out shopping?

Answer: If at all possible they should go home at once and Simon should be required to spend four minutes in time out as soon as they go through the front door. If this is impossible then Simon should be told calmly that he will lose so many minutes of his permitted television time that day or the next, or he should be told that he will lose so much of his weekly pocket money. This should be put into effect as soon as possible in a calm, matter-of-fact way. Donna should try to keep very calm, and *not* argue with Simon, but she must do as she has said she will.

The best true example of the application of the necessary firmness recounted to me was of a family going on holiday to the coast. Mum and then Dad asked several times for quiet behaviour from the children in the back of the car. When they continued in their rowdy behaviour, he gave one warning that if they were not quiet for the next 15 minutes when he was driving in a congested area he would turn the car round and they would all go home. The children did not believe him and pushed their luck. Dad said, 'Right, that's it; you've had one warning. We're going home.' He turned the car round and the whole family went home in stunned disbelief. The next day the journey to the coast was accomplished in near silence!

Evaluation takes place at the end of the intervention. It is the systematic comparison of the state of affairs at the beginning, in respect of both Donna's feelings of depression and Simon's difficult behaviour, with the state of affairs at the end. If any scales have been employed to measure any of these circumstances, for example the Beck Depression Inventory or the Strengths and Difficulties Questionnaire, then these can be completed again and the start and end scores compared.

There are bound to be difficulties in attempting to help parents change patterns of behaviour that have been established over many months and years of a child's life. If the assessment has been carried out accurately, however, and the caregivers are actually attempting to carry out the principles that have been discussed and incorporated into the plan, then it is highly likely that the child's behaviour difficulties will begin to subside and more positive behaviours to increase.

10

HELPING FAMILIES WITH CHILDREN WITH ATTENTION DEFICIT HYPERACTIVITY DISORDER

DIFFICULTIES OF ARRIVING AT DEFINITIONS AND DIAGNOSES

As explained in Chapter 9, there is a broad consensus that a distinct syndrome, with organic underpinnings, has been distinguished from the overarching category of conduct disorder. This syndrome has been variously named. At the time of writing the World Health Organization in its International Classification of Diseases, 10th edition (ICD-10), published in 1992, uses the term 'hyperkinetic disorder' and this has in the past been used in the UK. However, it is fast being overtaken by the American term, 'attention deficit hyperactivity disorder' (ADHD) which is included in the Diagnostic and Statistical Manual of Psychiatric Disorders, 4th edn (DSM-IV) published by the American Psychiatric Association in 1994. The term 'attention deficit disorder' (ADD) is sometimes used to describe broadly the same condition, as is 'attention deficit hyperkinetic disorder' (AD-HKD).

Descriptions of ADHD

There is increasing consensus that the syndrome of ADHD includes three main characteristic behaviours: attention deficit (short attention span), overactivity and impulsiveness. These are also features of most children's behaviour but where they are severe and continuing and where they are manifested in many different settings a diagnosis of ADHD may be considered. Of the many descriptions, that of Taylor (1994) seems among the clearest:

- *Attention deficit.* The behaviours involved are those of orientating only briefly to tasks imposed by adults, changing activities rapidly when spontaneous choice is allowed, orientating towards irrelevant aspects of the environment and playing for brief periods only.
- *Overactivity.* Overactivity means an excess of movements. The idea is simple but there is a wide range of activity in the normal population and no very clear point at which activity level becomes excessive. Overactivity can refer to an increased tempo of normal activities, an increase in purposeless, minor movements that are irrelevant to the task in hand (fidgeting), or an amount of movement of the whole body that is excessive for the situation (restlessness). The excess of movements is there even when hyperactive children are in bed and asleep (Porrino et al., 1983), so it is unlikely to be secondary to attention deficit.
- *Impulsiveness.* This means acting without reflection. In different contexts this may imply getting into dangerous situations because of recklessness, thoughtless rule breaking or impetuously acting out of turn when with other children.

Taylor goes on to remind us that: All these styles of behaviour are present to some degree in many normal children...Clinical definition of an affected individual therefore needs to be based upon a firm idea of what is expected of children at that age and of that developmental level...

Diagnosing ADHD

This is ordinarily a task for a child psychiatrist or a paediatrician and will usually involve observations at first hand, rather than the practitioner simply taking the word of parents or teachers. Similarly, a child must meet criteria for both inattentiveness and hyperactivity/impulsiveness (see Box 10.1). A child who is only inattentive or only hyperactive will not usually receive this diagnosis.

Additionally, many diagnosticians require that because some very active children show situation-specific behaviour, for example they are constantly moving and on the go at home with mother or father but are models of quiet behaviour with Gran, who 'won't put up with all this jigging-about behaviour', their hyperactivity should be assessed independently in at least two settings, typically home and school.

Conduct disorders and ADHD do overlap substantially and some researchers consider that they are the same disorder from different perspectives. Taylor (1994), however, considers that the indications that ADHD is often associated with developmental delays in motor, language and cognitive skills, while conduct disorders are not, suggest a different aetiology. Further, children who were found to be both hyperactive and conduct disorered when

---

Box 10.1: Features of children with attention deficit hyperactivity disorder. Criteria for ADHD according to *Diagnostic and Statistical Manual IV* (1994)

The child shows either maladaptive inattention or hyperactivity-impulsivity, or both, for at least six months, as marked by the following:

1. Inattention: at least six of the following
   fails to pay close attention to details or makes careless errors in schoolwork
   has trouble keeping attention on tasks or play
   doesn't appear to listen when being told something
   does not follow through on instructions . . .
   has trouble organizing activities and tasks
   dislikes/avoids tasks that involve sustained effort
   loses materials needed for activities
   is easily distracted
   is forgetful
2. Hyperactivity-impulsivity: at least six of the following often apply
   squirms in seat or fidgets
   inappropriately leaves seat
   inappropriately runs or climbs
   has trouble playing quietly or engaging in leisure activity
   appears driven or on the go
   talks excessively
3. Impulsivity
   answers qustions before they have been completely asked
   has trouble awaiting his turn
   interrupts or intrudes upon others

---

referred at age seven or eight continued to be at risk of conduct disorder when followed up: by contrast, those with conduct disorder at age seven did not become hyperactive when followed up (Taylor et al., 1991). This author concludes that 'hyperactivity is one of the routes into conduct disorder' (see Rutter, Taylor & Hersov, 1994, p. 289).

These behaviours are common in most young children, but that it becomes a problem when the characteristics are exaggerated, compared with other children of the same age.

PREVALENCE OF ADHD

Because of the looseness of definition of the term, several researchers have found different patterns of prevalence. An early working party of the British

Psychological Society (1996) reported that in the United States, where ADHD was an inclusive psychiatric category, rates of 2 %–10 % had been reported, but that European diagnostic practice was more stringent and suggested a prevalence rate of 0.5 %–1.0 % of the total child population. Since then, however, there has been a convergence of the two main diagnostic manuals, ICD-10 and DSM-IV, and this had led to revised figures of 6 %–8 % in the United States and 3 %–5 % in the United Kingdom (Myttas 2001).

RESEARCH INTO ADHD

Research into Origins

The evidence suggests that a multifactorial model encompassing many contributory factors is necessary to understand ADHD. Some of the major ones are considered below.

Genetic and organic influences

Goodman & Stevenson (1989) undertook an analysis of data from teacher and parent questionnaires on a large sample of twins from the general population and concluded that the greater frequency with which hyperactivity is found in monozygotic rather than in dizygotic twins indicates a genetic contribution to the disorder. Other researchers, such as Rutter, Giller and Hagell (1998), go further and write 'The genetic component for this behavior is preponderant, acounting for some 60 %–70 % of the variance or possibly even more'. There is now a general consensus that genetic factors are deeply implicated in the disorder.

Socioeconomic and structural factors

As indicated, there is a higher prevalence of children who appear to exhibit the behaviours characteristic of ADHD in the inner cities than elsewhere. This suggests that features accompanying the disadvantage that often characterises families living in the inner city, such as high levels of stress for parents and reduced play opportunities, may be contributing to the manifestation of the syndrome.

Factors highlighted by a cognitive-behavioural analysis

The unwitting and unintentional rewarding of demanding and restless behaviour in children and inconsistent management by isolated and exhausted parents almost certainly make a major contribution to the persistence of very active behaviour (Barkley, 1995; Sutton, 1995).

What Affects the Prognosis for a Child with ADHD?

As indicated, longitudinal studies have shown that there are many continuities in patterns of behaviour between infants as they grow into children, adolescents and adults. Lyon (1996), in a detailed analysis of a multifactorial model, has reported:

> The prognosis of an AD/HD child depends upon how nature and nurture interact with one another. It is when a high level of hyperactivity...combines with other risk factors that a negative outcome becomes likely. Conversely, decreasing the number of risk factors greatly increases the likelihood of a good outcome. The risk factors are as follows:

- Depressive or mental illness in mother.
- Anti-social father.
- Previous failed marriages.
- Lack of mutual support within marriage.
- High level of negative expressed emotion in family.
- Parents who are overly directive, issuing many commands to their child.
- Parents who initiate fewer interactions.
- A high level of hyperactivity when the child is young.
- Low self-esteem (created by failure in other areas).
- Poor social skills (as a result of social ineptness, and/or because of language difficulties).
- Aggression.
- Conduct disorder.
- Social, academic or learning difficulties at school.

RESEARCH CONCERNING THE MANAGEMENT OF ADHD

A Multifactorial Model

There is common agreement that, just as there is no single model of the aetiology of ADHD, so there is no single model of effective intervention. The British Psychological Society (1996) has concluded that a multidimensional conceptualisation of both causation and intervention is necessary (Figure 10.1). While acknowledging this multidimensionality, we can still distinguish some common approaches in trying to help parents of affected children, their teachers and the children themselves. Four major approaches will be examined: adjusting the diet of the individual child, cognitive-behavioural strategies, problem-solving approaches and adapting the environment to the child.

Research Focusing upon Dietary Factors

The working party mentioned above noted the links that have been made between ADHD and substances in the diet of the affected child. It reports

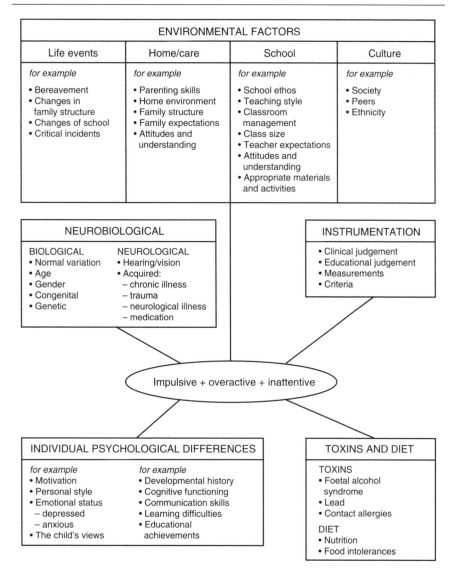

Figure 10.1   Areas of information to be considered in assessment of ADHD

Source: Reproduced by permission from British Psychological Society (1996). *Attention Deficit Hyperactivity Disorder (ADHD): A Psychological Response to an Evolving Concept.* Leicester: BPS.

two well designed studies (Egger, Carter, Graham, Gumley & Soothill, 1985; Carter et al., 1993), which found associations between certain specific substances in the child's diet and subsequent behaviour difficulties. These were children with 'multiple food intolerances' and parents had already noted the tendency for their children's behaviour to deteriorate when they had eaten specific allergens, including chocolate and certain food additives. In these circumstances the advice of a nutritional expert is essential. Following the working party's conclusion that the field of the impact of diet upon children's difficult behaviour was 'under-researched and controversial', a major study (Bateman et al., 2004) showed that there is indeed an effect of diet upon children's behaviour. The work in Southampton involving 277 hyperactive 3 year olds has been summarised as follows:

> Children were given dietary challenges in the form of a drink containing colourings and preservatives and a placebo drink. The parents, blind as to which drink was being given, reported more hyperactive behaviour while their children received the drink with additives than when they had the placebo drink. This was a carefully conducted trial and has considerable implications for public health intervention, for example policies on drinks permitted in schools.
> (Gardner, Lane & Hutchings, 2004)

In view of the relative ease with which a child's diet can be influenced, by contrast with his behaviour, it seems common sense for practitioners to work with parents towards eliminating substances that may be exacerbating a child's behaviour difficulties.

Research Focusing upon Cognitive-behavioural Approaches

The working party cited above reviewed the evidence for a range of ways of managing affected children. It considered the review by Fiore, Becker and Nero (1993), who examined 150 studies of intervention most of which were based upon cognitive-behavioural principles. The authors identified seven strategies of intervention, four of the most successful of which are paraphrased as follows:

1. *Positive reinforcement or token reinforcement.* These strategies appeared to result in reduced activity, increased 'time on task' and improved academic performance. The methods were seen as cost-effective, could be applied fairly easily to individuals or groups and were relatively familiar to most educators.
2. *Behaviour reduction strategies.* Mildly aversive short and immediate procedures (reprimands or redirection) seemed effective with primary-age children, especially when combined with positive reinforcement.
3. *Response cost.* A combination of positive and negative reinforcement procedures through the use of tokens was seen as promising for teachers. This would represent the next step if positive reinforcement did not result in sufficient effects.
4. *Parent or family training.* Some studies demonstrated effectiveness in reducing activity level and conflict intensity with an increase in 'on task'

behaviour and compliance. Parents reported reduced stress and better interaction and communication with their children. Medication formed part of most treatment strategies.

Research Focusing upon a Problem-solving Approach

This approach has been found particularly relevant to the management of ADHD because of the multiplicity of complex situations that a child with ADHD generates and because of their impact upon other people. To recap, the essence of the approach as suggested by Falloon, Laporta, Fadden and Graham-Hole (1993) is that one goes through the following steps:

1. Pinpoint the problem or goal.
2. List all possible solutions.
3. Highlight likely consequences of each course of action.
4. Agree on 'best' strategy.
5. Plan and implement this strategy.
6. Review results.

This approach has been found effective, by comparison with other approaches, for handling a range of complex situations and is certainly of relevance for the management of children with ADHD. It could only be employed, however, with children with a level of cognitive development adequate to understanding the steps of the approach.

RESEARCH FOCUSING UPON ORGANISATIONAL STRATEGIES

Burcham, Carlson and Milich (1993) in their review of studies in the United States, which address the management of children with ADHD from the perspective of how to structure and organise the experiences from which children can best benefit, found that settings that proved helpful to children and their families were those in which there were 'positive attitudes and understandings of ADHD arising from staff development, support at authority policy level and provision of coordinated intervention through teams of professional workers'. In other words, money and resources have to be made available to develop individualised care and educational programmes for children and to see that they are faithfully monitored and evaluated.

Barkley (1995), an American psychologist who has specialised in the field of ADHD and who has written a particularly helpful book for parents, *Taking Charge of AD/HD*, has concluded that the two most effective strategies for managing children with this difficulty are time out/calm down time (see p. 62) and response cost (see p. 230). Lyon (1996), a British educational psychologist who has specialised in this area, while agreeing with Barkley, favours three additional strategies:

1. *Helping the child to learn to relax.* A simple tape can be used for this, and all family members can enjoy resting together. The child may need quiet, soothing encouragement to rest calmly until a ringer sounds, and can earn some simple but satisfying reward for this. This time can gradually be extended from, say, 2 minutes to 5 or 10.
2. *Managing the environment.* Arranging the house or classroom to minimise upset and damage which can arise from restless and impulsive behaviour.
3. *Problem solving.* As children grow older, involving them in the task of how to manage the difficulty, much as one would if a child had diabetes or was enuretic. This essentially identifies times or situations that cause stress for the child and his or her caregivers and draws upon the child's creativity, experience and thoughtfulness as a means of solving the problems created by restlessness and overactivity.

HELPING PARENTS WITH CHILDREN WITH FEATURES OF ADHD

At present in the United Kingdom it is usually necessary for a diagnosis of ADHD to be made by a paediatrician or senior medical officer. General practitioners are not usually in a position to make this diagnosis and to prescribe medication. As indicated, it is desirable that the child's behaviour should be observed in each of the main settings where the child spends time: certainly independent measures in the home and school environment are called for. When such a diagnosis of ADHD *has* been made and if medication *is* prescribed, then there is the necessity for close liaison among those who have responsibility for the child. By contrast with medical approaches, I shall be focusing here upon the psychological support and management of the child and his family. The same steps as those in the ASPIRE process – Assessment, Planning, Implementation, Review and Evaluation – are followed.

Parents of a child who exhibits features of ADHD are likely to be exhausted. Their restless, impulsive child may have worn them out by sheer liveliness, demands and inability to settle to any sustained period of playing, reading or writing alone. Further, they are likely to have few friends and relations willing to invite the child to their house or to babysit. Many seek a medical diagnosis in order to give a respectable explanation for their child's difficult behaviour. It is crucial to allow parents to give voice to their frustration, anger and exasperation and to their distress as they see their child getting into social and educational difficulties. This relationship building constitutes Step 1 of the approach.

Assessment

Step 2 – Gather information

Where there is concern about whether a child is displaying features of ADHD, a medical examination is essential. As services for this group of children improve, so there are likely to be improved screening and diagnostic tools available for both parents and teachers. The authors of the BPS Working Party Report (British Psychological Society, 1996) identify two of the most commonly used scales:

1. *The Child Behaviour Checklist for Parents* (Achenbach, 1991) and the Teacher's Report Form (Achenbach & Edelbrock, 1986), which together give three scales dealing with social competence (activities, social behaviour and school behaviour) and nine scales dealing with specific childhood diagnostic categories. The inventory is regarded as one of the most comprehensive and has been subjected to psychometric standardisation in many languages.
2. *The Conners Parent and Teacher Rating Scales* (Conners, 1973; Goyette, Conners & Ulrich, 1978) have become widely used inventories. They include a 48-item scale for parents with five factors: impulsive-hyperactive, learning problems, conduct problems, psychosomatic factors and anxiety. The 39-item Teacher Rating Scale collects complementary information from the school setting.

If it is difficult for health visitors, social workers and school nurses to gain access to these scales, then hyperactivity features as one of the sub-scales on the Strengths and Difficulties Questionnaire (Goodman, 1997) and this is readily available on the Internet In any case, as multidisciplinary initiatives increase it is likely that any child thought to display ADHD will be offered first, a coordinated assessment and then a coodinated care plan.

Ideally, the child and family need one person as key worker, both as contact practitioner and to monitor the working of the plan. While working towards such a plan, the following basic information can be gathered, using the standard assessment framework, see page 8, with the now familiar domains.

The example of Leonie, aged five years

Consider Leonie, an African-Caribbean little girl, aged five. It is beyond the scope of this book to consider the detailed assessment that would be required both to arrive at a decision whether Leonie may be considered to have a diagnosis of ADHD, and what the detailed action plan may be, but we may nevertheless be able to be helpful to the families concerned. Some children may be seen by paediatricians or child psychiatrists as suffering so clearly from ADHD as to require medication. This has the effect of stimulating the inhibitory systems within the brain and may benefit certain children. Increasingly, however, medication is being supplemented by training parents in cognitive-behavioural methods so that they have strategies in place to manage the child if medication is reduced or withdrawn.

Leonie then is an exceptionally active child, who slept poorly from birth and whose parents, Valerie and Michael, are desperate for help. They had thought that things would improve when Leonie went to school but the opposite has happened: the teachers at two schools have complained about her restlessness and so her parents have removed her and persuaded another school to take her. Both parents are beginning actively to dislike their child and they say they are tempted to tell her so. No-one will invite her to play with their children and no-one will babysit. As a result the parents have lost all their friends. They have sought help from their GP, but he has told them there is nothing he can do: the child is not ill. He says he will refer her to the child psychiatrist, who has a long waiting list. Leonie says, 'I try to keep still, but my body won't let me'.

Michael tells you of a recent incident involving a visit from his mother. When Leonie's grandma brought a box of chocolates for the family, Leonie jumped up, grabbed it, shouted, 'I don't like these chocolates! They're crap!' and threw them out of the window. Valerie tried to play down the incident, but Michael was furious and shouted, 'you're a spoiled brat!' He had a huge row with Leonie, who kept cheeking him back, and then with Valerie about Leonie. Leonie seemed quite pleased to have got everyone so worked up. Grandma left in tears.

It is not typically within our sphere of knowledge and skill to make a diagnosis of ADHD. However, since there are many patterns of behaviour which are common to ADHD and to generally uncontrolled or disruptive behaviour, we may well be able to offer some initial help pending a fuller assessment by paediatrician or child psychiatrist (see Box 10.2).

Step 3 – Identify problem behaviours

Having gathered relevant background information and identified major organic or developmental factors which may be affecting Leonie, the practitioner can move to asking Valerie and Michael, her parents, to identify *specific* problems in the child's behaviour. The following can be pinpointed:

1. Leonie is extremely restless: she runs everywhere and finds it hard to sit still.

Box 10.2: Preliminary assessment of Leonie's difficulties

1. *The child's developmental needs, including,*
   - Information from the child's parents and, depending on age, from the child.
   - At what age Leonie began to display very active behaviour.
   - Information as to whether either parent or other close relative displayed very active behaviour similar to Leonie's.
   - Psychological assessment:
     - measurements of intellectual ability
     - reports of levels of attainment
     - tests of attention and impulsiveness
     - social adjustment
   - Information from the child's teacher(s) about classroom behaviour/ performance.
   - Information from rating scales completed by both parents and teachers.
2. *Family and environmental factors*
   Assessment of this domain will include details of the family's history and functioning, the stresses imposed on family members by the child's condition and the extent to which parents can draw upon community and other resources to help them in managing their restless and impulsive child.
3. *Parenting capacity*
   Here the assessment will focus upon the capacity of the parents to set boundaries for their child, to give basic care and guidance and to continue to offer love and affection despite the ongoing demands and frustrations posed by their child. A sophisticated assessment will also focus upon the interactions between parents and child in terms of A–B–C.

---

2. She is very impulsive: she seldom seems to think ahead or plan and, as the incident over the box of chocolates shows, does not seem able to control her actions.
3. She has a very short attention span, of perhaps half a minute, so she moves quickly from one activity to another.

Whatever Leonie may have inherited, her behaviour has become unacceptable to both her parents and her teachers. Similarly, whether or not a formal diagnosis of ADHD is made, there needs to be a concerted effort on the part of her parents and teachers to help her calm and control her behaviour.

Step 4 – Identify a positive profile

When asked if Leonie shows any positive forms of behaviour, her parents initially say 'no', but then acknowledge that she still shows a few behaviours that they like very much:

1. She is very affectionate. The only time she does sit still is when she is sitting on her Mum's or Dad's lap. This can last for five minutes or more.
2. While sitting on someone's lap, she will look at story books for up to five minutes.
3. She will sit quietly for a few minutes if doing a jigsaw or watching television.

When the worker talks to Leonie, she says she hates being 'so jumpy' but she 'can't help it'. When asked about sitting on her parents' laps, she smiles and says that it is 'lovely'. She doesn't feel so jumpy then.

Step 5 – Clarify what Leonie's parents really want

Leonie's parents are quite clear what they want: they want Leonie to 'calm down'. They have been to see their GP repeatedly and he has agreed to refer Leonie to the local paediatrician. There is, however, a lengthy waiting list. Meanwhile they are begging for help from anyone who has clear suggestions about what to do. They pinpoint the following goals:

1. That Leonie will learn to sit quietly for 3 periods of 15 minutes daily at home.
2. That Leonie will learn to sit quietly for 3 periods of 15 minutes daily at school.
3. That when Leonie feels 'jumpy' she will tell a grown-up and talk about how to deal with the 'jumpiness'.

Step 6 – Arrive at a formulation: key ideas shared with parents

When the practitioner has gathered as much relevant information as possible from parents, teachers and the child, all of which will contribute to the framework for assessment, it may be possible to explore the current situation with Leonie's parents. It is likely that the practitioner will discuss both developmental and environmental contributions to the present state of affairs. Parents who have been expecting a primarily medical formulation may find it difficult to accept that circumstances within the environment contribute at all to the difficulties but as there appear to be few children for whom an exclusively medical diagnosis is made it is probably wise to refer to both developmental and environmental factors when discussing the child's difficulties.

As stated in Chapter 9, we have several main responsibilities to those who seek our help:

1. Within the limits of our professional competence, to discuss with the parents a rationale for why the problems may have developed in the first place, taking into account all the available evidence. We cannot discuss genetic factors without specialist training but with appropriate supervision from, for example, a paediatrician, we may be able to help a family understand that a child's genetic endowment is important. He or she is not being deliberately naughty. The impact of environmental factors may be best described in terms of 'stresses' with which the family is having to cope.
2. According to our role and the decisions made concerning the use of medication, to clarify that we shall be liaising with medical and other personnel.
3. To teach the parents some basic strategies for managing Leonie in order to complement the effects of any medication which may be prescribed.

We can convey empathy for the parents who are finding their lives increasingly centring around Leonie. We can also show concern for Leonie herself, who is likely to be an unhappy little girl with no friends at school and little affection at home. She is unable to find her own way out of her predicament. Even though medication, if prescribed, is likely to calm Leonie's behaviour down somewhat, it is unlikely to relieve the problem of her overactive behaviour permanently and it certainly will not provide her with ready-made friends. Liaison among all concerned is essential. The paediatrician may or may not consider medication appropriate but in any case a coordinated strategy of offering a brief period of medication, supplemented by support for the parents by training them in cognitive-behavioural strategies, may provide the most constructive response to ADHD.

Step 7 – Gather data as an aid to assessment

Leonie's parents have identified three positive and three negative behaviours whose frequency can be recorded. It will be wise to start with the least complex of the three behaviours because the practitioner herself needs to experience success in her efforts to help parents before tackling deeply entrenched and longstanding difficulties. Thus, starting with trying to extend Leonie's period of calm behaviour would probably be most appropriate.

In this first week Leonie's parents should gather 'baseline' counts of both the negative, restless, roaming-about behaviour and of positive, calm, settled behaviour. An instance of calm behaviour is: 'Leonie is provided with story books, bricks and Lego and is encouraged to settle to play with them. She plays with them for a period of three minutes.'

An instance of restless behaviour is: 'Leonie is provided with story books, bricks and Lego and is encouraged to settle to play with them. She ignores them and roams or runs about restlessly for a period of three minutes.'

Box 10.3: Preliminary assessment/formulation of Leonie's difficulties

1. *In terms of Leonie's developmental needs*
   (a) It seems at least possible that a medical diagnosis of ADHD will be made.
   (b) She *is* very active and may have inherited a predisposition to this, as Valerie has a sister who has great difficulty in concentrating.
   (c) Leonie has already had two changes of school.
2. *In terms of family and environmental factors*
   (a) The whole family is becoming increasingly isolated because of Leonie's difficulties. Even Valerie's sister wants nothing to do with the child.
3. *In terms of parenting capacity and management of A–B–C factors*
   (a) Both Valerie and Michael are loving parents, very concerned for their daughter and wanting to do anything which will help her 'calm down'.
   (b) However, just in order to cope with Leonie, her parents have reacted to her as situations arose. They have had no structure or plan for managing her so have probably been unintentionally rewarding the very behaviour they find so difficult, e.g. by having a long drawn out row with her over the box of chocolates incident.

Because of the impossibility of observing her behaviour all day, the observation periods might take place for one hour in the morning and one hour in the evening, say, 7.00–8.00 a.m. and 6.00–7.00 p.m. Her parents should continue to handle her just as before, not attempting to do anything differently. Appendix 6 would be a suitable chart on which to collect the data and the completed charts for one week might look something like Table 10.1.

Step 8 – Planning

The parents and practitioners together are now partners in a shared effort to help Leonie. She too can be involved as fully as her understanding permits, and her 'jumpiness' can be discussed with her as one might discuss the management of diabetes or epilepsy with another child. The baseline information in itself is likely to offer the parents some surprises. When this has been discussed and its implications explored, we can guide Valerie and Michael in a systematic attempt to pay clear, explicit and immediate attention to the positive aspects of Leonie's behaviour, especially the few brief intervals when she is calm and settled. We should ask them to tell her clearly and directly after each instance of settled behaviour that when she behaves in this way they are very pleased with her – giving her a quick cuddle or some other show of affection and appreciation.

Table 10.1 Number of three-minute periods of Leonie's very calm and very restless behaviour in two sample daily hours over one week

CHARTING BEHAVIOURS				Name: Leonie			Week begining:	
Behaviour	*Sunday*	*Monday*	*Tuesday*	*Wednesday*	*Thursday*	*Friday*	*Saturday*	*Total*
Behaviours to encourage and praise								
Morning 7.00–8.00 a.m.				√√	√√			
Afternoon								
Evening 6.00–7.00 pm.		√		√				6
Behaviors to discourage								
Morning 7.00–8.00 a.m.	√√√	√√ √√	√√	√√√	√√√	√√	√√	
Afternoon								
Evening 6.00-7.00 pm.	√√√	√√	√√	√√√	√√	√√	√√	36

We have learned that Leonie loves cuddles, so these may be a good means of extending her attention span. Intervals of drawing, using playdough, playing with bricks or copying shapes could be rewarded by a short interval of sitting on her mummy's or daddy's knee to look at a story book together. A chart would helpfully show Leonie's extending capacity to settle to a quiet activity as the rewards take effect.

In respect of the negative or misbehaviour, there are two main strategies for dealing with these as we saw in Chapter 2. The first is to ignore the irritating, demanding behaviour so that by avoiding reinforcing it with attention it gradually extinguishes, or dies away. If this is insufficient to reduce misbehaviour, then it may be necessary to practise time out or calm down, that is, removing the child from the satisfactions of being in the centre of things. It will be difficult to ignore Leonie but the principle *must* be observed in some way or there is no opportunity for her to learn the necessity of inhibiting her restless behaviour.

As with most families with a child displaying ADHD, Leonie has almost certainly received a great deal of intermittent/occasional attention with the effect that some of her behaviours have been arbitrarily reinforced – often not the ones her parents and teachers would wish. Valerie and Michael will probably need help in learning how deliberately to ignore certain patterns of behaviour and a five-year-old child can be helped to understand that however much she throws herself about or interrupts her mother, she will be ignored. They may be very interested in the possibility of all family members learning to relax and to extend the relaxing period little by little. They may think that it would be of benefit to everyone to round this off by a family story time in which Leonie is rewarded for her relaxing practice by sitting on her Daddy's lap for a story.

Helping the parents explain the plan to Leonie

We should therefore advise Leonie's parents to set aside a few minutes to explain the new approach to her in a confident, matter-of-fact way and, if necessary, go through the steps in a practice session. If Leonie can be helped to see her difficulty not as 'naughtiness' but as a problem to be managed, much as some children have to manage being hearing or visually impaired, then a plan can be developed that avoids connotations of blame in favour of a focus upon the *management* of the difficult behaviur.

We strongly recommend that practitioners should write down the specific steps which parents should take in specific circumstances, for example as shown in Box 10.4. A plan for helping Leonie is shown in Box 10.4.

Helping the parents explain the plan to Leonie's teachers

It is apparent that an essential part of the intervention to help Leonie will be to inform her teachers and to seek their cooperation. They are likely to

---

Box 10.4: Plan devised by Mr and Mrs Green, Leonie and the practitioner

Name of child: Leonie   Age: Five years
To help improve Leonie's restless (or 'jumpy') behaviour we have agreed to focus on the following behaviours:
  Positive: Sitting quietly doing a jigsaw or playing with dough.
  Negative: Demanding, overactive behaviour; making constant requests.
Action plan agreed with parent(s)
In the light of the record of Leonie's patterns of behaviour for one week, it is agreed:

1. *To encourage positive behaviour:*
   (a) When Leonie has sat quietly for three minutes doing a jigsaw, her mother will come and sit by her and together help fit in some more pieces and praise her achievement.
   (b) When Leonie has looked at a story book quietly for three minutes, her mother or father will come and sit by her and they will look at it together for a further 3 minutes.
2. *To discourage negative behaviour:*
   (a) If Leonie keep on making demands, she will be given one warning and then placed in time out/calm down for four minutes.
   (b) Each time Leonie runs indoors, she will lose 1 of the 5p pieces which she has been given each Saturday out of the total of 10 for the week (response cost).
3. In addition, either Valerie or Michael will relax on the floor or sofa with Leonie for a few minutes each evening: (5 minutes the first week, 6 the second, up to a maximum of half an hour). They will use a relaxing tape provided by the social worker/health visitor. If Leonie can achieve this, she will earn the right to watch 15 minutes of a suitable children's video, which she can choose.

This will be reviewed on
Signed................. Signed .... Date.................

---

be interested in the written plan and, because most teachers seek the wellbeing of their pupils, will probably cooperate so long as this does not make too many demands upon them and does not interfere with the wellbeing of other pupils. A simple version of the plan, involving a brief note to be sent home each evening highlighting Leonie's *achievements*, rather than her shortcomings, may be very helpful.

Step 9 – Implement the plan

Over the next few days, it will be important for the worker to be in touch with Leonie's parents as they begin to put the plan into effect. Sometimes a weekly contact is sufficient but, in line with cognitive-behavioural theory, it will probably be appropriate to offer more immediate contact – say within two or three days after embarking on the new regime. This is to reinforce the parents' efforts to alter their patterns of responding to Leonie. They will have been warned that her restless behaviour is likely to grow worse before it improves and they should be encouraged to follow the guidelines devised with her of how to respond to their daughter's difficult behaviour. They should also continue to keep records to see if the behaviour gets worse or better.

Step 10 – Review and evaluate the intervention

To review this intervention will require monitoring it on a regular basis – usually weekly or twice weekly – to see how far it is being successful. This has two main purposes:

1. To consider the quantitative data – that is, the counts of positive and negative behaviours that Valerie and Michael are recording on the charts.
2. To consider the qualitative information – that is, their accounts of their experiences in trying to respond differently to Leonie's troublesome behaviour. They are likely to have some questions for which they will be seeking answers.

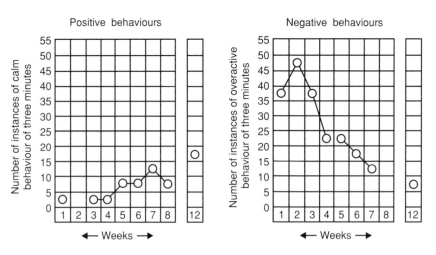

SHOWING THE INCREASE OR DECREASE WEEK BY WEEK

Figure 10.2   Leonie's calm and overactive behaviour during two sampled hours over eight weeks and at three months' followup

Evaluation takes place at the end of an intervention. It is the systematic comparison of the state of affairs at the beginning, in respect of both the parents' moods and Leonie's difficult behaviour, with the state of affairs at the end. If any scales have been employed to measure any of these circumstances, for example the Beck Depression Inventory or the Strengths and Difficulties Questionnaire, then these can be completed again and the pre- and post-scores compared. Figure 10.2 illustrates how committed parents can achieve improvements given a supportive and structured approach. Far more practitioners are needed now who are trained to offer the knowledge and skills required to bring about such outcomes.

11

HELPING FAMILIES WHOSE CHILDREN WET OR SOIL

ENURESIS/BED WETTING: DEFINITION AND PREVALENCE

This first part of this chapter will focus mainly upon nocturnal enuresis, of which one commonly used definition is: 'Repeated involuntary passage of urine during sleep in the absence of any identified physical abnormality in children aged above five years' (Shaffer, 1994). Primary enuresis refers to bed wetting when a child has never been dry; secondary enuresis is bed wetting when a child has achieved dryness but has lost it again.

Prevalence of Enuresis

Differences in definition have led to discrepancies in statistics. However, Morgan (1988) has devised a graph, shown as Figure 11.1, which, although early, is still an indication of the extent of nocturnal enuresis and accords with data from international studies. Several studies have shown that bed wetting (more than once a week) is higher in boys, but shows a steady decline as children get older. Around one in six of five year olds regularly wet the bed, but by the time these children are aged 11, this figure has dropped to about 1 in 20.

Concerning daytime wetting, 2%–4% of children aged five to seven wet at least once a week during the day and a further 8% are wet at least once a month. Daytime wetting is more common in boys than girls and about half those children who wet during the day are also wet at night.

RESEARCH CONCERNING THE ORIGINS OF BED WETTING

It is clear that, as with so many children's difficulties, enuresis is the outcome of many interacting variables. We shall briefly examine some of the major

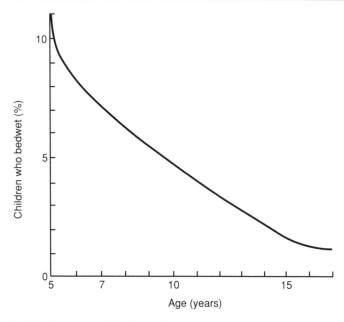

Figure 11.1   The frequency of bed wetting

> *Source*: Reproduced by permission from Morgan (1998). *Help for the Bedwetting Child*. London: Cedar.

contributory factors, as shown by a range of studies, but other variables may be implicated in the future.

Socio-economic Variables

In an early study, Miller et al. (1960), who observed 750 children in Newcastle for a period of several years, noted that children who wet the bed were more likely to:

- come from large families
- be second children
- come from socioeconomic classes four and five
- be subject to overcrowding in the home

The Contribution of Genetic and Medical Factors

There have been a number of efforts to establish whether genetic variables make a contribution to nocturnal enuresis. Bakwin (1971; 1973) reported that of children who wet the bed 70 % have a parent or sibling who was late in becoming dry. Bakwin (1971) also found from an examination of 338 pairs of same-sex twins that identical twins were almost twice as likely to be bedwetters as nonidentical twins. Together, these bodies of evidence suggest strongly that there is a genetic contribution to the condition.

There are indications that about 16 % of children with a urinary tract infection will present as bed wetters and that successfully treating the infection will stop the enuresis in about 30 % of them.

Psychological Factors: the Association with Stress

It is important to distinguish between primary enuresis, when the child has never been dry, and secondary enuresis, when the child has been dry but has lapsed. It is usually appropriate to look for stress factors contributing to secondary enuresis. From the National Children's Bureau longitudinal study (Douglas, 1973) of over 4,300 children, there seems to be some association between the number of stressful events in the first 4 years of the children's lives and patterns of enuresis. There were correlations/associations between bed wetting and the following life events:

- break-up of the family through death, divorce or separation.
- temporary separation from the mother.
- the birth of a younger brother or sister.
- moving house or home.
- admission to hospital.
- accidents.

The contribution of environmental factors towards secondary enuresis has been confirmed by Shaffer (1994) from his review of case-control comparison studies. The implication of these findings is that stressful situations affect some, but by no means all, children. Those most likely to be affected by stress may be those who already have a genetic vulnerability.

Summary of the Research Findings

The review of the evidence of how children become dry, although early, is still valid today; MacKeith, Meadow and Turner (1973) reported:

> We conclude that children become dry at night in the following way. At birth some partial mechanisms are already present. In the next four years, maturation takes place in the central nervous system, making the behaviour of nocturnal bladder control possible. This behaviour is not dependent on training or learning. It is destined to emerge during the first four years, providing nothing acts

at the time of maturation to inhibit its emergence. Such negative factors may be transient or continuing stresses, amongst which unsuitable toilet training is probably important. The emergence of nocturnal bladder control cannot be accelerated, but it can be retarded. A few children become dry at night by the age of one year, a large proportion in the second and third years ... In children under the age of five, but not in older children, delayed maturation is one of the factors leading to the delayed appearance of nocturnal dryness ... Genetic factors probably play a part by affecting either the age of maturation of necessary mechanisms or the development of nocturnal bladder capacity.

RESEARCH CONCERNING THE MANAGEMENT OF BED WETTING

There have been many studies investigating various forms of intervention in terms of their short- and long-term effectiveness. McGonaghy (1969) compared five forms of treatment: prescription of imipramine; prescription of amphetamine; prescription of placebo; random waking (to control for the giving of attention) and behavioural training, using the bell and pad. He found the last approach to be the most effective, followed by the prescription of imipramine. This conclusion has been confirmed by more recent reviews, for example, Clayden, Taylor, Loader, Borzykowski and Edwards (2002), who wrote 'It is puzzling that medication is so often preferred to the alarm when the latter is more effective, safer and less expensive'.

An example of the research which contributed to the view of Clayden et al. (2002) is the work of Turner (1973) who reviewed 17 studies of behavioural treatment for enuresis, involving 1,067 children, where the criterion for success was 7 consecutive dry nights. He found success rates of 64.8%–100%. All children were followed up for periods ranging from 1 to 63 months and while there was an average relapse rate of 27% across the studies, many of these relapsed children, some of whom had wet only once in 7 months, responded to a second intervention with bell and pad. The enuresis alarm is typically offered when the child has reached the age of 7 years and when other approaches have been tried but not found helpful. However, parents may need help and ongoing support in their management of the alarm, as indeed may the child concerned.

HELP FOR FAMILIES WITH CHILDREN WHO WET THE BED

An Example: Andrew

Andrew is a six year old who has only very occasionally been dry at night. This little boy seems healthy. He is settled at school but is upset that he cannot go and visit his cousins because he wets the bed. His mum is at home and his dad is at sea for long spells. Andrew always goes to sleep in his own bed but often if he wets, while his dad is away, his mum lets him come to sleep in her bed. This is not allowed when his dad is home from sea. There is a lot of tension between Andrew and his dad, who thinks that Andrew is becoming too 'soft' and who thinks a good spanking might cure the wetting. He was smacked whenever he wet the bed and it 'did him no harm'. Andrew's mum wet the bed until she was nine, and the parents think he may well have inherited this pattern from her. Andrew has a sister, Jane, aged four, who is already dry at night.

Assessment

As has been discussed in previous chapters, parents will need time, empathy and understanding to enable them to say just how many difficulties the child's enuresis causes both for the child and for other family members. Not least, wetting is very expensive because of the cost of washing and drying bedclothes and nightwear, so if information and support can be given concerning any services available this will be important. This is Step 1.

Step 2 – Gather Information

The child's developmental needs

A wide range of information will be sought concerning the child's earliest years and about the patterns of becoming dry at night of siblings and both parents, if this is available. Such information will include:

- Has Andrew ever been dry at night?
- If so, for how long? (Is this primary or secondary enuresis?)
- Does the wetting show any pattern at all; for example, is it better or worse at weekends?
- Does diet seem to play any part in Andrew's wetting?
- How does Andrew feel about his wetting?
- Does he have any ideas about what makes it better or worse?
- What was the pattern of becoming dry of Andrew's parents?

Family and environmental factors

- It seems to be important that Andrew's Dad is away at sea for long periods, and that when he does come home, he shows his disappointment at Andrew's wetting. This is understandable but nevertheless may contribute to Andrew's anxiety.
- Andrew has been invited to stay at his auntie's house but he doesn't want to go while he still wets the bed.

Parenting capacity

- Both parents are very proud of Andrew, his thoughtfulness and his kindness to other children.
- Andrew's mum wet the bed until she was nine and so seems to assume that he will do the same. His daddy was dry from early childhood. Andrew's parents respond very differently to his wetting: his mum comforts him and says that as she used to wet, he probably will do the same; she lets him come into the big bed if he wets, rather than change the bed in the middle of the night; his Dad becomes very cross and says Andrew is a baby and he is not to come into the big bed. In summary, it is *how the parents respond to the child's wetting* that is the particular focus of interest here: does their response cause more stress for the child, or less?

Aids to Assessment

It is essential when a child wets the bed that he or she is examined by a doctor or another appropriately trained person so that a range of medical factors, such as urinary infections, can be eliminated. It may be embarrassing for a child, particularly an older child, to have to be seen by a doctor for bed wetting but the problem is so common and help so generally accessible that parents should be encouraged to take their child to the doctor just as they would for an injection or a chest infection. In other words, bed wetting is a normal and common occurrence but it is one very seldom openly acknowledged. It is therefore helpful if parents can talk frankly about their child's difficulties to friends, just as they would if their child had, say, eczema or slept poorly. There is help available for most who seek it.

It is important always to check how easy is it for the child to reach the bathroom in the middle of the night? Is the light switch easy to reach and is he or she confident about using the toilet? For children who wet during the daytime, what is the state of the school lavatories? Are they well supplied with toilet paper? Do they offer privacy?

A further area that anecdotal evidence suggests is important is the timing of the child's intake of fluids. If it is difficult to obtain plenty of water to drink at school, children may be drinking the greater part of their fluid intake in the early evening, rather than having a balanced intake of fluid throughout the day. This is an important matter, well worth exploring, if necessary, with the school governors. It can usefully be part of a broader exploration of the place of commercial drinks machines within schools.

Step 3 – Identify Problem Profile

1. Andrew, aged six, wets the bed almost every night.
2. He occasionally wets during the day when he is anxious.

3. When his daddy is home he hides wet pyjamas as he is afraid he will be told off.

Step 4 – Identify Positive Profile

Upon being asked about Andrew's strengths and positive behaviours, his parents are able to agree that there are several:

1. He is a cheerful and friendly little boy, who shares his toys readily with other children, although not so well with his sister Jane.
2. He can already read several short stories.
3. He can concentrate for long periods, building high and complicated structures with wooden or plastic bricks.

Step 5 – What are the Goals for Andrew?

When asked gently what he would like to happen, Andrew says, 'I just want not to wet the bed'. His mum agrees that that would be nice but says that she would be satisfied if she could be reassured that Andrew would eventually become dry and if only he would not hide his wet pyjamas.

Step 6 – Arrive at a Formulation

The overall formulation might be as shown in Box 11.1. Points that may arise in the discussion of this preliminary formulation include:

1. Andrew is *not* being naughty: he would be dry if he could. He is, however, sometimes being placed in a situation that does not make it any easier for him to become dry at night as he is often 'rewarded' for being wet by being allowed to come into his mum's bed – only to be rejected when his dad returns. This conflict is hard for a six year old.
2. He is genuinely afraid of his dad's threats. These are serving to make him more anxious and more likely to wet. It will help him if his dad ceases to show his crossness to Andrew.

These points are discussed tactfully and tentatively with the parents. Their contributions and reactions are taken directly into account. The formulation is provisional but provides some working hypotheses.

It is now the turn of the practitioner, having gathered information, to give information: that bed wetting is a very common phenomenon among young children, that many children are upset and worried by it, that they are unable

Box 11.1: Preliminary assessment/formulation of Andrew's bed wetting

1. *In terms of Andrew's developmental needs*
   (a) Organically, Andrew may well have inherited a genetic tendency to bed wetting, as his mother had a similar history.
   (b) Andrew has had a urine test and there is no evidence of a medical problem.
   (c) Andrew has had to cope with the arrival of a younger sister and one who is now already dry.
   (d) While many children have to cope with a dad who is at home only occasionally, it places extra stress upon them as they have to adjust and readjust.
2. *In terms of family and environmental factors*
   There seem no special factors to note in this domain. The family has close links in the community and there is a supportive wider family network.
3. *In terms of parenting capacity and the impact of immediate variables (A–B–C)*
   (a) Unintentionally, his mother has been rewarding Andrew for wetting the bed, as when her husband is away she allows him to come into her bed.
   (b) When Andrew's daddy returns, Andrew is not allowed to sleep in his parents' bed.

to stop it by willpower and that cognitive-behavioural theory has much to offer. This, of course, may not be the language chosen but nevertheless it is important to convey to parents that there is a substantial body of knowledge about bed wetting that has proved helpful to many children and families and that the practitioner is knowledgeable and experienced in this field. It is helpful to instil confidence that we know what we are doing!

Step 7 – Gather Baseline Data

Andrew's mum will probably be able to make a game of gathering counts of one positive and one negative behaviour. His daddy clearly approves of his construction skill, so this might be the positive behaviour on which to focus, whereas wetting might be the appropriate undesirable one. Two charts could be completed (see Appendix 6) for one full week to provide baseline information. A useful anecdotal suggestion is that only a child's behaviour in the desired direction should be recorded – for example, a wet night should be left blank upon the chart but dry nights or parts of nights could feature a star, an animal sticker or something chosen by the child. The whole thrust of the work is towards instilling more confidence in child and parents, a greater sense of achievement for all and more positive attention from parents into the child's life.

Step 8 – Planning

The following plans, or similar ones, should be explored with the parents and Andrew:

Step 9 – Implement the Plan

After due discussion and adjustment of the above plan, it will be put into effect. The *whole* approach must be kept positive, with real appreciation of any progress Andrew is able to make towards being dry and with minimal attention to any accidents. Any dry nights, or parts of nights, should be commended and the whole matter should be dealt with in as matter-of-fact a way as possible. As suggested, only successes, whether for a full night or for the hours before Andrew is woken at his parents' bedtime, should be entered on the chart; these records will demonstrate whether progress is being made.

If at the end of an agreed period, say eight weeks, there is no indication of progress, then it may be appropriate to stop attempts to help Andrew become dry at night until he is seven years old and then consider using the *waking alarm*. This works so that the child is conditioned to wake, first to the sound of a buzzer or bell that rings when he begins to pass urine and then to the changes in the sphincter muscles of the bladder.

It is necessary to introduce the waking alarm in such a way that all those involved see and understand it. As its uses become more widely publicised, some parents are likely to know other families where it has been used successfully. The alarm must be introduced with confidence – preferably by someone very familiar with it.

One of the most recent designs is particularly helpful in that the device which wakes the child can be placed discreetly in the child's pyjama pocket. Parents and child should receive a careful demonstration and Andrew can experiment with a doll so that he becomes familiar with the device. The routine that will be followed at night should be gone through at least twice so that everyone knows what will happen and what to do. Dry night clothes and bed clothes should be made available. If the device can first be used on a Friday or Saturday night, or during the holidays, this reduces the anxiety that a child may feel. The worker should be in touch the morning after the first occasion it is used to give support and to see how the family fared. Whatever has happened, the approach should anticipate gradual improvement as the process of learning to wake at signals from the sphincter muscles takes effect.

Box 11.2: Plan to help the Johnson family

Parents   Diana and Mark Johnson, 28 High Street, Anytown
Children   Andrew   Age six
                     Jane   Age four
Sure Start worker   Susan Westgate, Sure Start Centre, Anytown.

Agreement between Diana, Mark and Andrew Johnson and Susan Westgate

Overall aim: To work towards Andrew's being dry 50 % of nights
Our goals are: To increase the number of times (currently 10 %) of dry nights
               To increase the number of times when Mark praises Andrew's
               skill in building with blocks and Lego.

Diana and Mark agree to:

1. Praise Andrew warmly when he builds with his blocks.
2. Explain that from now on Andrew will sleep in his own bed each night. This will be explained tactfully (this is so that there will be no reward for his wetting the bed).
3. Discuss with Andrew whether he wants them to wake him at, say, 10.30 p.m. when they go to bed.
4. Mark promises that when he comes home from sea, he will not tell Andrew off, even if he has been wet.
5. Mummy will take him and Jane out, swimming/to the harbour/birdwatching for two hours on either Saturday or Sunday, regardless of whether he has been able to be dry or not.
6. For his part, Andrew promises to tell his mummy if he wets the bed and to put his wet pyjama bottoms into the laundry basket.

In return, Susan agrees to:

1. Visit the family weekly and telephone midweek.
2. Spend 15 minutes with Andrew each time she comes looking at the sticker chart. Remember that it is possible that Andrew's wetting may get worse before improving.

Other points:

1. The above agreement will be reviewed in a fortnight.
2. If the above plan is not helpful, Susan will discuss the possible use of the 'waking alarm' with all members of the family.

Step 10 – Review and Evaluation

This review or monitoring will be based upon the evidence gathered; progress is unlikely to be smooth, as events of the day are likely to interact with the effects of the alarm. For example, if Andrew has a difficult day at school and feels he cannot cope with his new reading book, this anxiety might affect his waking at night in response to the alarm. The process will take longer for some children than for others but parents should remain positive, encouraging and optimistic that the child will become dry in due course.

There is extremely encouraging evidence that effective treatment using the waking alarm brings about a number of additional beneficial side effects for the children. Shaffer (1994) reports that many studies (e.g. Moffatt, Kato & Pless, 1987) have shown that children who have been successfully helped by the alarm become 'more assertive, independent and happy and that they gain in self-confidence'. If this intervention with bed wetting is successful it is highly likely that Andrew's daytime confidence will also improve. The greater sensitivity to the bladder, which a child develops when undergoing training with the alarm, seems to carry over into daytime situations so that the child becomes more sensitive to the signals of a full bladder. A spare pair of pants and trousers should be available in Andrew's school bag for the occasions when the inevitable accident occurs.

ENCOPRESIS/SOILING

A Definition/Description and Prevalence

It is reported by Hersov (1994) that: 'The term "faecal soiling" is used to describe disorders of bowel function and control, excluding constipation without soiling, occurring in children over a certain age in the absence of any structural abnormality or disease.'

He continues that the age at which faecal incontinence is considered abnormal varies and that an early study by Whiting and Child (1953) reported much variation in the age at which control is achieved by children in different cultures. In the United Kingdom almost all the children in the groups studied had achieved bowel control by night and by day by the age of two-and-a-half, Hersov suggests that 4 years is a more realistic minimum age for diagnosing abnormality of bowel control.

As to prevalence, an early study by Bellman (1966), in which the parents of 8,863 children aged 7 years were asked about this particular difficulty, found that among children of 7 and 8 years the frequency was 1.5%, with over 3 times as many boys affected as girls. This figure has been confirmed by other studies, for example Rutter et al. (1975a) in the Isle of Wight studies. Several studies have also found a close association between soiling and enuresis.

RESEARCH INTO THE ORIGINS OF SOILING

Classification

Several researchers have attempted to devise a scheme of classification for soiling. That which will be followed here is by Herbert (1991), who distinguished four types:

1. *Primary encopresis*, where there is a genuine failure to gain bowel control. Here the failure to gain control is associated with the child having learning disabilities or, more probably, with inconsistent or inadequate help in enabling the child to gain control. As in teaching any new skill, it is important to take a positive approach to helping children to recognise the signs that they need to use the toilet or potty, to commend them when they are successful and to miminise the importance of the inevitable accidents.
2. *Secondary encopresis*, where the child has acquired control in toileting but has then lost it or failed to exercise it. Many such instances arise in which control has been adequately established but breaks down under stressful circumstances such as the birth of a sibling or starting school, or a traumatic event such as an accident. If parents can handle this situation sensitively, the child usually regains control within weeks or months. Punitive responses are particularly unhelpful and are likely to make matters worse. Smearing faeces is often an indication of considerable distress on the part of a child and again it is counterproductive to respond with heavy punishments.
3. *Retentive encopresis*, marked by retention of faecal matter, accompanied by soiling due to leakage of fluid from around the faeces. Here the faeces are abnormal in appearance and the problem may be associated with a medical disorder, such as ulcerative colitis. Sometimes children become severly constipated and the overflow is of associated fluid. These circumstances seem to arise from anxiety on the part of the child because of a previous very painful episode of passing a motion, or sometimes from an intense conflict that has arisen between parent and child about the use of the toilet. This reluctance may be associated with just one person or it may have generalised into an unwillingness to use the potty or toilet at all.
4. *Non-retentive encopresis* refers to the involuntary voiding of faeces resulting in soiling. This is best understood as a difficulty on the part of the child in recognizing the cues offered by the sphincters and in taking action thereon.

The Timing of Training

An early study by Sears, Maccoby and Levin (1957) showed that too early training can be less effective than training that begins later. They found that mothers who began training before the child was 5 months needed an average of 10 months before cleanliness was established, whereas mothers who began at 20 months or older required only 5 months. There seems to be increasing consensus that the optimum time to start is when the child is about 2 years old.

Constipation and Retention

Gabel (1981) found that constipation and retention of faeces are features of most forms of encopresis. They both render the ordinary signals of the need to pass a motion ineffective and typically cause fear and avoidance in the child. Constipation can be a factor in any of the four major types of soiling and must be dealt with as part of the total intervention strategy.

RESEARCH INTO THE MANAGEMENT OF SOILING

It is important that all children who are soiling should be medically examined, ideally by a paediatrician, in order to establish the form of encopresis and also to screen for medical conditions that may be contributing to the overall difficulty. The possibility of anal fissures will probably be considered. If these can be eliminated, then a carefully planned approach in order to enable the child to excrete the hardened stools is likely to be suggested; this may involve laxatives or, occasionally, enemas. As Clayden, Taylor, Loader, Borzykowski and Edwards (2002) suggest, 'Different treatment approaches are required for the young child who has never been toilet trained, the child with impacted faeces and overflow soiling, the child who is frightened to defecate or to use the toilet, and the child who is intentionally defecating in inappropriate places'.

In all cases it will be necessary to monitor the child's diet in order to ensure that he or she is receiving sufficient fibrous material and sufficient fluid as part of a balanced intake.

Doleys (1978), in a review of the treatment of children who soil, reported that 93 % of cases were successfully helped by the use of behavioural methods. After careful assessment, a wide range of strategies based on the principles of cognitive-behavioural theory were selectively employed to help children who were soiling, and a combination of positive and negative reinforcement, integrated with an approach involving dietary monitoring, seemed to be particularly helpful. Other studies and reviews of studies of cognitive- behavioural treatment have supported this conclusion (Buchanan, 1992; McGrath, Mellon & Murphy, 2000).

HELP FOR FAMILIES WITH CHILDREN WHO SOIL

An Example: Colin, Aged Five Years

This is an unhappy little boy. He was toilet trained by the time he was 3 years old, but then began to soil when his Mum began a series of admissions to hospital because of mental health problems. His Daddy died from AIDS 18 months ago and Colin still asks for him. He will go to the toilet when told to but does not perform and then soils immediately he leaves the bathroom. He has plenty of clean clothes to put on but hides dirty pants all over the house. He lives with his nana, his mother's mother, and sees his Mum two afternoons a week. Nana finds the soiling a great strain. She tends to talk with Colin about how hard her life has been and how hard it is now that her daughter has been diagnosed as suffering from schizophrenia. Colin does not like these talks.

Colin had settled well at school but after two episodes of soiling there his nana was asked not to bring him any more until he had been dependably clean for three weeks.

Assessment

If parents of children who suffer from enuresis need support, the support needed by those whose children soil is much greater! Encopresis is not a disorder that attracts a lot of concern and understanding. It is known that children who soil are often the butt of unpleasant comment from other children or adults and their self-esteem is likely to be fragile. Support for the whole family is Step 1.

Step 2 – Gather Information

The assessment will be in line with the dimensions of the Common Assessment Framework (see page 87). First, information is needed concerning the child's general developmental history and then in respect of overall toilet training, what age it was begun and what happened as it progressed. Are the current soiling episodes primary or secondary? It is unlikely that informants' memories will be wholly accurate but it is of course vital to hear what they think happened. If the child is old enough, his or her view of the difficulty must also be explored. As with enuresis, the parents' own histories should be sought. The assessment should include information about the toileting patterns of other children, if any, of the family and also about the child's relationships with all family members. Why do the parents or carers think the child soils? How do they feel about the soiling? How have they tried to cope with it?

Aids to assessment

An older child, say above the age of five years, may be able to give some pointers as to why, say, secondary encopresis is occurring. For example, a child who has established control but who loses it on the birth of a new

---

Box 11.3: Preliminary assessment of/rationale for Colin's soiling

1. *Colin's developmental needs*
   (a) Medical checks show nothing of note, but much retention of hardened faeces.
   (b) Colin has had several major distressing events in his short life:
       ● The loss of a much-loved daddy.
       ● The frightening changes in his mummy.
       ● Her having to go to hospital when ill.
   (c) He has had to get used to living with his nana.
   (d) Because of the soiling, his nana has been asked not to bring him to school. Colin is really sad about this as he does enjoy school.
2. *In terms of the family circumstances*
   ● Colin's nana is *very* upset by her daughter's illness.
   ● She finds caring for Colin very stressful particularly in view of his soiling.
3. *In terms of parenting capacity, including A–B–C*
   (a) Through sheer frustration, his nana has been shouting at Colin and telling him that he is a very bad and ungrateful child. This gives him a great deal of attention.
   (b) She has threatened to tell Colin's mummy how bad he has been; this adds to his anxieties.

---

sibling may be able either to say or to draw something of how he or she feels about the arrival of the 'intruder'. The aim is to enable the child to accept his or her own feelings, to have these feelings accepted by an understanding and caring adult and to be able to talk without condemnation of, say, jealousy of the new arrival.

Step 3 – Identify Problem Profile

There are many problems to choose from but his Nana has no doubt about which are the most urgent.

1. Colin frequently soils.
2. He smears faeces on the walls of his bedroom.
3. He hides dirty pants all over the house.

Step 4 – Identify Positive Profile

Upon being asked about Colin's strengths and positive behaviours, his nana says that apart from his soiling he is a child who 'tugs at your heart strings':

1. He is very affectionate: he comes and sits on her lap, wanting cuddles.
2. He is helpful to her in the house: fetches things and finds things that are lost.
3. He helps her clean up the messes he makes – he seems to enjoy doing so.

Step 5 – What are the Goals for Colin?

When asked gently what he would like to happen, Colin says, 'I want my Daddy; I want my Mummy'. His nana gets very upset and says she can see why Colin is upset but she can't understand why he has to show his upset by soiling. At the very least she wants him to stop smearing the faeces and to stop hiding dirty pants.

Step 6 – Arrive at a Formulation

The overall formulation might be as shown in Box 11.3. In discussing this preliminary assessment the practitioner is likely to suggest that Colin is a very unhappy little boy. The soiling and smearing are signs of his distress: he is *not* just being naughty. His distress arises from a double bereavement: a total one in respect of his daddy and a partial one, which he cannot understand, concerning his mummy. There appears to be nothing medically wrong with Colin but he is under acute stress that is reflected in patterns of soiling and smearing.

Step 7 – Gathering Baseline Data

Colin's Nana indicates that the negative behaviour she wants to target is:

Episodes of smearing faeces.

and the positive behaviour is:

Coming and sitting on her lap and looking at story books with her.

The practitioner then asks nana to keep a week's records, on charts adapted from Appendix 6, of the number and timing of each of these two behaviours. At the end of one week there should be data available concerning both the episodes of smearing and the times Colin has come for a cuddle.

Step 8 – Planning

The practitioner can now discuss with Colin's nana that it seems to her that Colin is not deliberately playing her up at a time when she can least cope, but that the soiling seems to be a reaction to feelings of great insecurity. Skill will be needed to enlist her willingness to go on putting up with the smearing and soiling, but Colin's nana is more likely to cooperate if she is assured of continuing support.

Involving the child in the plan

Colin will need to be brought into the plan. He will need both understanding and a firm limit set to the extent and consequences of his soiling. He will need help and time from an understanding person to whom he can put questions and with whom he can talk about his mummy and daddy. He may well welcome there being someone who is not shocked or disgusted by his behaviour but instead seems to understand it and to know how to manage it. The plan shown in Box 11.4, which incorporates elements of direct work with Colin and draws upon cognitive-behavioural principles, might help.

Step 9 – Implementation of the Plan

It may be necessary for Colin to receive treatment in the form of laxatives or suppositories to relieve the constipation, for until this is cleared he is likely to soil his clothes through leakage of fluid around the impacted faeces. This medical oversight is likely to be provided by a paediatrician, general practitioner, health visitor or practice nurse. When the constipation is relieved a diet that will ensure sufficient fibre and fruit will be necessary and when regularity, without soiling, is established for three weeks, Colin will be able to go back to school.

A simple agreement can be devised along the lines discussed in Chapter 12. This might include clauses such as those shown in Box 11.3. The first week provides a baseline against which future progress can be assessed. Thereafter the practitioner remains in touch for as long as the agreement indicates, offering encouragment to Colin and his nana and taking practical steps to reduce the pressures upon Colin. This may involve being in touch with Colin's school, liaising with the paediatrician and monitoring developments. The course of the intervention is likely to be 'two forward and one back'. It is unlikely to go smoothly.

Step 10 – Review and Evaluation

These steps will be grounded upon the evidence which is gathered. The chart will show week by week whether Colin is managing to recognise the sphincter promptings that he needs to go to the toilet and whether, in the event of an accident, he can tell his nana about it calmly. Such a plan is likely to need

Box 11.4: A possible plan for helping Colin and his nana

- Nana will try to offer two spells daily when Colin and she can look at story books together.
- She will try to make no angry comment when Colin smears, but will help him wash the walls and freshen up the room.
- She will ask Colin to go to the toilet and sit on it for 5 minutes with a story book, about 10 minutes after each meal. If he performs, she will show her pleasure; if not she will say nothing.
- Colin will be asked to tell his nana if he does have an accident and soils his pants.
- She will provide a bucket of cold water into which Colin agrees to place his pants if he soils.
- The practitioner, Jan, agrees to meet with Colin for half an hour twice weekly to talk about his Mummy and Daddy. She will mark the days on the calendar.

Table 11.1 An alternative three-way agreement for helping Colin and his nana

Colin's nana will	Colin will	Jan (practitioner) will
1 Provide Colin with clean pants daily plus a spare pair.	Go to the toilet when he feels the urge to do so.	Arrange to see Colin for two 20-minute periods weekly to play or to talk about anything he wants.
2 Talk with Colin about happy things they have done together.	Tell his nana if he does have an accident.	Explore resources from the Family Fund.
3 If Colin has an accident, but does tell Nana, she will not be cross with him.	Keep a simple chart, prepared by Jan, on which to record days when his pants/bed are clean.	Monitor progress as shown on the chart, attending primarily to 'no accident days'.
4 When Colin has no accident on a given day, she will tell him how pleased she is with him.	Put a sticker on a chart for each 'no accident!' day. Three stickers in a week means a small treat – e.g. a trip to the park.	Meet with Colin and his nana for a further 20 minutes each Tuesday, to give everybody encouragement.
5 If Colin does have an accident, but has not told her, she will not arrange a small treat that week.	Amuse himself instead.	Find some story books for Colin.

recasting at least every fortnight and perhaps even weekly. This review or monitoring will also indicate whether events during the day are interacting with the efforts to support Colin.

It is likely that there will be an improvement if the participants are able to keep to the clauses of the agreement *but it will take time*. Soiling is often the mark of a troubled child and while there is good evidence that help can be given it takes time to foster the necessary neurological and muscular developments. Emotional support is vital but so is a good understanding of cognitive-behavioural theory. Here the practitioner is essentially a troubleshooter, someone who, with a good experience of the general principles of devising agreements, and in liaison with other colleagues, can adapt the cognitive-behavioural principles to suit the particular circumstances that occur.

12

PARENT EDUCATION AND TRAINING: VALUES AND RESEARCH

This chapter will focus upon a number of fields at the leading edge of research into working with families to prevent children's distress and unhappiness:

1. The value base of the work: ethical issues.
2. Support for families within a multicultural society.
3. The content and process of effective programmes of parent training.
4. Methods and structures of parent training.
5. Devising agreements to support practice.
6. Maintaining improvement.

THE VALUE BASE OF THE WORK: ETHICAL ISSUES

The Value Base of the Work

The principles set out in Box 12.1 were devised by a group of social workers who attended a training workshop organised by myself with the support of the then Central Council for the Education and Training of Social Workers.

Ethical Issues

Any approach that deliberately makes use of principles of cognitive-behavioural theory lays itself open to the charge that it is unethical and manipulative. This accusation must be taken seriously, for we should recall that workers in the so-called 'Pin-down' scandal in the United Kingdom, where misbehaving children in the care of the local authority were deprived of liberty

---

Box 12.1: The value base of helping families with troubled children

1. All children and young people are intrinsically valuable. They are to be cared for and respected.
2. The overall aim of the work is to enable parents to continue to care for their children.
3. Diverse family patterns are to be acknowledged and respected.
4. Cultural diversity is to be acknowledged and respected.
5. Each child is unique, with a unique history and background.
6. Families benefit from being respected and empowered.
7. Parents' existing strengths, knowledge and experience should be built upon.
8. Practice must be actively antidiscriminatory.
9. The involvement of fathers and grandparents as well as mothers in promoting their children's wellbeing is invaluable.
10. Children are the responsibility of the wider society as well as of their families.

---

and basic human rights, also claimed to be using cognitive-behavioural approaches.

There is no doubt that the principles can be used unethically. To avoid this, organisations that seek to publicise the appropriate use of the principles in an ethical way have devised ethical guidelines. The most highly developed of these, namely those developed by the British Association for Behavioural and Cognitive Psychotherapy, are given as Appendix 11. It will be noted that two of the clearest statements are that, 'The aims and goals of assessments/interventions will be discussed with service users at the outset...' and 'Assessments/interventions will be planned in such a way that effectiveness can be evaluated'. It is to these ends that I have insisted on:

1. asking service users what are *their* goals for our work together; and
2. asking that records be kept so that these data can be used for monitoring and evaluation of progress towards these goals.

The area of greatest potential abuse lies in using time out/calm down. This is the brief period of time during which a child is placed in a safe but dull and boring place immediately after misbehaving. It is infinitely more effective than smacking. The sanction lies in the child's being *ignored and bored*, and is discussed in Chapter 2, p. 62. The effectiveness of the approach was well known to our Victorian forebears and is also known to later generations, for when I enquire among the present generation of grandparents as to what punishments were used for naughty children, often the response is, 'I was sent to stand in the corner' or 'I was sent to sit on the stairs'. It is extremely sad that this folk wisdom has been lost to later generations, many of whom have instead resorted to smacking or hitting, both of which are less effective as deterrents and far more dangerous to the child. Different forms of time out are explored on p. 61. There are a number of dangers.

The first is that parents have such difficulty in praising or appreciating their child that they do not employ this approach at all but instead resort only to a punitive use of time out. To counter such a possibility I ask people who attend my training sessions actually to be present sufficiently often at the outset of a programme of work with a child for them to *see and hear* the parent praising the child and to give support and coaching in this, if necessary. Further, a number of health visitors with whom I have worked have reported that they have been so concerned about this issue that they have decided against teaching the use of time out: they teach only the approach involving praise and appreciation of the child.

A second danger is that parents assume that if a 3-minute exclusion is effective, then a 30-minute one will be even more the case. This is not so. Research by Hobbs, et al. (1978) found that for most children aged 4–9 years, 4 minutes was the most effective length of time, repeated each time the target misbehaviour occurred.

A third danger is that parents or childminders will allow a child for whom time out is used to be stigmatised or labelled as a 'bad' or 'naughty' child. This is entirely contrary to the spirit of what I am proposing: the intention is that this sanction should be used firmly but discreetly to manage children to prevent the escalation of disruptive or destructive behaviour which infringes the rights of others. Once the time out interval is over, the child should be received back warmly into the group: wherever possible the incident is over and done with.

SUPPORT FOR FAMILIES IN A MULTICULTURAL SOCIETY

This issue has close links with the previous one. It is very important for professional people to realise the power their professional role bestows upon them in the eyes of many members of society and the responsibilities that this imposes upon them. We as practitioners carry statutory responsibility that requires us to protect children against exploitation of any kind, as well as against neglect and abuse, but we may be in danger of imposing our own values and viewpoints upon families who seek our help in relation to matters that have nothing to do with child protection but which are in fact culturally determined. Thus, the timing of going to bed, whether one sits at a table to eat or not, what implements, if any, we use to eat food, are all cultural conventions and it is vital that we respect diversity of practice in these matters.

Our society increasingly looks to science as a source of wisdom in under-standing our needs, our development and our difficulties, and indeed this book is intended to make a contribution to that perspective – but research has its limitations. For example, there is no clear evidence from research that children should go to bed at a certain time. In many cultures throughout the world, it is natural and normal for children to go to bed at roughly the same time as the adults in their families: it is Western families that are statistically very odd in insisting that their children go to bed at mid-evening.

To consider the needs of families belonging to ethnic and other minorities, there are a number of steps that workers can take to be sensitive and sup-portive. These have been discussed in relation to the work of Forehand and Kotchik (1996) (see p. 75).

THE CONTENT AND PROCESS OF EFFECTIVE PROGRAMMES OF PARENT TRAINING

Much of the research concerning parent training deals with children who are displaying serious behaviour problems because so many families seek help for this problem; so this will be the main focus considered here.

In the first edition of this book I referred to the work of Barlow (1997) who undertook a review of the effectiveness of parent-training programmes in improving behaviour problems in children aged 3 to 10 years, and reports that 'There is still insufficient evidence to show that parent-training curric-ula are the decisive factor in producing change'. She considered that there is a need for further research comparing parent-training programmes with parent support/discussion groups, in which no parent-training curriculum is implemented. Since then, however, there have been an abundance of re-views and papers upon effectiveness of various strategies and a wide range of practitioners and reviewers have come to endorse cognitive-behavioural approaches as the most effective theoretical approaches for helping children with behaviour problems and indeed many other difficulties. (Scott, 2002; Richardson & Joughin, 2002). We can now turn to the more specific fields of content and process.

CONTENT AND CHARACTERISTICS OF EFFECTIVE PARENT EDUCATION PROGRAMMES

In a review of the components of effective interventions, Scott (2002) has clar-ified several which the evidence suggests are crucial and Hutchings, Gard-ner and Lane (2004) have added others which they believe to be key. See Box 12.2.

> **Box 12.2:** Characteristics of effective parent training programmes (Scott, 2002)
>
> *Content*
>
> Structured sequence of topics, introduced in set order over 8–12 weeks.
> Subjects include play, praise, incentives, setting limits and discipline.
> Emphasis on promoting sociable self-reliant child behaviour and calm parenting.
> Constant reference to parent's own experience and predicaments.
> Theoretical basis informed by extensive empirical research and made explicit.
> Detailed manual available to enable replicability.
>
> *Delivery*
>
> Collaborative approach acknowledge parents' feelings and beliefs.
> Difficulties normalised, humour and fun encouraged.
> Parents supported to practise new approaches during sessions and through homework.
> Parents and children seen together in individual family work; just parents in some group programmes.
> Creche; good quality refreshments and transport provided if necessary.
> Therapists supervised regularly to ensure adherence and to develop skills.
>
> In addition, Hutchings et al. (2004) point out the effectiveness of roleplay, rehearsal and videotape feedback in strengthening parent behaviours (Webster-Stratton, 1998). They also highlight the findings of Dadds, Schwartz and Sanders (1987) that where major difficulties existed between adults in a family, a 'partner support' programme was needed to achieve sustained improvements.

The Choice of Concepts to Be Taught

This, happily, has been broadly agreed by most of the major researchers in the field, although inevitably different trainers have different emphases. Gordon and Davidson (1981), in an early review of the core concepts and skills proposed by a range of practitioners, reported what they found to be the common core of parent education programmes using behavioural approaches (Box 12.3). Later trainers have tended to include broadly the same content and I used a very similar curriculum in my own research (Sutton, 1992, 1995).

Studies are ongoing to discover which particular features of training carry the greatest probability of bringing about change: for example, brief lectures, videotaped programmes, modelling or roleplay. There are indications that modelling, that is, *providing parents with an example* of how to respond to a

Box 12.3: The common core of many parenting education programmes (after Gordon & Davidson, 1981)

Session 1 – The contribution of play to promoting positive interactions between parent and child. Learning to define and measure behaviour.
Session 2 – Graphing (i.e. recording) behaviours.
Session 3 – Using consequences to change behaviour.
Session 4 – How to apply reinforcement to behaviour; the great importance of praise.
Session 5 – Using good teaching procedures; modelling.
Session 6 – How to decrease undesired behaviour.
Session 7 – What to do regarding specific behaviours.
Session 8 – How to maintain improvements.

child's difficult behaviour, is particularly effective. This could not be tested in my own research, however, because one of the methods of training parents was by telephone and it was not possible to provide visual models of how to respond to a child.

THE PROCESS AND PRACTICALITIES OF PARENT TRAINING

However well defined the key components of a core curriculum may be, this is likely to be lost upon individuals or members of groups who do not feel safe and appreciated. In other words, the process of preparing for and facilitating a group is extremely important. Box 12.4 shows some of the most important features to be borne in mind.

With increasing attention being paid to issues of effectiveness and cost-effectiveness research has been directed towards examining the efficacy of different practice methods of working with families. For example, what are the merits of group, as against individual, training and is it possible to train people by 'distance learning'? How many parents can be trained together and still achieve positive results? And what is the most effective structure of training – what is the optimal number and length of sessions?

Methods of Training

These were reviewed by O'Dell (1985), who reported a number of studies comparing the impact of training parents in groups with that of training them on an individual family basis. A range of outcome measures were used. Pointing out that 'group training' can mean anything from working with just 2 parents to working with 20, and that there are innumerable variations

Box 12.4: Preparing for and facilitating a group or working with individual parents/carers

Preparing for a group

1. Consider the type of advertising that will be used: posters, cards in libraries, health centres, schools, playgroups, information to other practitioners.
2. Where will the group be held? Schools may have unfortunate associations for some parents. A more neutral setting such as a health or community centre may be more acceptable.
3. Preliminary home visits are essential: one is absolutely necessary, two are highly desirable; three may lead to the beginning of trust among some anxious families.
4. Arrangements for the care of young children should be made well in advance.

Facilitating the group

1. The choice of facilitator is of the greatest importance. He or she should possess the core ingredients for effective counsellors: warmth, empathy and respect for others and able to offer unconditional positive regard (Rogers, 1951; Truax and Carkhuff, 1967).
2. Issues of confidentiality, child protection and possible disclosure of sensitive material should be discussed with participants before the group begins.
3. The plan for the group should be lighthearted, with plenty of opportunity for laughter.

in group structure, O'Dell concluded that the evidence generally suggested that group training was as effective as individualised training. Barlow (1999) has gone further and from her review suggests that group methods are more effective in the long term than individualised training.

There are reports of great diversity in size of group. At one end there are many single case studies reporting highly focused work with individuals, whereas at the other is the approach of Rinn, Vernon and Wise (1975), who reported a training programme which met their criteria for success in that over 1,100 parents attended 5, once weekly, 2-hour sessions at a community mental health centre. The teaching consisted of conveying general principles with minimal attempts to offer individualised guidance. Groups ranged in size from 16 to 90, with a mean of 41! Further, Brightman, Baker, Clark and Ambrose (1982) worked with 66 families having children with physical and learning disabilites, seeking to enable parents to teach their children self-help skills and to manage behaviour problems. The outcomes for 3 methods of training were compared: group format, individualised format and waiting-list control. All children improved on some measures but both group and individually trained families did better than controls on other measures and these improvements were equally maintained at 6 months, followup.

The majority of studies, however, report work with smaller groups of participants. In my own research I compared 4 active models of intervention: group training, home visit training, training by telephone and a waiting-list control, with 5 to 7 participants in the groups. This was as many as I could cope with in order to give individualised attention to all. I found that all 3 active training methods achieved equally good outcomes by comparison with the waiting-list control, both at the end of training and some 12–18 months later; parents trained by the home visit method were doing very slightly better than those trained by the other 2 methods.

In the light of these data, it is obviously cost-effective for family members to be trained by methods which require the least investment of trainer time. In my study, the mean time taken per child in the home visit method was 5 hours, 47 minutes; in the group method, 4 hours, 30 minutes; and in the telephone method, 3 hours 9 minutes. It seems likely from this and other studies that group methods will become increasingly popular and also that training by telephone will be developed, particularly in view of the saving of travel costs and time to families who live in distant places.

The Number and Length of Sessions

There are diversities reported concerning these issues. The numbers reported as achieving effective results are very variable but there seems to be a broadly emerging consensus that for optimum effect parents meeting in groups should have no less than seven to eight training sessions of about two hours each, and that there should also be ongoing booster meetings at about monthly intervals thereafter in order to maintain the improvement. This last is very important, as a number of studies, including my own, have shown that, although it is a relatively straightforward matter to help parents manage their behaviour-disordered children more effectively, 'slippage' occurs after the withdrawal of weekly support and the difficult behaviour tends to reappear as parents slip back into old habits of managing their children. This, of course, is exactly what we should expect within the cognitive-behavioural framework: behaviour (that is, parents' newly learned skill of praising their children) which is not rewarded tends to 'extinguish'; to maintain it, practitioners must continue to reinforce it.

DEVISING AGREEMENTS TO SUPPORT PRACTICE

Theoretical Principles for Writing Agreements

As research increases in the field of helping troubled children, it becomes apparent that there are major difficulties in helping parents to alter their patterns of interacting with their children and, indeed, with older children, in helping them keep to undertakings that they have made. In response to these challenges, a number of researchers, such as Herbert (1981) and Hudson and Macdonald (1986), have advocated devising agreements, discussed and signed by all those participants who are old enough to understand, which have the effect of encouraging the signatories to follow through on agreed courses of action. Indeed 'behaviour contracts' are now common features of the understandings that many schools develop in liaising with the parents of their pupils.

The evidence for the usefulness of agreements in supporting parents is substantial: Hazel (1980) demonstrated their usefulness in enabling young people to move from residential care to foster care and claimed that the written agreements reduced the level of breakdown of the foster placements, whereas Sheldon (1980) has made a very strong case with clear examples for the benefits of 'contingency contracts'.

There are three levels of agreement: primary, secondary and tertiary (Table 12.1) and there are a number of important ideas intrinsic to agreements. First, they are based on the notion of a cost–benefit analysis – that people are motivated to behave in ways that increase their benefits, be they in material terms, in respect of advancing of their values or those of other people important to them. Thus, everybody should be able to anticipate gaining something from the agreement. This is why writing an agreement may take a long time; it is better to ensure that everybody is satisfied at the outset, rather than trying to save time at the risk of being unclear or of failing to think of what might go wrong. Second, agreements are expressed in positive terms – in terms of what people should do rather than what they should not do. With practice, it becomes possible to express almost anything in a positive form! Third, the agreement should be devised in such a way as to enable participants to advance by way of small successes. Agreements do not typically bring about dramatic overnight changes; they provide a strategy for people

Table 12.1 Types and examples of agreement

Level of agreement	Participants	Example
Primary	An offender and a court representative	A probation order made by a court with an offender
Secondary	Two people	A 'service' agreement made between two people, typically a client and a professional.
Tertiary	Three or more parties	A 'contingency' contract among a mother, her 10-year-old son and a teacher.

Source: Adapted from Sheldon (1980). *The Use of Contracts in Social Work.* Birmingham: British Association of Social Workers.

Box 12.5: Essential steps in devising an agreement (after Sheldon, 1980)

1. Discuss whether using an agreement is socially acceptable to those involved. It may be familiar for business arrangements but not for personal ones. If so, invite people to try the idea out.
2. Focus upon actions or behaviours rather than attitudes or feelings.
3. Select one or two behaviours initially. Avoid working with too many problems. Start with a simple goal; early success is vital.
4. Describe those behaviours in a very clear way. Vagueness may seem to make the negotiation easier but all the participants then interpret the agreement differently. This can lead to confusion and anger.
5. Write the agreement so that everyone understands it. Make the wording clear, brief and simple and write in each person's first language.
6. The benefits for each person must be worth the costs as he or she perceives them.
7. The agreement should be written in positive language, specifying things that are to be done rather than those which are not to be done.
8. Collect records. It is essential to know whether the situation is getting better or worse. Information can be collected on simple daily charts.
9. Renegotiate the agreement. A series of short-term agreements is generally more effective than one long-term one.
10. The artificiality and short-term nature of the agreement should be explained.
11. The penalty for failure to fulfil the agreement on each person's part should be clear.
12. Everyone concerned should sign the agreement, which should be dated.
13. As soon as a stable position has been maintained for several months, begin to phase out the agreement.

to achieve small gains, which gradually add up to improvement. There are bound to be failures and disappointments but so long as the general trend is toward improvement, then people's motivation and morale are likely to rise. Finally, it should be emphasised that writing agreements is a skill that may be learned. Sample agreements are discussed later in his chapter and forms for framing such agreements are shown as Appendices 12 and 13. When writing a agreements it is essential to go through the stages shown in Box 12.5

Examples of Written Agreements

Figure 12.1 illustrates an example of an agreement devised between two people in respect of a mother with a small child for whom she is seeking help;

A. The agreement

This agreement is drawn up between:

Name: *Tracey Harris* Address: *The Cedars Hostel* and

Name: *Jenny Cooper* worker from (Agency): *Middleshire Soc. Services*

Address: *17 Lay Lane, Middleton* Telephone no.: *74682*

B. What we are trying to do together:

Our overall aim is *to increase Tracey's feeling of control over her life.*

Our particular goals or objectives are:

1. To *enable Tracey to feel better in health.*
2. To *ensure she has claimed all her welfare rights entitlements*
3. To *help Tracey manage Kevin's misbehaviour*
4. To *give Tracey info. about parent & child drop-in centres.*

C. In order to work towards these goals, we have made some agreements:

Agreed by *Tracey* (client)   Agreed by *Jenny* (worker)

1. To *go to the GP serving the hostel for a check-up.*
2. To *go to the welfare rights office to check her entitlements.*
3. To *respond to Kevin's misbehaviour in a consistent manner as suggested by Jenny.*

1. To *phone Tracey's health visitor and liaise with her.*
2. To *get a list of parent & child drop-in centres & crèche facilities.*
3. To *visit Tracey for 3 x 30 minutes to suggest practical ways of managing Kevin.*

D. Other points to be noted

1. The above agreement is to be reviewed and updated every *1* weeks
2. The agreement can be changed if both parties agree to this
3. Failure on *—* 's part to keep the agreement may result in

— Our next meeting is on 24th October.

Signed *Tracey Harris* Signed *Jenny Cooper* Date *17 October*

Figure 12.1 An example of an agreement between two people

Source: Reproduced from Sutton (1994). *Social Work, Community Work and Psychology*. Leicester: British Psychological Society.

Appendix 13 provides a form for framing such an agreement. Box 12.6 provides an example of an agreement devised between several people, one of whom is a child of 10 but the same principles could be adapted for a much younger child and his or her extended family.

Box 12.6: Example of an agreement between several people: a young person, his family and an educational welfare officer

A. The agreement
This agreement is drawn up between:
1. *David Morrison*   3. *Ronald Henderson* (step-father)
2. *Rosemary Morrison* (mother)   4. *Mr Roberts* (form teacher)
and *Melanie Jones (educational welfare officer)*
    Agency: Northshire Educational Welfare Officers' Dept.
    Address: Park House, Speedwell Road, Northchester, Northshire
    Telephone no: Northchester 2345

B. What we are trying to do together
1. *To improve the relationship between David and Ronald*
2. *To enable David to attend school on a daily basis*
3. *To ensure that David has enough suitable clothing for school activities*
4. *To enable David to take further his interest in athletics*

C. To work towards these goals
The worker (*Melanie*) agrees:
1. *To meet with David each Tuesday at 5.00 p.m. for half an hour and with the whole family fortnightly at 5.30 p.m. for an hour to highlight successes and to troubleshoot problems*
2. *To seek funds so that David can buy necessary sports equipment*
3. *To talk to Mr Renton, the coach, about opportunities for David in athletics*

First family member (*David*) agrees:
1. *To meet Melanie each Tuesday at 5.00 p.m. at a place he chooses*
2. *To attend school daily and remain there after registration*
3. *To ignore people calling him names, but to report bullying to the year head*
4. *To say 'hello' to Ronald each day and not ignore him*

Second family member (*Rosemary*) agrees:
1. *To tell David she is pleased with him each day he attends school*
2. *To put aside _p. daily towards new clothes/equipment for him*
3. *To read any homework David asks her to and say what she likes about it before she criticises it*

Third family member (*Ronald*) agrees:
1. *To say 'hello' to David each day*
2. *To speak quietly and calmly if he asks David to do anything, e.g. help clear up*
3. *To thank David if he does what he is asked*
4. *To avoid criticising David's friends*

Form teacher (*Mr Roberts*) agrees:
1. *To spend five minutes each day looking at David's work with him*
2. *To encourage David to follow up his interests and abilities in athletics*

Other points to be noted:
1. *The above agreement is to be reviewed each week*
2. *The agreement can be changed if everyone agrees*

Signed _____   Signed _____
Signed _____   Signed _____
Signed _____   Date _____

MAINTAINING THE IMPROVEMENT

Studies have repeatedly shown that very substantial help can be given to troubled children, usually by working alongside their parents. A major issue, however, which continues to confront researchers, is how to ensure that improvements are maintained – whether in terms of increased confidence in anxious or depressed children through more regular patterns of sleeping, weight gain and improved diet, or in calmer and more restrained behaviour of children with conduct disorders. The challenge lies in the fact that many parents are being helped to manage their children in different ways, to notice their strengths rather than their weaknesses, their good behaviour rather than their bad and their successes rather than their failures, but that this teaching and their learning inevitably takes place over a very short period, usually a matter of a few weeks, with perhaps a few booster sessions. This new learning has to compete, as it were, with years of deeply ingrained habits of managing their children and, as we all know from the difficulties we experience in following New Year's resolutions, the new intentions, the new learning, tend all too easily to fall away.

In my own work I found that although, with boosters, parents were able to maintain gains for up to 12 months, by 18 months after the end of training the gains were beginning to slip. This pattern has been noted in other studies. On the other hand, Kazdin (1995) noted, in his review of the studies, that 'gains were often maintained for between 1 and 3 years after treatment' and Long, Forehand, Wierson and Morgan (1994), who followed up a cohort of young people with serious behaviour problems some 14 years after their parents had received training in principles of positive parenting, found them to be indistinguishable from the general population of young people. In other words, the impact of training was to enable their parents to cope better with a very troubled group of youngsters.

Other means of helping parents to maintain their newly learned strategies in managing their children will be the focus of future research studies. There are some indications that joining a support group enables parents to maintain their progress but this is not a universal finding.

CONCLUDING REMARKS

This continues to be an exciting time to be attempting to help troubled children – exciting but enormously frustrating. This is because there is at last a body of theory for helping children that has been repeatedly tested and from which many thousands of children and their families are already benefiting. (This theory has been shown to be of help to adults, too, who have difficulties in living.) It is a frustrating time, however, because so few people have been adequately trained in the theoretical principles and because the pace of disseminating knowledge and skill continues to be extremely slow. Courses have to be planned, validation from professional bodies and universities has to be won, supervisors have to be engaged and students have to be trained. Such processes take years. This book has been written to speed those processes along a little. I hope it will be of benefit to the practitioners who read it, to the families with whom they work and to the children whose distress may thereby be alleviated.

APPENDIX 1   FORM FOR ASSESSMENT OF CHILD BEHAVIOUR DIFFICULTY

(Reproduced with permission of De Montfort University)

CONFIDENTIAL
ASSESSMENT OF CHILD BEHAVIOUR DIFFICULTY

A GENERAL AND MEDICAL DETAILS

1 Name of child .... Boy/Girl ....

2 Age .... Date of birth ....

3 Address ....

.... Telephone no. (if available) ....

4 Family composition

Mother's name .... Date of birth ....

Father's name .... Date of birth ....

Please list all children, including referred child, with ages

1 .... (age) ....   3 .... (age) ....   5 .... (age) ....

2 .... (age) ....   4 .... (age) ....   6 .... (age) ....

5 Difficulties being experienced with the child

1 ....   3 ....

2 ....   4 ....

6 Living circumstances of household (brief information about accommodation, etc.)

....

....

7 Any other information the parents think is relevant ....

8 Were there any medical difficulties at birth or during the first year of life?

....

9 Any major illnesses/hospital admissions? ....

10 Have you been worried about his/her development? ....

11 If so, what worried you? ....

12 Is your child allergic to colourings/other substances? ....

13 If you exclude these substances, what happens? ....

14 Is your child having medicine/tablets for the problems? ....
If so, what? ....

15 What seems to be their effect? ....

B FAMILY CIRCUMSTANCES

16 What age was the child when the difficulties began? ....

17 Did anything happen around that time that might be linked with the onset of the difficulties?

a) ....

b) Anything else? ....

18 Have there been any events in the family which made things worse? e.g. bereavement, loss of employment, parental separation

a) ....

b) ....

19 What other stresses are you or other household members under?

a) ....

b) ....

20 Why do you think the misbehaviour happens? ....

....

21 In what ways have you tried to deal with the misbehaviour or difficulty?

1 .... 3 ....

2 .... 4 ....

C SETTINGS IN WHICH THE CHILD MISBEHAVES

22 People involved: with whom does the misbehaviour happen? ....

Is there anyone with whom it never happens? ....

23 Places involved: where does the misbehaviour happen? ....

24 Times involved: when does the misbehaviour happen? ....

25 Can you think of any reason for the child's misbehaving, such as being afraid or jealous?

....

26 What usually brings the misbehaviour to an end? ....

27 What usually happens immediately after a misbehaviour? ....

28 What are some of your child's good behaviours or things that he or she does that you like?

1 .... 2 ....

29 Which of your child's behaviours would you like to see more of?

1 .... 2 ....

D CONCERNING BEDTIME/SLEEPING DIFFICULTIES

30 How old was the child when bedtime/sleeping difficulties began? ......

31 Did anything seem to set them off? e.g. illness? ....

32 Where does the child ordinarily sleep? e.g. cot ....

33 Where does the child ordinarily fall asleep? ....

34 Is this usually alone, or is anyone with him or her? ....

35 How have you tried to deal with the difficulty? ....

36 Would you tell me about the child's pattern of sleeping?

a) What time does he or she wake up in the morning? ....

b) Does the child have any naps during the day? If so, please tell me how many ....

From .... to .... and From .... to ....

c) What time does the child begin to get ready for bed? ....

d) By what time is the child actually in bed? ....

e) Does he or she get out of bed after being settled down? If yes, what happens? ....
....

f) What time does he or she typically go to sleep? ....

g) Does he or she wake in the night? .... If yes, how many times? ....

h) What happens when he or she wakes? ....

i) Is anything said to the child when someone goes to him or her? ......

j) Is the room usually light or dark when the child goes to sleep? ....

37 What is the worst thing about your child's sleeping difficulties? ....
....

38 Is there any other information which you think is relevant to these difficulties? ....
....

E CONCERNING EATING DIFFICULTIES

39 How old was the child when the eating difficulties began? ....

40 Did anything seem to set them off? e.g. illness? ....

41 Where does the child ordinarily eat? e.g. at a table ....

42 Is this usually alone, or is anyone with him or her? ....

43 How have you tried to deal with the difficulty? ....

44 Would you tell me about the child's pattern of eating?

a) What does he or she typically eat at breakfast time? ....

b) What does he or she typically eat in the middle of the day? ....

c) What does he or she typically eat in the evening? ....

d) What is the child happy to eat between main meal times? ....

e) What are the child's favourite foods? ....

f) What are his or her favourite drinks? ....

g) Is there any food that he or she eats a very great deal of? ....

    h) When food is refused, what do you do? ....

    i) What worries you most about the child's eating difficulties? ....

45 What has been the overall impact of the behaviour difficulties on family/ household?

....

Thank you for giving me this information.

The assessor should then pass these assessment sheets to the person(s) who has supplied the information and ask that it be checked for accuracy. Invite the informant to sign the assessment, if he or she is willing to do so.

Signed: .... (Assessor)

Professional role: ....

Address: ....

....

Telephone number: ....

Signed: .... (Parent/Guardian)

Date: ....

APPENDIX 2 FORM FOR RECORDING 'LIFE EVENTS' FOR THE FAMILY AND CHILD

PARENTING POSITIVELY

Helping parents improve children's behaviour

'Life events' for the family and child

Events in the life of the parents/family   Events/impact in the life of the child

Year:			Child's age
e.g. 19....	Mother had post-natal depression	Grandma cared for baby for first year of life	1–6 months

APPENDIX 3 FORM FOR OBTAINING RATINGS ON THE LIFE EVENTS SCALE

Life Events

This form to be completed by the **client**.

Client's name: ....

Worker's name: ....

Encircle the number next to any items which have happened to you in the last six months. Add the numbers and insert the sum into the total box on the right.

Life event	Life change value
Death of spouse or partner	100
Divorce	73
Marital separation	65
Jail term	63
Death of close family member	63
Personal injury or illness	53
Marriage	50
Lost job	47
Marital reconciliation	45
Retirement	45
Change in health of family member	44
Pregnancy	40
Sex difficulties	39
Gain of new family member	39

TOTAL [　　　]

As with all scales, the ratings obtained from this checklist should be treated with caution and used only as clues to possible problems. Cultural issues should also be considered.

Business readjustment	39
Change in financial state	38
Death of close friend	37
Change to different line of work	36
Foreclosure of mortgage	30
Change in responsibilities at work	29
Son or daughter leaving home	29
Trouble with in-laws	29
Outstanding personal achievements	28
Partner begins or stops work	26
Begin or end school	26
Change in living conditions	25
Revision of personal habits	24
Trouble with boss	23
Change in residence	20
Change in school	20
Change in recreation	19
Change in church/temple activities	19
Change in social activities	18
Change in sleeping habits	16
Change in eating habits	15
Vacation	13
Christmas or major religious festival	12
Minor legal violations	11

Adapted with permission from a table by Holmes, T.H. and Rahe, R. (1967). 'Social Readjustment Rating Scale', *Journal of Psychosomatic Research, 227*. Published by Pergamon Press, Oxford.

APPENDIX 4   FORM FOR COMPILING SUMMARY OF INFORMATION RELEVANT TO ASSESSMENT

PARENTING POSITIVELY
Helping parents improve children's behaviour

Summary of information relevant to assessment

Name of child . . . .   Date. . . . .

Predisposing factors for this child/family
1 . . . .
2 . . . .
3 . . . .

Organic/developmental factors affecting the child
1 . . . .
2 . . . .
3 . . . .

Immediate factors
Behaviour difficulties
1 . . . .
2 . . . .
3 . . . .

A–B–C analysis

Antecedents	*Behaviour*	*Consequences*
1	1	1 . . . .
2	2	2 . . . .
3	3	3 . . . .

APPENDIX 5   FORM FOR NOTING A–B–C SEQUENCES

PARENTING POSITIVELY
Helping parents improve children's behaviour

The A–B–C sequence

The following sheet is blank to give you opportunities of noting the A–B–C sequences for yourself.

	Antecedent (What happened just before the behaviour)	**Behaviour** (The specific behaviour identified)	**Consequences** (What happened just after the behaviour)
1	*Example*		
2			
3			
4			
5			
6			

APPENDIX 6   FORM FOR CHARTING BEHAVIOURS

CHARTING BEHAVIOURS   Name: . . . . Week beginning: . . . .

Behaviour	Sunday	Monday	Tuesday	Wednesday	Thursday	Friday	Saturday	Total
Positive behaviour. Follows request in one minute.								
Morning								
Afternoon								
Evening								
Negative behaviour. Does not follow request in one minute.								
Morning								
Afternoon								
Evening								

APPENDIX 7   FORM FOR EIGHT-WEEK CHARTING OF POSITIVE AND NEGATIVE BEHAVIOURS

SHOWING THE INCREASE OR DECREASE WEEK BY WEEK

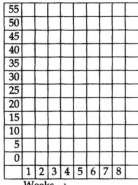

Positive behaviours

Number of instances of beginning to follow a request within one minute

Weeks →

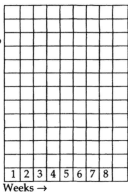

Negative behaviours

Number of instances of not beginning to follow a request within one minute

Weeks →

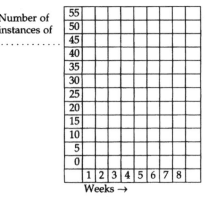

Number of instances of
. . . .

Weeks →

Weeks →

Number of
instances of
. . . .

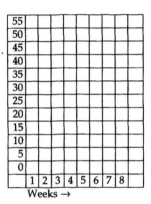

Weeks →

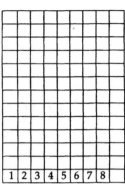

Weeks →

Number of
instances of
. . . .

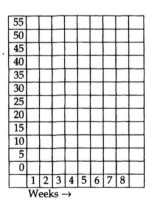

Weeks →

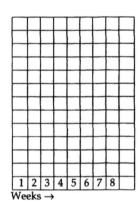

Weeks →

Number of
instances of
. . . .

Weeks →

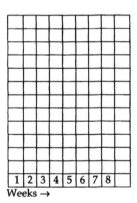

Weeks →

APPENDIX 8   FORM FOR PLANNING WITH PARENTS

PARENTING POSITIVELY

Helping parents improve children's behaviour

Planning with parents

Name of child .... Date of birth ....

To help improve patterns of behaviour, we have agreed to focus on the following:

Positive behaviour

1 ....

2 ....

Negative behaviour

1 ....

2 ....

Action plan agreed with parent(s)

1 ....

2 ....

3 ....

4 ....

This will be reviewed on ....

Signed .... Signed ....

Date ....

APPENDIX 9 PARENTING POSITIVELY: SOME NOTES FOR PARENTS

DE MONTFORT UNIVERSITY

PARENTING POSITIVELY

Helping parents improve children's behaviour

Some Notes for Parents

1. Work out some house or family guidelines: for example, 'All toys must be put away before bedtime'. Everyone helps each other to carry out the guidelines.
2. Find three behaviours each day for which you can praise a child. Catch them being good!
3. Reward behaviour you want to encourage, by attending to it and showing how pleased you are with it.
4. Ignore small misbehaviours: whining, pestering, tantrums. Turn your back on the child.
5. Try to be consistent. If you promise to threaten something, you must carry out the promise or threat.
6. Speak directly and firmly to your child when giving instructions.
7. Encourage others who care for the child to use these same guidelines.
8. Take a day at a time.
9. You'll have some bad days. Try to commend yourself for what you have already achieved.
10. Try to find someone you can confide in when it all seems to be falling apart. *Don't give up.*

APPENDIX 10   WEEKLY SLEEP CHART

SLEEP CHART

Name: . . . .   Date: . . . .

Shade in the times of sleep, and mark with small crosses any periods of prolonged crying.

	7 a.m.	8	9	10	11	noon	1 p.m.	2	3	4	5	6	7	8	9	10	11	12	1 a.m.	2	3	4	5	6
Sunday																								
Monday																								
Tuesday																								
Wednesday																								
Thursday																								
Friday																								
Saturday																								

Example:

	7 a.m.	8	9	10	11	noon	1 p.m.	2	3	4	5	6	7	8	9	10	11	12	1 a.m.	2	3	4	5	6
Sunday																								
Monday																								

APPENDIX 11 GUIDELINES FOR GOOD PRACTICE OF BEHAVIOURAL AND COGNITIVE PSYCHOTHERAPY

INTRODUCTORY STATEMENT

1. All members of the British Association for Behavioural and Cognitive Psychotherapies are required to endeavour to adhere to these guidelines.
2. Most BABCP members will already be members of the helping professions and hold appropriate qualifications. They should, therefore, be bound by a code of practice by virtue of their belonging to a profession and so a detailed statement of general ethical/legal principles is not included in these guidelines. It is expected that all members of BABCP approach their work with the aim of resolving problems and promoting the well-being of service users and will endeavour to use their ability and skills to their best advantage without prejudice and with due recognition of the value and dignity of every human being.
3. The term 'worker' and 'service user' are used throughout to designate the person responsible for helping and the person being helped respectively and should be taken to subsume similar relationships, e.g. doctor/patient, therapist/client, teacher/student etc. as appropriate. Similarly 'assessments/interventions' is used to subsume training, treatment, programme etc.

I ASSESSMENT AND BEHAVIOUR/COGNITIVE CHANGE PROCEDURES

(i) The worker will ensure that any intervention procedures adopted will be based upon evaluation and assessment of the service user and the environment. The worker will also strive to ensure that any assessments/interventions will be in the best interests of the service user, minimising any possible harm and maximising benefits over both the short and long term whilst at the same time balancing these against any possible harmful effects to others.

(ii) Assessments/interventions will always be justified by the available public evidence taking into account all possible alternatives, the degree of demonstrated efficacy, discomfort, intervention time and cost of alternatives.

(iii) Assessments/interventions will be planned and implemented in such a way that effectiveness can be evaluated.

(iv) The aims and goals of assessments/interventions will be discussed and agreed with service users at the outset and may be renegotiated, terminated or a referral made to another worker at the request of either party if the goals are not being met after a reasonable period of time or if they later appear to be inappropriate.

(v) On both ethical and empirical grounds assessments/interventions used will be of demonstrable benefit to the service users both short and long term and will not involve any avoidable loss, deprivation, pain or other source of suffering. It is recognised, however, that circumstances might exist where long term benefits could only be achieved by interventions which involve relatively minor and transient deprivation. Workers will ensure that no such assessments/interventions are used where effective alternatives exist or where long term benefit does not clearly outweigh the short term loss. The design of such assessments/interventions by virtue of the aims would minimise any suffering involved and ensure that dangerous or long term deprivation will not occur. Whenever there is room for doubt about justifying the use of such interventions, workers will always seek advice from an appropriately qualified and experienced colleague who is in a position to give an independent and objective opinion.

2 CONSENT

(i) It is understood that consent to particular assessments/interventions is an ongoing process which places emphasis upon the service user's role in the continual evaluation of the assessments/interventions.

(ii) Where a worker sees a service user only for evaluative or diagnostic procedures, this will be explained clearly to them.

(iii) Upon team agreement regarding the best procedure to implement, the aims, rationale and alternatives of assessments/interventions will be explained to the service user at the start as explicitly and as fully as is consistent with therapeutic effectiveness and the person's best interests. If the assessments/interventions are experimental rather than established and proven, this will be communicated to the service user. If this has been fulfilled, the service user gives consent to the intervention and this is recorded.

(iv) For people unable to give informed voluntary consent, written consent will be obtained from a relative after informing them as described above. If no relative is available, consent will be obtained from an advocate or other responsible professional.

(v) Retroactive consent will only be considered sufficient in emergency situations such that any delay in intervention would lead to permanent and irreversible harm to the person's well being.

(vi) If a service user, when capable of informed consent, or other appropriate person when 2(iv) applies, chooses to withhold consent, the intervention does not proceed. This applies equally to involuntary service users or those referred from the courts.

(vii) Where a service user is within an institution, whether voluntary or otherwise, interventions may take the form of institutional management or specific programmes in which all members take part in these circumstances informed consent may be difficult to achieve but the conditions of 1(iv) are taken as minimum requirement. People are informed of the extent to which they are free to withdraw from any aspect of assessments/interventions. In addition, those responsible for the procedures have the responsibility for collecting objective evidence for their continuing efficacy.

3 QUALIFICATION AND TRAINING

(i) No workers represent themselves as having qualifications or skills they do not possess.

(ii) Workers recognise the boundaries to their competence both from formal training and from work experience and if faced with a situation outside their competence, either refer the person to a colleague who has the required skills or, if taking on the situation themselves, ensure that they receive supervision and training from a competent other.

(iii) Workers expect to continue to develop expertise after formal training has finished and take reasonable steps to keep up-to-date with current research and practice, e.g. reading current research, by attending appropriate courses and receiving regular practice supervision from an appropriately qualified and experienced person.

4 INTERPROFESSIONAL RELATIONSHIPS

(i) Workers in a multi-disciplinary setting keep their colleagues informed of their decisions, consult with them when appropriate and establish clearly the limits of their involvement with a particular service user.

(ii) Where workers have in practice overall responsibility for service users, they recognise aspects where their own professional competence ends and consult other professionals as appropriate.

5 CONFIDENTIALITY

 (i) Information acquired by a worker is confidential within their understanding of the best interest of the service user and the law of the land. Written and oral reports of relevant material are made available to other persons directly involved.
 (ii) The service user's consent is required where information is passed beyond the normal limits of persons concerned or made available for the purpose of research.
(iii) The service user's consent is required if they are presented to an individual or group for teaching purposes and it is made clear that refusal would have no implication for intervention.
(iv) If an intervention is being published, personal details are restricted to the minimum required for describing the intervention.
 (v) If a video tape, film or other recording is made, consent in writing is required specifying whether the recording may be shown to: (a) other professionals; (b) students; (c) the lay public.

6 RESEARCH

 (i) If a service user is asked to be tested or interviewed as part of a research project, it is made explicit when the procedures used are not of direct therapeutic benefit to that individual and formal consent is obtained.
(ii) When service users are in a research project where interventions are being compared or a control condition included, if one intervention or condition emerges as the most effective it is subsequently made available to those in the less effective control groups.

7 EXPLOITATION OF SERVICE USERS

(i) Workers have a clear responsibility not to exploit service users in financial, sexual or other ways. Though some interventions entail workers and service users socialising together, a clear distinction between personal and professional relationships is still made.

8 PRIORITIES

(i) Workers will often have to decide areas in which to specialise and this choice is made with due regard to the priorities involved taking into account the known efficacies of interventions available and the overall benefit conferred on service users in general.

9 ADVERTISING

(i) Membership of BABCP does not confer any professional status or qualification. Workers will not refer to their membership of BABCP in advertising or elsewhere to imply any such professional status or qualification.

(ii) Workers accredited by BABCP as Behavioural and/or Cognitive Psychotherapists to meet the criteria for registration with the Behavioural and Cognitive Psychotherapy Section of the United Kingdom Council for Psychotherapy, are free to advertise or otherwise announce that fact.

APPENDIX 12   FORM FOR FRAMING AN AGREEMENT BETWEEN A WORKER AND A CLIENT

A. The agreement

This agreement is drawn up between:

Name: .... Address: .... and

Name: .... worker from (agency): ....

Address: .... Telephone no: ....

B. What we are trying to do together

Our overall aim is ....

Our particular goals or objectives are:

1. To ....

2. To ....

3. To ....

C. In order to work towards these goals, we have made some agreements:

Agreed by .... (client)   Agreed by ....(worker)

1. To ....   1. To ....

    ....

2. To ....   2. To ....

    ....

3. To ....   3. To ....

    ....

D. Other points to be noted

1. The above agreement is to be reviewed and updated every .... days

2. The agreement can be changed if both parties agree to this

3. If the agreement does not work, i.e. if either party does not keep to the agreement, then ....

Signed .... Signed .... Date ....

APPENDIX 13 FORM FOR FRAMING AN AGREEMENT IN ONE-TO-ONE OR FAMILY WORK

This form to be completed by the worker in discussion with the client and the family. It is all-purpose and can be adapted to a wide range of situations.

A. The agreement

This agreement is drawn up between:

1. .... 3. ....

2. .... 4. ....

and .... worker from: ....

Agency: ....

Address: ....

.... Telephone no: ....

B. What we are trying to do together

We have talked about what we can work towards together, and agree that our goals are to:

1. ....

2. ....

3. ....

4. ....

C. To work towards these goals

The worker agrees to:

1. ....

2. ....

3. ....

The following members of the family agree to:

First person (name) ....

1. ....

2. ....

3. ....

Second person (name) ....

1. ....

2. ....

3. ....

Third person (name) ....

1. ....

2. ....

3. ....

Fourth person (name) ....

1. ....

2. ....

3. ....

D. Other points to be noted

The above agreement is to be reviewed every .... weeks.

The above agreement can be changed if everyone agrees.

Signed: .... Signed: ....

Signed: .... Signed: ....

Date: ....

REFERENCES

Achenbach, T. M. (1991). *Manual for the Child Behaviour Checklist 4-18 and 1997.1 Profile.* Burlington, VT: University of Vermont, Department of Psychiatry.

Achenbach, T. M. & Edelbrock, C. S. (1986). *Manual for the Child Behaviour Checklist and Revised Child Behaviour Profile.* Burlington, VT: University of Vermont, Department of Psychiatry.

Adcock, M. (2000). The core assessment process – how to synthesise information and make judgments. In J. Howarth (ed.). *The child's world. Assessing children in need.* London: Department of Health.

Allen, D. M. & Tarnowski, K. J. (1989). Depressive characteristics of physically abused children. *Journal of Abnormal Child Psychology, 17*, 1–11.

American Psychiatric Association (1994). *Diagnostic and statistical manual of mental disorders* (4th ed). (DSM-IV). Washington, DC: American Psychiatric Association.

Armstrong, K. L., Quinn, R. A. & Dadds, M. R. (1994). The sleep patterns of normal children. *Medical Journal of Australia, 161*, 202–206.

Aro, H. M & Palosaari, U. (1992). Parental divorce, adolesunce and transition to young adulthood: a follow-up study. *American Journal of Orthopsychiatry, 62*, 601–615.

Atkinson, R. L., Atkinson, R. C., Smith, E., Bern, D. J. & Hilgard, E. (1990). *Introduction to Psychology* (10th edn). New York: Harcourt, Brace, Jovanovich.

Bakwin, H. (1971). Enuresis in twins. *American Journal of Diseases in Children. 121*, 222–225.

Bakwin, H. (1973). The genetics of bedwetting. In I. Kolvin, R. MacKeith and R. S. Meadow (Eds). *Bladder Control and Enuresis.* Clinics in Developmental Medicine, Nos 48/49. (pp. 73–77). London: Heinemann/Spastics International Medical Publications.

Bandura, A. (1986). *Social foundations of thought and action. A social cognitive theory.* Englewood Cliffs, NJ: Prentice Hall.

Bandura, A. & Walters, R. H. (1959). *Adolescent aggression.* New York: Ronald.

Barkley, R. (1995). *Taking charge of AD/HD.* New York: Guilford.

Barlow, J. (1997). *Systematic review of the effectiveness of parent-training programmes in improving behaviour problems in children aged 3–10 years.* Oxford: University of Oxford, Health Services Research Unit, Department of Public Health.

Barlow, J. (1999). *Effectiveness of parenting training programmes in improving behaviour problems in children aged 3–10 years.* (2nd edn). Oxford: Health Services Research Unit.

Barrett, P. M. (1998). Evaluation of cognitive behavioural group treatment for childhood anxiety disorders. *Journal of Clinical Child Psychology, 27*, 459–468.

Bateman, B. J. et al. (2004). The effects of a double blind placebo controlled artificial food colourings and benzoate preservatives challenge on hyperactivity in a general population sample of pre-school children. *Archives of Disease in Childhood, 89*, 506–511.

Baumrind, D. (1971). Current patterns of parental authority. *Developmental Psychology Monographs, 1*, 1–102.

Beck, A.T. (1976). *Cognitive Therapy and the Emotional Disorders*. International Universities Press: New York.

Bee, H. (1992). *The developing child*, (6th edn). London: Harper Collins.

Beidel, D. C. & Turner, S. M., (1997). At risk for anxiety. 1 Psychopathology in the offspring of anxious parents. *Journal of the American Academy of Child and Adolescent Psychiatry, 36*, 918–924.

Bellman, M. (1966). Studies on encopresis. *Acta Paediatrica Scandinavica* (suppl), *170*, 1–151.

Bernstein, G. & Garfinkel, B. (1986). School phobia: the overlap of affective and anxiety disorders. *Journal of the American Academy of Child and Adolescent Psychicitry, 25*, 235–241.

Bithoney, W. & Newberger, E. H. (1987). Child and family attributes of failure-to-thrive. *Developmental and Behavioural Paediatrics, 8*, 32–36.

Bosco, J. J. & Robin, S. S. (1980). Hyperkinesis: prevalence and treatment. In C. K. Whalen and B. Henker (eds). *Hyperactive children: the social ecology of identification and treatment*. New York: Academic Press.

Boswell, G. (1995). *Violent victims. The prevalence of abuse and loss in the lives of Section 53 offenders*. London: The Prince's Trust.

Botting, B., Rosato, M. & Wood, R. (1998). Teenage mothers and the health of their children. *Population Trends. 93*, 19–28.

Bowlby, J. (1979). *The making and breaking of affectional bonds*. London: Tavistock.

Brennan, P. A., Grekin, E. R., & Mednick, S. A. (1999). Maternal smoking during pregnancy and adult male criminal outcomes. *Archives of General Psychiatry, 56*, 215–224.

Brightman, R. P., Baker, B., Clark, D. & Ambrose, S. A. (1982). Effectiveness of alternative parent training formats. *Journal of Behavior Therapy and Experimental Psychiatry, 13*, 113–117.

Brinch, M., Isager, T. & Tolstrup, K. (1988). Anorexia nervosa and motherhood: reproduction pattern and mothering behaviour of 50 women. *Acta Psychiatrica Scandinavica, 77*, 611–617.

British Psychological Society (1996). *Attention deficit hyperactivity disorder (ADHD): A psychological response to an evolving concept*. Leicester: British Psychological Society.

Brown, C. & Harris, T. (1978). *The social origins of depression*. London: Tavistock.

Browne, K. & Hamilton-Glachritsis, C. (2005). The influence of violent media on children and adolescents: a public-health approach. *The Lancet, 365*, 702–710.

Buchanan, A. (1992). *Children Who Soil. Assessment and Treatment*. Chichester: Wiley.

Bull, J., McCormick, G., Swann, C. & Mulvihill, C. (2004). *Ante- and post-natal home-visiting programmes: A review of reviews*. London: Health Development Agency.

Burcham, B., Carlson, L. & Milich, R. (1993). Promising school-based practices for students with attention-deficit disorder. *Exceptional Children, 60*, 174–180.

Butler, N. R. & Golding, J. (eds). (1986). *From birth to five. A study of the health and behaviour of Britain's five year olds*. London: Pergamon.

Carter, C. M., Urbanowicz, M., Hemsley, R., Mantilla, L., Strobel, S., Graham, P. J. & Taylor, E. (1993). Effects of a 'few foods' diet in attention deficit disorder. *Archives of Disease in Childhood, 69*, 564–568.

Caspi, A., Moffitt, T., Newman, D. L. & Silva, P. A. (1996). Behavioral observations at age 3 predict adult psychiatric disorders. *Archives of General Psychiatry, 53*, 1033–1039.

Caspi, A., Taylor, A., Moffitt, T. E., & Plomin, R. (2000). Neighbourhood deprivation affects children's mental health: environmental risks identified in a genetic design. *Psychological Science, 11*, 21–36.

Caspi, A., et al. (2002). Role of genotype in the cycle of violence in maltreated children. *Science, 297*, August, 851–854.

Clayden, G., Taylor, E., Loader, P., Borzykowski, M. & Edwards, M. (2002). Wetting and soiling in childhood. In M. Rutter and Taylor, E. (eds). *Child and adolescent psychiatry*. (4th edn.). Oxford: Blackwell.

Cleaver, H., Unell, I. & Aldgate, J. (1999). *Children's needs – parenting capacity*, London: The Stationery Office.

Cohen, N. J., Davine, M., Hordezky, M. A., Lipseu, L. & Isaacson, B. A. (1993). Unsuspected language impairments in psychiatrically disturbed children: prevalence and language and behavioral characteristics. *Journal of the American Academy of Child and Adolescent Psychiatry, 32*, 595–603.

Communities that Care (1998) *Communities that care. A new kind of prevention programme*. London: Communities that Care.

Conners, C. K. (1973). Rating scales for use in drug studies with children. *Pharmacology Bulletin, 9*, 24–29.

Cooper, C. (1985). 'Good-enough', border-line and 'bad-enough' parenting. In M. Adcock & R. White (eds). *Good-enough parenting: A framework for assessment.* London: British Agencies for Adoption and Fostering.

Cooper, P. J. & Murray, L. (1998). Postnatal depression. *British Medical Journal, 316*, 1884–1886.

Cross, M. (1997). Challenging behaviour or challenged comprehension. *Royal College of Speech and Language Therapists Bulletin*, September, 11–12.

Crow, I., France, A., Hacking, S. & Hart, M. (2004). *Does 'Communities that Care' work? An evaluation of a community based risk prevention programme in three neighbourhoods.* York: Joseph Rowntree Foundation.

Dadds, M. R., Schwartz, S. & Sanders, M. R. (1987). Marital discord and treatment outcome in the treatment of childhood conduct disorders. *Journal of Consulting and Clinical Psychology, 55*, 396–403.

Dahl, M. & Kristiansson, B. (1987). Early feeding problems in an affluent society: (iv) impact on growth up to two years of age. *Acta Paediatrica Scandinavica, 76*, 881–888.

Davie, R., Butler, N. & Goldstein, H. (1972). *From birth to seven*. London: Longman.

Davis, H., Day, C. & Bidmead, C. (2002). *Working in partnership with parents: The parent advisor model*. London: Harcourt Assessment The Psychological Corporation.

Davis, H. & Spurr, P. (1998). Parent counselling: an evaluation of a community child mental health service. *Journal of Child Psychology and Psychiatry, 39*, 365–376.

Dawson, G., Groter-Klinger, L., Panagiotides, H., Hill, D. & Spieker, S. (1992). Frontal lobe activity and affective behaviour in infants of mothers with depressive symptoms. *Child Development, 63*, 725–737.

Dawson, G., Ashman, S. & Carver, L. (2000). The role of early experience in shaping behavioural and brain development and its implication for social policy. *Development and Psychopathology, 12*, 695–712.

Department for Education and Skills (2004). Permanent exclusion from schools. *DFES Statistical Bulletin and Statistics of Education*. London. The Stationery Office.

Department of Health & Social Security (1988). *Present day practice in infant feeding, third report*. DHSS Report on Health and Social Subjects, No. 32. London: HMSO.

Department of Health (1995a). *Child and adolescent mental health services: together we stand*. London: HMSO.

Department of Health (1995b). *Child protection: messages from research*. London: HMSO.

Department of Health (1998). *Health and personal social services statistics for England* (1997 ed). London: HMSO.

Department of Health (1999). *Modernising health and social services. National priorities guidance*. 1999/2000-2001/2002. London: Department of Health.

Department of Health (2002a). *Survey of the Mental Health of Children and Adolescents.* London: HMSO.

Department of Health (2000b). *Framework for the assessment of children in need and their families.* London: HMSO.

Department of Health (2003). *Every child matters.* London: HMSO.

Department of Health, Social Services Inspectorate and Department for Education (1995) *A handbook on child and adolescent mental health.* London: HMSO.

Dodge, K. A. (1980). Social cognition and children's aggressive behavior. *Child Development, 51,* 162–170.

Dodge, K. A. & Frame, C. L. (1982). Social cognitive biases and deficits in aggressive boys. *Child Development, 53,* 620–635.

Doleys, N. M. (1978). Assessment and treatment of enuresis and encopresis in children. In M. Hersen, R. M. Eisler & P. M. Miller (eds). *Progress in Behavior Modification.* (vol. 6, pp. 85–121). New York: Academic Press.

Douglas, J. (1989). Training parents to manage their child's sleep problem. In C. E. Schaefer & J. M. Briesmeister (eds). *Handbook of parent training. Parents as co-therapists for children's behaviour problems.* New York: Wiley.

Douglas, J. W. (1973). Early disturbing events and later enuresis. In I. Kolvin, R. C. MacKeith & S. R. Meadows (eds). *Bladder control and enuresis.* Clinics in Developmental Medicine, Nos 48/49. London: Heinemann/Spastics International Medical Publications.

Douglas, H., Rheeston, M. & Robinson, K. (2001). *The Solihull Approach Resource Pack.* Birmingham. Solihull NHS Primary Care Trust and University of Central England in Birmingham.

Durand, B. M. & Carr, E. G. (1991). Functional communication training to reduce challenging behaviour: maintenance and application in new settings. *Journal of Applied Behavior Analysis, 24,* 251–254.

Earls, F. (1982). Cultural and national differences in the epidemiology of behaviour problems in pre-school children. *Culture, Medicine and Psychiatry, 6,* 45–56.

Earls, F. & Jung, K.G. (1987). Temperament and home environment characteristics as early factors in the development of childhood psychopathology. *Journal of the American Academy of Child and Adolescent Psychiatry, 26* (4) 491–498.

Earls, F. (1994). Oppositional-defiant and conduct disorders. In M. Rutter, F. Taylor & L. Hersov (eds). *Child and adolescent psychiatry* (3rd edn). Oxford: Blackwell Scientific.

Earls, F. & Mezzacappa, E. (2002). Conduct and oppositional disorders. In M. Rutter, F. Taylor & L. Hersov (eds). *Child and adolescent psychiatry.* (3rd edn). Oxford: Blackwell Scientific.

Egger, J., Carter, C. M., Graham, P. J., Gumley, D. & Soothill, I. F. (1985). Controlled trial of oligoantigenic treatment in the hyperkinetic syndrome. *Lancet, 9* (March), 540–545.

Eisenberg, L. (1958). School phobia: a study in the communication of anxiety. *American Journal of Psychiatry, 114,* 712–718.

Elliott, D., Huizinga, D. & Morse, B. (1986). Self-reported violent offending. *Journal of Interpersonal Violence, 1,* 472–514.

Emmet, N. (1987). A feedback loop suggested by social learning theory. In C. Sutton (ed). *A handbook of research for the helping professions.* London: Routledge & Kegan Paul.

Falloon, I. R. H., Boyd, J. L. & McGill, C. W. (1984). *Family care of schizophrenia.* London: Guilford.

Falloon, J. R. H., Laporta, M., Fadden, G. & Graham-Hole, V. (1993). *Managing stress in families: Cognitive and behavioural strategies for enhancing coping skills.* London: Routledge.

Farmer, E. & Owen, J. (1995). *Child Protection Practice: Private Risks and Public Remedies.* London. HMSO.

Farrington, D. (1995a). Intensive health visiting and the prevention of juvenile crime. *Health Visitor, 68*(3), 100–102.

Farrington, D. (1995b). The development of offending and anti-social behaviour from childhood: key findings from the Cambridge Study in Delinquent Development. *Journal of Child Psychology and Psychiatry, 360*, 924–964.

Farrington, D. (1996). *Understanding and preventing youth crime.* York: Joseph Rowntree Foundation/York Publishing Services.

Farrington, D. & West, D. J. (1993). Criminal, penal and life histories of chronic offenders. Risk and protective factors and early identification. *Criminal Behaviour and Mental Health, 3*, 492–523.

Ferber, R. (1986). *Solve your child's sleep problems.* London: Dorling Kindersley.

Fiore, E.A., Becker, E.A. & Nero, R.C. (1993). *Research Synthesis on Education Interventions for Students with ADD.* NC. Research Triangle Institute.

Forehand, R. & Kotchik, B. (1996). Cultural diversity: a wake-up call for parent training. *Behavior Therapy, 27*, 187–206.

Forehand, R. & MacDonagh, T. S. (1975). Response contingent time out. An examination of outcome data. *European Journal of Behaviour Analysis and Modification, 1*, 109–115.

Forsyth, B.W. (1989). Colic and the effect of changing formulas: a double-blind multiple, cross-over study. *Journal of Pediatrics, 115*, 521–526.

Gabel, S. (1981). *Behavioral Problems in Childhood. A Primary Care Approach.* New York. Grune & Stratton.

Gardner, F., Lane, E. & Hutchings, J. (2004). Three to eight years. In C. Sutton, D. Utting & D. Farrington (eds). *Support from the start.* Norwich: HMSO, Department for Education and Skills.

Garmezy, N. (1983). Stressors of childhood. In N. Garmezy & M. Rutter (eds). *Stress, coping and development in children.* Stanford, CA: Centre for Advanced Study in the Behavioural Sciences. New York: McGraw Hill.

Gerhardt, S. (2004). *Why love matters. How affection shapes a baby's Brain.* New York: Brunner-Routledge.

Ghate, D. & Hazel, N. (2002). *Parenting in poor environments: Stress, support and coping.* London. Jessica Kingsley.

Goldston, D. B., Tumquist, D. & Kuutson, J. (1989). Presenting problems of sexually abused girls receiving psychiatric services. *Journal of Abnormal Psychology, 98*, 314–317.

Goodman, R. (1997). The Strengths and Difficulties Questionnaire, *Journal of Child Psychology and Psychiatry, 38*(5), 581–586.

Goodman, R. & Stevenson, J. (1989). A twin study of hyperactivity. II. The aetiological role of genes, family relationships and perinatal adversity. *Journal of Child Psychology and Psychiatry, 30*(5), 691–709.

Gordon, S. B. & Davidson, N. (1981). Behavioral parent training. In A. Gurman & D. Kniskern (eds). *Handbook of family therapy.* New York: Brunner/Mazel.

Gordon, D. A. (2003). Intervening with troubled youth and their families: Functional Family Therapy and Parenting Wisely. In J. McGuire (ed.). *Treatment and rehabilitation of offenders.* Chichester: Wiley.

Goyette, C.H., Conners, C.K. and Ulrich, R.F. (1978). Normative data on revised Conners parent and teacher rating scales. *Journal of Abnormal Child Psychology, 6*, 221–236.

Hagell, A. (2002). *The mental health of young offenders. Bright futures: working with vulnerable young people.* London: Mental Health Foundation.

Hampton, D. (1996). Resolving the feeding difficulties associated with non-organic failure to thrive. *Child Care, Health and Development, 22,* 261–121.

Harrington, R. (1994). Affective disorders. In M. Rutter, F. Taylor & L. Hersov (eds). *Child and adolescent psychiatry,* (3rd edn). Oxford: Blackwell Scientific.

Harrington, R. (2002). Affective Disorders. In M. Rutter & E. Taylor (eds). *Child and Adolescent Psychiatry.* (4th ed). Oxford: Blackwell Scientific.

Hart, B. & Risley, T. R. (1995). *Meaningful differences.* London: Brooks Publishing Co.

Hazel, N. (1980). *Bridge to Independence.* Oxford. Basil Blackwell.

Henderson, A. (2000). *The good sleep guide for you and your baby.* Muir of Logie: ABC Health Guides.

Henggeler, S. W. (1999). Multisystemic Therapy: An overview of clinical procedures, outcomes and policy implications. *Child Psychology and Psychiatry Review, 4,* 2–10.

Henry, B., Caspi, A., Moffitt, T. & Silva, P. A. (1996). Temperamental and familial predictors of violent and nonviolent criminal convictions: age 3 to age 18. *Developmental Psychology, 32,* 614–623.

Herbert, M. (1978). *Conduct disorders of childhood and adolescence: A social learning perspective.* Chichester: Wiley.

Herbert, M. (1981). *Behavioural treatment of problem children.* London: Academic Press.

Herbert, M. (1987). *Behavioural treatment of children with problems.* London: Academic Press.

Herbert, M. (1991). *Clinical child psychology. Social learning, development and behaviour.* Chichester: Wiley.

Herbert, M. (1998). *Clinical Child Psychology. Social Learning, Development and Behaviour* (2nd ed). Chichester: Wiley.

Hersov, F. (1977). Emotional disorders. In M. Rutter & F. Hersov (eds). *Child and adolescent psychiatry.* Oxford: Blackwell Scientific.

Hersov, L. (1985). Emotional disorders. In M. Rutter & F. Hersov (eds). *Child and adolescent psychiatry* (4th ed). Oxford: Blackwell Scientific.

Hersov, L. (1994). Faecal soiling. In M. Rutter, F. Taylor & L. Hersov (eds). *Child and adolescent psychiatry.* Oxford: Blackwell Scientific.

Hobbs, S. A., Forehand, E. & Murray, R. G. (1978). Effects of various durations of Time Out on the non-compliant behavior of children. *Behavior Therapy, 9,* 652–656.

Hobcraft, J. & Kiernan, K. (1999). *Childhood poverty, early motherhood and adult social exclusion.* CASE paper 28. London: Centre for Analysis of Social Exclusion, London School of Economics.

Hollin, C. (1991). Cognitive behaviour modification with delinquents. In M. Herbert (ed). *Clinical child psychology: Social learning, development and behaviour.* Chichester: Wiley.

Holmes, T. H. & Rahe, R. H. (1967). The social readjustment rating scale. *Journal of Psychosomatic Research, 11,* 213–218.

House of Commons Health Committee (1997). *Child and adolescent mental health services.* London: HMSO.

Howlin, P. (1998). Practitioner review: psychological and educational treatments for autism. *Journal of Child Psychology and Psychiatry, 39*(3), 307–322.

Hudson, B. & McDonald, G. (1986). *Behavioural social work. An introduction.* Basingstoke: Macmillan.

Huesmann, L. R., Moise-Titus, J., Podolski, C. L. & Eron, L. D. (2003). Longitudinal relations between children's exposure to TV violence and their aggressive and violent behavior in young adulthood 1977–1992. *Developmental Psychology, 39,* 201–221.

Hunt, C. (1994). Infant sleep position and sudden infant death syndrome risk: a time for change. *Pediatrics, 94,* 105–107.

Hutchings, J., Gardner, F. & Lane, E. (2004). Making evidence-based interventions work. In C. Sutton, D. Utting & D. Farrington (eds). *Support from the start.* London. DfES.

Illingworth, R. S. & Lister, J. (1964). The critical or sensitive period, with special reference to certain feeding problems in infants and children. *Journal of Pediatrics, 65,* 839–849.

Iwaniec, D. (1995). *The Emotionally abused and neglected child.* Chichester: Wiley.

Iwaniec, D. (2004). *Children who fail to thrive: A practice guide.* Chichester: Wiley.

Iwaniec, D., Herbert, M. & McNeish, A. S. (1985a). Social work with failure-to-thrive children and their families. Part 1: Psychosocial factors. *British Journal of Social Work, 15,* 243–259.

Iwaniec, D., Herbert, M. & McNeish, A. S. (1985b). Social work with failure-to-thrive children and their families. Part 2: Behavioural social work intervention. *British Journal of Social Work, 15,* 375–389.

Kallarackal, A. M. & Herbert, M. (1976). The adjustment of Indian immigrant children. In *Growing up: A new society social studies reader.* London: IPC.

Kazdin, A. (1987). Treatment of antisocial behavior in children: current status and future directions. *Psychological Bulletin, 102,* 187–203.

Kazdin, A. (1993). Treatment of conduct disorder. Progress and directions in psychotherapy research. *Development and Psychopathology, 5,* 277–310.

Kazdin, A. (1995). *Conduct disorders in childhood and adolescence.* London: Sage.

Keefe, M. (1996). A longitudinal comparison of irritable and nonirritable infants. *Nursing Research, 45,* 4–9.

Keefe, M. R., Froese-Fretz, A. & Kefzer, A. M. (1997). The REST regime: an individualized nursing intervention for infant irritability. *American Journal of Maternal Child Nursing, 22,* 16–20.

Keenan, K. & Wakschlag, L. (2004). Are oppositional defiant and conduct disorder symptoms normative behaviors in preschoolers? A comparison of referred and non-referred children. *American Journal of Psychiatry, 161,* 356–358.

Kendall, P. C. (ed.) (1991). *Child and Adolescent Therapy: Cognitive-Behavioral Procedures.* London: Guilford .

Kendler, K. S., Karkowski, L. M. & Prescott, C. A. (1999). Fears and phobias: reliability and heritability. *Psychological Medicine, 29,* 539–553.

Kerr, S., Jowett, S. & Smith, L. (1997). Education to help prevent sleep problems in infants. *Health Visitor, 70,* 224–225.

Klein, R. G. & Pine, D. S. (2002). Anxiety disorders. In M. Rutter, F. Taylor & L. Hersov (eds). *Child and Adolescent Psychiatry* (3rd edn). Oxford: Blackwell Scientific.

King, N. J., Hamilton, D. I. & Ollendick, T. J. (1988). *Children's Phobias.* London: Academic Press.

Klackenberg, C. (1987). Incidence of parasomnias in children in a general population. In C. Guilleminault (Ed.). *Sleep and its disorders.* New York: Raven Press.

Klein, R. & Pine, D. S. (2002). *Anxiety disorders. In M. Rutter & E. Taylor (eds). Child and Adolescent Psychiatry.* (4th edn). Oxford. Blackwell Publishing Co.

Kolvin, I., Miller, F.J., Fleeting, M. & Kolvin, P.A. (1988). Social and parenting factors affecting criminal offence rates. (Findings from the Newcastle Thousand Family Study 1947–1980). *British Journal of Psychiatry, 152,* 80–90.

Lachenmeyer, J. & Davidovicz, H. (1987). Failure to thrive: a critical review. *Advancement of Clinical Child Psychology. 10,* 335–358.

Lahey, B. B., Piacentini, J. C., Macburnett, K., Stone, P., Hartdagen, S. E. & Hynd, G. W. (1988). Psychopathology in the parents of children with conduct disorder and hyperactivity. *Journal of the American Academy of Child and Adolescent Psychiatry, 27,* 163–170.

Lahey, B. B., Russo, M. F., Walker, J. L. & Piacentini, J. C. (1989). Personality characteristics of the mothers of children with disruptive behaviour disorders. *Journal of
Consulting and Clinical Psychology, 57*(4), 512–515.

Lane, T.W. & Davis, T.E. (1987). Child maltreatment and juvenile delinquency. Does a
relationship exist? In J.D. Burchard and S.N. Burchard (eds) *Prevention of Delinquent
Behaviour. Primary Prevention of Psychopathology.* Newbury Park. CA. Sage.

Lane, E., Gardner, F., Hutchings, J. & Jacobs, B. (2004). Nine to 13 years. In C. Sutton, D.
Utting & D. Farrington (eds). *Support from the Start. Working with Young Children and
their Families to Reduce the Risks of Crime and Antisocial Behaviour.* London: Department
for Education and Skills.

Lindberg, L., Bohlin, G. & Hagekull, B. (1991). Early feeding problems in a normal
population. *International Journal of Eating Disorders, 10,* 395–405.

Lochman, J. E., White, K. & Wayland, K. (1991). Cognitive-behavioral assessment and
treatment with aggressive children. In P. Kendall (ed.). *Child and adolescent therapy:
Cognitive-behavioral procedures.* New York: Guilford.

Loeber, R. (1990). Development and risk factors of juvenile antisocial behavior and
delinquency. *Clinical Psychology Review, 10,* 1–41.

Long, P., Forehand, R., Wierson, M. & Morgan, A. (1994). Does parent training with
young non-compliant children have long-term effects? *Behaviour Research and Therapy, 32*(1), 101–107.

Lyon, J. (1996). *The nature and identification of attention deficit/hyperactivity disorder
(AD/HD).* Hurstpierpoint: International Psychology Services.

Maccoby, E. E. & Martin, J. A. (1983). Socialisation in the context of the family: parent-
child interaction. In P. H. Mussen (ed.). *Handbook of child psychology. Vol. 4.* Chichester:
Wiley.

MacKeith, R., Meadow, R. & Turner, K. (1973). How children become dry. In I. Kolvin,
R. C. MacKeith and S. R. Meadow (eds). *Bladder Control and Enuresis.* Spastics International Medical Publications. Oxford: Heinemann Medical.

Main, M., Kaplan, N. & Cassidy, J. (1985). Security in infancy, childhood and adulthood.
A move to the level of representation. *Monographs of the Society for Research in Child
Development, 50,* 66–104.

Main, M., & Soloman, J. (1990). Producers of identifying infants as disorganized/
disoriented during the Ainsworth Strange Situation. In M. T. Greenberg, D.
Cicchetti & E. M. Cummings (eds). *Attachment in the preschool years theory research
and intervention.* Chicago: University of Chicago Press.

Martin, C. & Pear, J. (1992). *Behavior modification: What it is and how to do it.* Hemel
Hempstead: Prentice Hall.

Maslow, A. (1970). *Motivation and personality.* New York: Harper & Row.

McGonaghy, N. (1969). A controlled trial of imipramine, amphetamine, pad and bell
conditioning and random awakening in the treatment of nocturnal enuresis. *Medical
Journal of Australia, 2,* 237–239.

McGrath, M.L., Mellon, M.W. & Murphy, L. (2000). Empirically supported treatments
in pediatric psychology: constipation and encopresis. *Journal of Pediatric Psychology,
25,* 225–254.

Mendlowitz, S. L., Manassis, K., Bradley, S., Scapillato, D., Mietzis, S. & Shaw, B. F.
(1999). Cognitive behavioral group treatment in childhood anxiety disorders: the
role of parent involvement. *Journal of the American Academy of Child and Adolescent
Psychiatry, 38,* 1223–1229.

Mental Health Foundation (1999). Bright Futures. *Promoting children and young people's
mental health.* London: Mental Health Foundation.

Miller, F.J., Court, S.D., Walton, W.S. & Knox, E.G. (1960). *Growing Up in Newcastle upon
Tyne.* Oxford. Oxford University Press.

Minde, K. & Minde, R. (1986). *Infant psychiatry. An introductory text.* London: Sage.

Mischel, W. (1973). Towards a cognitive social learning reconceptualization of personality. *Psychological Review, 80,* 272–283.

Mitchell, S. & Rosa, P. (1981). Boyhood behaviour problems as precursors of criminality: a fifteen-year follow-up study. *Journal of Child Psychology and Psychiatry, 22,* 19–33.

Moffatt, M.E.K., Kato, C. & Pless, I. (1987). Improvements in self concept after treatment of nocturnal enuresis: randomized control trial. *Journal of Pediatrics, 110,* 647–652.

Moffitt, T. & Caspi, A. (2003). Preventing the inter-generational continuity of antisocial behaviour: implications of partner violence. In D. P. Farrington & J. W. Coid (eds). *Early prevention of adult antisocial behaviour.* Cambridge: Cambridge University Press.

Moffitt, T., Mednick, S. & Gabriella, W. (1989). Predicting careers of criminal violence. Descriptive data and predispositional factors. In D. Brizer & M. Crowner (eds). *Current approaches to the prediction of violence* (pp. 13–34). Washington, DC. American Psychiatric Press.

Morgan, R. (1988). *Help for the bedwetting child.* London: Cedar.

Morris, S., I. St James-Roberts, Sleep, J. & Gillham, P. (2001). Economic evaluation of strategies for managing crying and sleeping problems. *Archives of Disease in Childhood, 84,* 15–19.

Murray, L. Cooper, P. J., Wilson, A. & Romaniuk, H. (2003). Controlled trial of the short- and long-term effect of psychological treatment of post-partum depression. *British Journal of Psychiatry, 182,* 420–427.

Myttas, N. (2001). Understanding and recognizing ADHD. *Practice Nursing, 12,* 278–280.

NHS Advisory Service (1995). *Child and adolescent mental health services.* London. HMSO.

National Statistics Online (2004). Retrieved October 15, 2005 from www.statistics.gov.uk/cci/nugget.asp?id =1229.

Nezu, A. M. & Perri, M. (1989). Social problem-solving therapy for unipolar depression: an initial dismantling investigation. *Journal of Consulting and Clinical Psychology, 57,* 408–413.

Nikolopoulou, M. & St James-Roberts, I. (2003). Preventing sleeping problems in infants who are at risk of developing them. *Archives of Disease in Childhood, 88,* 108–111.

Oaklander, V. (1988). *Windows to Our Children.* Highland, NY: Gestalt Journal Press.

O'Connor, T. G., Heron, J., Golding, J., Beveridge, M. & Glover, V. (2002). Maternal antenatal anxiety and children's behavioural/emotional problems at 4 years. *British Journal of Psychiatry, 180,* 502–508.

O'Dell, S. (1985). Progress in parent training. In M. Hersen, R. M. Eisler & P. Miller (eds). *Progress in behavior modification: Vol. 19.* New York: Academic Press.

Offord, D. R., Boyle, M. C. & Racine, Y. A. (1991). The epidemiology of antisocial behavior in childhood and adolescence. In D. J. Pepler & K. H. Rubin (eds). *The development and treatment of childhood aggression.* Hillsdale, NJ: Erlbaum.

Olds, D. L. et al. (1998). Long-term effects of nurse home visitation on children's criminal and antisocial behaviour. *Journal of the American Medical Association, 80,* 1238–1244.

Olds, D. L. et al. (2004). *Pediatrics, 114,* 1550–1559.

Ollendick, T. & King, N. (1991). Fears and phobias of childhood. In M. Herbert (ed.). *Clinical child psychology: Social learning, development and behaviour.* Chichester: Wiley.

Olweus, D. (1979). Stability of aggressive reaction patterns in males: a review. *Psychological Bulletin, 86,* 29–34 .

Onozawa, K., Glover, V., Adams, D. Modi, N. & Kumar, R. C. (2001). Infant massage improves mother-infant interaction for mothers with postnatal depression. *Journal of Affective Disorders, 63*, 201–207.

Open University (1980). *Systems organization: The management of complexity.* T243 Block 1: Introduction to Systems Thinking and Organization. Milton Keynes: Open University Press.

Patterson, G. (1974). Intervention for boys with conduct problems: multiple settings, treatment and criteria. *Journal of Consulting and Clinical Psychology, 42*, 471–481.

Patterson, G. (1976). *Living with children.* Champaign, IL: Research Press.

Patterson, G. (1975). *Applications of social learning to family life.* Champaign, IL: Research Press.

Patterson, C., Dishion, T. J. & Chamberlain, P. (1993). Outcomes and methodological issues relating to treatment of antisocial children. In T. R. Giles (ed), *Handbook of effective psychotherapy.* New York: Plenum.

Patterson, C. & Stoolmiller, M. (1991). Replications of a dual failure model for boys' depressed mood. *Journal of Consulting and Clinical Psychology, 59*, 481–498.

Pollitt, E., Eichler, A.W. & Chan, C.K. (1975). Psychosocial development and behaviour of mothers of failure-to-thrive children. *American Journal of Orthopsychiatry, 45*, 525–537.

Porrino, L, Rapoport, J. I., Behar, D., Sceery, W., Jesmond, D. & Bunney, W. E. (1983). A naturalistic assessment of the motor activity of hyperactive boys: I. Comparison with normal controls. *Archives of General Psychiatry, 40*, 681–687.

Puckering, C., Rogers, J., Mills, M., Cox, A. D. & Mattsson-Graf, M. (1994). Process and evaluation of a group intervention for mothers with parenting difficulties. *Child Abuse Review, 3*, 299–310.

Quillin, S. & Gleen, L.L. (2004). Interaction between feeding method and co-sleeping on maternal-newborn sleep. *Journal of Obstetric & Gynecological Neonatal Nursing, 33*, 580–588.

Quine, L. (1996). *Solving children's sleep problems.* Huntingdon: Beckett Carlsson.

Radke-Yarrow, M., & Sherman, T. (1990). Hard growing. Children who survive. In J. Rolf, A. Masten, D. Cicchetti, K. Nuechterlein & S. Weintraub (Eds.). *Risk and protective factors in the development of psychopathology.* Cambridge: Cambridge University Press.

Raine, A., Brennan, P. & Mednick, S. A. (1994). Birth complications combined with maternal rejection at age 1 year predisposes to violent crime at age 18 years. *Archives of General Psychiatry, 51*, 984–988.

Richardson, J. & Joughin, C. (2002). *Parent training programmes for the management of young children with conduct disorders: Findings from research.* London: Royal College of Psychiatrists.

Richman, N. (1981). A community survey of characteristics of one to two year-olds with sleep disruptions. *Journal of the American Academy of Child Psychiatry, 20*, 280–291.

Richman, N. (1985). Disorders in pre-school children. In M. Rutter & L. Hersov (eds). *Child and adolescent psychiatry: Modern approaches* (2nd edn). Oxford: Blackwell Scientific.

Richman, N. Stevenson, I. & Graham, I. (1982). *Pre-school to school: A behavioural study.* London: Academic Press.

Rinn, R. C., Vernon, J. C & Wise, M. J. (1975). Training parents of behavior-disordered children in groups: a three years' programme evaluation. *Behavior Therapy, 6*, 378–387.

Roberts, S. (1993). Tackling sleep problems through a clinic-based approach. *Health Visitor, 66*(5), 173–174.

Robins, L. N. (1966). *Deviant children grown up*. Baltimore, MD: Williams & Wilkins.

Robins, L. N. (1981). Epidemiological approaches to natural history research: anti-social disorders in children. *Journal of Consulting and Clinical Psychology, 50*, 226–233.

Robins, L. N. & Price, R. K. (1991). Adult disorders predicted by childhood conduct problems: results from the NIMH Epidemiologic Catchment Area project. *Psychiatry, 54*, 116–132.

Rogers, C. R. (1951). *Client-centred therapy*. Boston, MA: Houghton Mifflin.

Rose, S., Rose, S. A. & Feldman, J. F. (1989). Stability of behaviour problems in very young children. *Development and Psychopathology, 1*, 5–19.

Rutter, M. (1978). Family, area and school influences in the genesis of conduct disorders. In L.A. Hersov, M. Berger & D. Shaffer, (eds). *Aggression and Antisocial Behaviour in Childhood and Adolescence*. Oxford. Pergamon.

Rutter, M. (1986). The developmental psychopathology of depression: issues and per-spectives. In M. Rutter, C. Izard & P. Read (eds) *Depression in Young People: Developmental and Clinical Perspectives*. New York: Guilford.

Rutter, M. (1987). *Helping Troubled Children* (2nd edn). Harmondsworth: Penguin.

Rutter, M. (1988). *Psychiatric Disorder in Parents as a Risk Factor for Children*. Commis-sioned Review for the American Academy of Child Psychiatry.

Rutter, M., Cox, A., Tupling, C., Berger, M. & Yule, W. (1975a). Attainment and adjust-ment in two geographical areas: I. The prevalence of psychiatric disorder. *British Journal of Psychiatry, 126*, 493–509.

Rutter, M., Yule, B., Quinton, D., Rowlands, 0., Yule, W. & Berger, M. (1975b). Attain-ment and adjustment in two geographical areas: III. Some factors accounting for area differences. *British Journal of Psychiatry, 126*, 520–523.

Rutter, M., Taylor, E. & Hersov, L. (1994). *Child and Adolescent Psychiatry* (3rd ed). Oxford: Blackwell Scientific.

Rutter, M. & Sandberg, S. (1992). Psychosocial stressors: concepts, causes and effects. *Journal of European Child and Adolescent Psychiatry, 1*, 3–13.

Rutter, M. , Giller, H. & Hagell, A. (1998). *Antisocial behavior by young people*. Cambridge: Cambridge University Press.

Sadler, S. (1994). Sleep: what is normal at six months? *Professional care of mother and child, 4*, 166–167.

Sampson, R. J., Raudenbush, W. & Earls, F. (1997). Neighborhoods and violent crime. A multilevel study of collective efficacy. *Science, 277*, 918–924.

Sanders, M. R. (1999). Triple P-Positive Parenting Program: Towards an empirically validated multilevel parenting and family support strategy for the prevention of behaviour and emotional problems in children. *Clinical Child and Family Psychology Review, 2*(2) 71–90.

Schachar, R. & Tannock, R. (2002). Syndromes of hyperactivity and attention deficit. (2002). In M. Rutter, F. Taylor & L. Hersov (eds). *Child and Adolescent Psychiatry. Third edition*. Oxford: Blackwell Scientific.

Scott, C. & Richards, M. P. M. (1990). Night waking in infants: effects of providing advice and support for parents. *Journal of Child Psychology and Psychiatry, 31*, 551–567.

Scott, S. (2002). Parent training programmes. In M. Rutter & E. Taylor (eds). *Child and Adolescent Psychiatry*. Oxford: Blackwell Science.

Scott, S., Knapp, M., Henderson, J. & Maughan, B. (2001a). Cost of social exclusion: Antisocial children grown up. *British Medical Journal, 323*, 191–193.

Scott, S., Spender, Q., Doolan, M., Jacobs, B., & Aspland, H. C. (2001b). Multicentre controlled trial of parenting groups for childhood antisocial behaviour in clinical practice. *British Medical Journal, 323*, 194–203.

Scragg, R. K. et al. (1996). Infant room-sharing and prone sleep position in sudden infant death syndrome. *Lancet, 347,* 7–12.

Sears, R.R., Maccoby, E.E. & Levin, H. (1957). *Patterns of Child Rearing.* Evanston. IL. Row Peterson.

Shaffer, D. (1994). Enuresis. In M. Rutter, F. Taylor & L. Hersov (eds). *Child and Adolescent Psychiatry* (3rd edn). Oxford: Blackwell Scientific.

Sheldon, B. (1980). *The use of contracts in social work.* Birmingham: British Association of Social Workers.

Skuse, D. (1994). Feeding and Sleeping Disorders. In M. Rutter, L. Hersov and F. Taylor (eds). *Child and adolescent psychiatry,* (3rd edn). Oxford: Blackwell Scientific.

Smith, M., Bee, P., Heverin, A. & Nobes, G. (1995). *Parental Control with the family: the nature and extent of parental voilence to children.* The Thomas Coram Research Unit, University of London.

Spivack, C., Platt, J. J. & Shure, M. (1976). *The problem-solving approach to adjustment.* San Francisco, CA: Jossey-Bass.

Steele, M. L., Marigna, M. K., Tello, J., Johnson, R. (1999). *Strengthening multi-ethnic families and communities: A violence prevention parent training program.* Los Angeles, CA: Consulting and Clinical Services.

Stein, A. & Barnes, J. (2002). Feeding and sleep disorders. In M. Rutter, F. Taylor & L. Hersov (eds). *Child and adolescent psychiatry.* (3rd edn) Oxford: Blackwell Scientific.

Stein, A., Woolley, H. & McPherson, K. (1999). Conflict between mothers with eating disorders and their infants during mealtimes. *British Journal of Psychiatry, 175,* 455–461.

Stevenson, J. & Goodman, R. (2001). Association between behaviour at age 3 and adult criminality. *British Journal of Psychiatry, 179,* 197–202.

Sutton, C. (1979). *Psychology for social workers and counsellors.* London: Routledge & Kegan Paul.

Sutton, C. (1992). Training parents to manage difficult children: a comparison of methods. *Behavioural Psychotherapy, 20,* 115–139.

Sutton, C. (1994). *Social work, community work and psychology.* Leicester: British Psychological Society.

Sutton, C. (1995). Parent training by telephone: a partial replication. *Behavioural and Cognitive Psychotherapy, 23,* 1–24.

Sutton, C. (2001). Resurgence of attachment (behaviours) within a cognitive behavioural intervention: evidence from research. *Behavioural and Cognitive Psychotherapy, 29,* 357–366.

Sutton, C. & Herbert, M. (1992). *Mental health: A client support resource pack.* Windsor: National Foundation for Educational Research, Nelson.

Sutton, C., Utting, D. & Farrington, D. (eds). (2004). *Support from the start: working with young children and their families to reduce the risk of antisocial behaviour.* Norwich: HMSO.

Sutton, C. & Precht, D. Key components of effective parenting programmes. What do some experienced facilitators think? Forthcoming.

Sykes, D. H., Hoy, E. A., Bill, J., Garth McClure, B., Halliday, H. & Reid, M. (1997). Behavioural adjustment in school of very low birthweight children. *Journal of Child Psychology and Psychiatry, 38,* 315–325.

Taylor, E., Sandberg, S., Thorley, G. & Giles, S. (1991). *The Epidemiology of Childhood Activity.* Maudsley Monographs, no. 33. Oxford. Oxford University Press.

Taylor, F. (1994). Syndromes of attention deficit and overactivity. In M. Rutter, E. Taylor & L. Hersov (eds). *Child and adolescent psychiatry* (3rd ed). Oxford: Blackwell Scientific.

Tellegen, A., Lykken, D. T., Bouchard, T. J. Jr, Wilcox, K. J., Segal, N. & Rich, S. (1988). Personality similarity in twins reared apart and together. *Journal of Personality and Social Psychology, 54,* 1031–1039.

Thoman, E. B. & Whitney, M. P. (1989). Sleep states of infants monitored in the home: individual differences, developmental trends and origins of diurnal cyclicity. *Infant Behaviour and Development, 12,* 59–75.

Thomas, A. & Chess, S. (1977). *Temperament and development.* New York: Brunner/Mazel.

Continuing concern over the number of black children excluded. (1999, July 9). *Times Educational Supplement.*

Tizard, B., Blatchford, P., Borke, J., Farquhar, C. & Plewis, I. (1988). *Young Children at school in the inner city.* Hillsdale, NJ: Erlbaum.

Tremblay, R. E., LeBlanc, M. & Schwarzmann, A. E. (1988). The predictive power of first-grade peer and teacher ratings of behaviour: sex differences in antisocial behaviour and personality at adolescence. *Journal of Abnormal Child Psychology, 16,* 571–583.

Truax, C. F. & Carkhuff, H. R. (1967). *Toward effective counselling and psychotherapy.* Chicago, IL: Aldine.

Turner, K. (1973). Conditioning treatment of nocturnal enuresis. In I. Kolvin, R. C. MacKeith & S. R. Meadow (eds) *Bladder control and Enuresis* (pp. 195–210). Oxford: Heinemann Medical.

Vela-Bueno, A., Bixler, E. O., Dobladez-Blanco, B., Rubo, M. E., Marrison, R. E. & Kales, A. (1985). Prevalence of night terrors and nightmares in elementary school children: a pilot study. *Research Communication in Psychology, Psychiatry and Behaviour, 10*(3), 177–188.

Wakschlag, L. S., Lahey, B. B., Loeber, R., Green, S. M., Gordon, R. A. & Leventhal, B. L. (1997). Maternal smoking during pregnancy and the risk of conduct disorder in boys. *Archives of General Psychiatry, 54,* 670–676.

Wallerstein, J. & Kelly, J. B. (1980). *Surviving the breakup. How children and parents cope with divorce.* London: Great McIntyre.

Watson, J. B. (1930). *Behaviourism.* New York: Norton.

Watson, J. B. & Raynor, R. (1920). Conditioned emotional reactions. *Journal of Experimental Psychology, 3,* 1–14.

Watson, D. L. & Tharp, R. G. (1981). *Self-directed Behaviour. Self-modification for Personal Adjustment.* Monterey, CA: Brooks-Cole.

Webster-Stratton, C. (1992). *The Incredible Years.* Toronto: Umbrella Press.

Webster-Stratton, C., Reid, M. J. & Hammond, M. (2001). Preventing conduct problems, promoting social competence: a parent and teacher training partnership in Head Start. *Journal of Clinical Child Psychology, 30,* 238–302.

Webster-Stratton, C. (1998). Parent training with low income families: promoting parental engagement through a collaborative approach. In J. Lutzker, (ed.) *Handbook of Child Abuse Research and Treatment.* New York: Plenum Press.

Webster-Stratton, C. & Herbert, M. (1994). *Troubled Families: Problem Children.* Chichester: Wiley.

Webster-Stratton, C., Reid, M. J. & Hammond, M. (2001). Preventing conduct problems, promoting social competence: a parent and teacher training partnership in Head Start. *Journal of Clinical Child Psychology, 30,* 238–302.

Weller, R. A., Weller, E., Fristad, M. & Bowes, J. (1991). Depression in recently bereaved prepubertal children. *American Journal of Psychiatry, 148,* 1536–1540.

Werner, F. E. & Smith, R. S. (1982). *Vulnerable but Invincible: A Study of Resilient Children.* New York: McGraw-Hill.

White, J. L., Moffitt, T. E., Earls, F., Robins, L. N. & Silva, P. A. (1990). How early can we tell? Predictors of child conduct disorder and adolescent delinquency. *Criminology, 28*, 507–533.

Whiting, J.W. & Child, I.L. (1953). *Child Training and Personality.* Newhaven, CT: Yale University Press.

Wigfield, R., Fleming, P. J. Berry, P. J., Rudd, P. T. & Golding, J. (1992). Can the fall in Avon's sudden infant death rate be explained by changes in sleeping position? *British Medical Journal, 304*, 282–283.

Widom, C. S. (1989). Does violence beget violence? A critical examination of the literature. *Psychological Bulletin, 106*, 3–28.

Wilde, E. J., Keinhorst, L. C., Dickstra, R. F. & Walters, W. H. G. (1992). The relationship between adolescent suicidal behaviour and life events in childhood and adolescence. *American Journal of Psychiatry, 149*, 45–51.

Wilson, H. (1980). Parental supervision: a neglected aspect of delinquency. *British Journal of Criminology, 20*, 203–235.

Wilson, H. (1987). Parental supervision re-examined. *British Journal of Criminology, 27*, 275–300.

Wolfgang, M., Figlio, R. F. & Sellin, T. (1972). *Delinquency in a Birth Cohort.* Chicago: University of Chicago Press.

World Health Organization (1992). *The ICD-10 Classification of Mental and Behavioural Disorders: Clinical Description and Diagnostic Guidelines.* Geneva: World Health Organization.

Young Minds (2003). Retrieved March 12, 2005, from www.youngminds.org.uk/briefings/03_12_13.php.

Yule, W., Udwin, O. & Murdock, K. (1990). The 'Jupiter' sinking: effects on children's fears, depression and anxiety. *Journal of Child Psychology & Psychiatry, 31*, 1051–1061.

Zoccolillo, M., Pickles, A., Quinton, D. & Rutter, M. (1992). The outcome of childhood conduct disorder: implications for defining adult personality disorder and conduct disorder. *Psychological Medicine, 22*, 971–986.

INDEX